Civil Society

Civil Society

Views and Reviews

Edited by

G.K. Rathod

Viva Books

New Delhi | Mumbai | Chennai | Kolkata | Bengaluru | Hyderabad | Kochi | Guwahati

First Published 2012

Viva Books Private Limited

- 4737/23, Ansari Road, Daryaganj, New Delhi 110 002
  Tel. 42242200, 23258325, 23283121, Email: vivadelhi@vivagroupindia.net
- 76, Service Industries, Shirvane, Sector 1, Nerul, Navi Mumbai 400 706
  Tel. 27721273, 27721274, Email: vivamumbai@vivagroupindia.net
- Jamals Fazal Chambers, 26 Greams Road, Chennai 600 006
  Tel. 28294241, 28290304, Email: vivachennai@vivagroupindia.net
- B-103, Jindal Towers, 21/1A/3 Darga Road, Kolkata 700 017
  Tel. 22816713, Email: vivakolkata@vivagroupindia.net
- 7, GF, Sovereign Park Aptts., 56-58, K. R. Road, Basavanagudi, Bengaluru 560 004
  Tel. 26607409, Email: vivabangalore@vivagroupindia.net
- 101-102, Moghal Marc Apartments, 3-4-637 to 641, Narayanguda, Hyderabad 500 029
  Tel. 27564481, Email: vivahyderabad@vivagroupindia.net
- First Floor, Beevi Towers, SRM Road, Kaloor, Kochi 682 018
  Tel. 0484-2403055, 2403056, Email: vivakochi@vivagroupindia.net
- 232, GNB Road, Beside UCO Bank, Silpukhuri, Guwahati 781 003
  Tel. 0361-2666386, Email: vivaguwahati@vivagroupindia.net

www.vivagroupindia.com

ISBN: 978-81-309-1779-5

Published by Vinod Vasishtha for Viva Books Private Limited, 4737/23 Ansari Road, Daryaganj, New Delhi 110 002.

Printed & bound by Sanat Printers, Kundli 131 028.

S0000/S1000

Contents

Acknowledgements

The editor and publisher would like to thank the following for permission to reproduce copyright material:

'Putting Civil Society in Its Place' by Bhikhu Parekh in *Exploring Civil Society: Political and Cultural Contexts* (pages 15–25) published by Routledge ©2004 Reproduced with permission of Talyor & Francis Books (UK).

'Nationalism and Civil Society' by Craig Calhoun in *Social Theory and the Politics of Identity* edited by Craig Calhoun (pages 304–335) published by Blackwell Publishing ©1994. Reproduced with the permission of Blackwell Publishing Ltd. (UK).

'Introduction to Civil Society and Government' by Robert C. Post and Nancy L. Rosenblum in *Civil Society and Government* edited by Nancy L. Rosenblum and Robert C. Post (pages 1–25) published by Princeton University Press © 2002. Reprinted by permission of Princeton University Press (NJ).

'Civil Society and the Politics of Identity' by Ellen Meiksins Wood in *Democracy against Capitalism: Renewing Historical Materialism* authored by Ellen Meiksin Wood (pages 238–263) published by Cambridge University Press (1995). Reproduced with permission of Cambridge University Press (UK).

'Civil Society and Democracy' by Baogang He in *Democratic Theory Today* edited by April Carter & Geoffrey Stokes (pages 203–227) published by Polity Press (2002). Reproduced with permission of Polity Press (UK).

'Civil Society by Marina Ottaway' in *Politics in the Developing World* edited by Peter Burnell and Vicky Randall (pages 120–135) published by Oxford University Press © 2005. Reproduced with permission of Oxford University Press (UK).

'Interpreting the Notion of Civil Society' by Jean Cohel in *Towards Global Civil Society* edited by Michael Walzer (pages 35–40) published by Berghahn Books © 1995. Reproduced with permission of Marion Berghan, Berghan Books, (New York).

'Reconceptualizing Sivil Society for Now: Some Somewhat Gramscian Turnings' by Kai Nielsen in *Towards Global Civil Society* edited by Michael Walzer (pages 41–68) published by Berghahn Books © 1995 Reproduced with permission of Marion Berghan, Berghan Books, (New York).

'Civil Society: Theory and Practice' by Michael Edwards. This shorter article from INFED is a summary of the Book *Civil Society* authored by Michael Edwards (Polity Press, 2009). Reproduced with permission of Michael Edwards, (New York).

'Civil Society Debates in India: Civil Society against Political Society?' By Bruno Jobert in *Changing Images of Civil Society from Protest to Governance* edited by Bruno Jobert and Beate Kohler-Koch (pages 70–86) Published by Routledge, Oxon. Routledge © 2008. Reproduced by permission of Taylor & Francis Books (UK).

'Civil Society: Active or Passive?' by Rob Jenkins in *Politics in the Developing World* edited by Peter Burnell and vicky Randall (pages 275–285) published by Oxford University Press © 2005. Reproduced with permission of Oxford University Press (UK).

'Religion in the Public Sphere' by K.N. Panikkar. Reprinted with permission of K.N. Panikkar.

1

Introduction

G.K. Rathod

Like democracy, many meanings are attached to the word civil society. As civil society is a contested word, we can never agree to define it in the same way because the very definition carries a different social, moral or political agenda. But somehow, nowadays at least, we cannot live without it.

A just society is one in which people work towards the common good, practice civic virtues of wisdom, courage, moderation and justice, and perform the occupational role to which they are best suited. Plato's ideal state is ruled by philosopher-kings who make decisions based solely on the common good. Socrates, for example, discussed the idea of civil society as a representation of a good society that was connected to the state and the ideal society. Plato, like Socrates retained the links between a civil society and the ideal society. He argued that the concept of a civil society was principally based upon the idea of 'goodness' and justice.

To Aristotle, man is by nature social and must live in an associated life. Society being an integral part of man's life, he cannot live without it. Laws should be the result of public deliberation among average citizens rather than experts, since people through discourse enhance their collective practical intelligence and ensure optimal satisfaction of all parties in the society. The second is that, subject to obeying rightly constituted laws, people should be able to live as they like, free from interference from the state. In this society, people are to be treated as equals.

For Locke, the state of nature is an alternative to a civil society that is legitimate political order based on rights of its members. A civil society is an effective remedy for the state of nature. With Locke, we begin out understanding of modern society. For Locke, civil society is the arena where the inconveniencies and insufficiencies of the state of nature are rectified through the mutuality of contract and consent (Seligmen).

Hobbes's Leviathan portrayed civil society as a coterminous with effective governing institutions embodied in commonwealth. Hobbes viewed civil society as opposed to a disorderly state of nature where distinctions between good and bad, moral and immoral, just and unjust did not exist but emerged only after the creation of the civil society. Though his sovereign was not a party to the contract, the ceaseless conflict and strife were inevitable so long men were guided by the contract. He described the route out of conflict to civil society embodied in compact or a contract.

Hegel placed great value on civil society chiefly because it was a necessary stage in the development of freedom. He saw civil society as another manifestation of the fundamental principle of the modern world: the right of subjectivity or individual freedom. To him the creation of civil society through individual freedom is a great achievement of the modern world. Hegel was as critical of radical utopians who would banish civil society as extreme liberals who would remove all restrictions from it. Although, he agrees with Adam Smith that the pursuit of self- interest creates some social order and interdependence, he denies that this is of common goods for all. To achieve such a good, Hegel argues that the market for civil society must be controlled and regulated by the state. Civil society was 'a wild beast that needs a constant and strict taming and mastery.'

Public-spirited citizenship, Ferguson insisted, was indispensable even in the best modern politics. The real moral danger in modern times, he said, was not wealth but political laziness. Society, for Ferguson is made of men who compete, fight, interact and rise to challenges. Civil society evolves from an early 'savage' phase of primitive tribes to 'barbarism' phase. Thus, civil society has remained associated with Ferguson's name.

The word 'civil society' emerged in eighteenth century and has gained popularity across the world. The language of civil society has been spoken by government officials, journalists, funding agencies, writers, academics and people across the globe. Civil society has remained a dream and an aspiration but it has not been realized fully in practice. Though the idea of civil society is inadequate for the solution to impasses of the contemporary world, it can be understood in several yet distinct ways. Left learning scholars (Arato, Cohen J and John Kean) were using the idea of civil society as a tool to critique both Western capitalist and Eastern communist (or State Socialist). Adam Seligman distinguished among political uses of civil society as a slogan, normative uses of the term as a vision of the good life and social scientific uses as an analytical concept to describe or explain social phenomena. Adam Ferguson termed civil society, not merely as an arena of civic association and free exchange but as a moral sphere and for him civil society was a space for mutual service, grounded in clearly defined moral principles. In his days, the term civil society referred to an orderly and peaceful society, under one government by law – civil society was civilized. It was refined thanks to the peace that the good government had provided but corrupted by its very refinement. Civil society, thus, underlined a problem more than a solution to this problem of good polity. It is a call indeed for competitive coexistence and toleration, for civility, and therefore, it is considered to be synonymous with a search for civility. However, there is no consensus about its meaning and existence in part of the world. Though the civil society idea is the fetish, it has worked some magic and kindled a reformist spirit. Some scholars believe that it is useful to understand forces reconfiguring the sovereignty of the nation-state, the meaning of citizenship, the identity of the modernist subject and the nature of public sphere. Civil society is a relational term because it has relation with many other interdependent terms. The ideal of civil society has stirred social and political aspirations across the globe in recent years.

The revival of concept of civil society took place in Eastern European countries. It was people's struggle against the authoritarian communist states. At the same time, the idea of civil society was also emerging in Western Europe and United States for different reasons. This idea also began to spread in other countries like, Philippines, South Korea, South Africa and India.

Democratic change in several countries cannot be comprehended without reference to civil society (Larry Diamond). The concept of civil society is indispensable to understanding of the dramatic changes that occurred in Latin America and Eastern Europe – especially to understanding the stakes of the transitions to democracy as well as self-understanding of the relevant actors (Jean Cohen). The civil society helps to understand the relationship between society and government. Civil society was the only viable way that the world could be reconstructed in terms of a meaningful order of the things. As it is explained by Muthiah Alagappa, civil society was the missing key to sustained political reform, legitimate states and governments, improved governance, viable state-society and state-economy relationships and prevention of the kind of political decay. Democracy advocates also view civil society as a site for the development of democratic culture with the goal of democratizing the remaining authoritarian regimes. To understand the political change taking place in Asia, he categorized the civil society into space, site and agency. Space indicates the location of civil society in relation to other spheres. The space conception permits the construction of civil society as a site for governance and strategic action. Neo-liberals have also appropriated the notion of civil society as a site for struggle to subvert and replace communist and authoritarian regimes. Civil society has been used to denote agency. This is a realm of power, inequality and struggle and conflicts among competitive interests. It is invariably competitive and heterogeneous. Agency applies to organizations that populate the civil society space, not to civil society as single entity.

We value civil society because it makes democracy possible and we value democracy because, if authentic it transforms domination into self-rule. Benjamin Barber sees civil society as 'free space' in which democratic attitudes are cultivated and democratic behaviour is cultivating a fact of civil society's putative function as a nurture of virtue. He also emphasizes that strong civil society on other hand, sees civil society as a key ingredient in reviving notion of active citizenship nurtured in 'strong democratic community'. By the later, Barber means a community characterized by active participation grounded in civil education, open arena of participation and real decision-making possibility for ordinary citizens. However, civil society requires strong state. The members of civil society must also be committed and vigilant citizens.

Charles Taylor argues that civil society exists over against the state in partial independence from it. It includes those dimensions of social life which cannot be confounded or swallowed up in the state. Civil society is not so much a sphere outside political power rather it penetrates deeply into this power fragment and decentralizes it (power). Its components are truly 'amphibious'. Tocqueville reformulates the ideals of publican freedom in a context of fragmented, decentralized power.

In the concept of civil society, it is suggested by Peter Wagner that society could organize itself in a civil manner. The concept was first proposed to explore the possibility and limits of collective self-determination on the eve of the gradual democratic revolution; it declined with the gradual normative acceptance and institutional consolidation of democracy and it re-emerged at a moment of quest for renewal of democratic impetus.

Marx raises questions and casts doubt about the possibility, meanings and demands of society itself. Through an examination of the idea of civil society, it might be possible to explore matters such as why we live in the societies we do and how we understand the delicate relationship between the demands of external source of authority and one's private interest. An exploration of civil society can help to clarify what might be seen as mysterious and difficult mechanism, of society, nature of social order as we wonder about societies in which we live. Civil society is best understood as confrontation with the very possibility of society itself – this society, our society. An existing image which could be examined to explain what it was that made the social world social (Keith Tester).

Modern civil society – one that is heterogeneous and often multiracial – has to establish different rules: Principle of toleration and need for plural communities to agree on rules governing procedure within framework of Constitutionalism. The ability to accept difference requires the cultivation of a moral imagination that sees reality in other human beings. We learn from the experience of civil society that otherness is intriguing, colourful, and not just scary. Living with difference is crucial to realize that there are two sides to this equation. Certainly, one element at work is an opposition to the fanatical insistence that there is only one way to the truth. In this sense, civil society has about it a measure of relativism, for it asserts that difference is unavoidable, instead desirable for those who insist that the ends of life are diverse. Other side of the picture, stressing the sharing of the belief that diversity is acceptable, is quite as important. Relativism is at discount here, for some differences are unacceptable in a civil society.

With a democracy what is necessary is that difference must not be a source of discrimination. It must be acknowledged, accommodated and above all, given equal position with a democratic polity. Some say that civil society is about pluralism but Chantal Mouffe's view does not allow a total pluralism and it is important to recognize the limits to pluralism, which are required by a democratic politics that aims at challenging a wide range of relation of subordination. Civil society does not only guide to live together but refers to a way of living together well. Steven DeLue contends that civil society is important for securing the way of life that most of us value and want to preserve, a way of life that allows people to place significance on their lives.

Civil society refers to the realm of interaction, institutions and social cohesion that sustain public life outside the spheres of the state and economy. More generally, civil society is a domain of public participation that is founded upon cooperation, empathy and reciprocity. In some conceptions, civil society is synonymous with social solidarity or community identity. Other conceptions equate civil society with individual rights and liberties that protect the individual and nourish public life. Another conception views civil society as a basis for public trust that promotes citizenship and enhances the stability of civic institution. In short, the notion of civil society is very broad and scholars use the concept to identify a wide range of empirical cases. There is no agreement on the analytical distinction between civil society and other related concepts including social relation.

Bhikhu Parekh in his essay in this volume briefly outlines the historical discourse on civil society and narrates central features of civil society. He analyses its explanatory and normative strengths and weaknesses and suggests its proper place in a well-ordered political community. The Western model of civil society has its obvious limitations. It should not be held up as an universal norm and used to mould the rest of the world in the Western image. He also highlights failure of the discourse on civil society to give an adequate account of the nature and role of the state. The state can use its coercive power to challenge vested interests and increase the freedom and opportunities of its citizens. Civil society is not wholly non-coercive. Civil society and the state are based on different principles and play a complementary role. A vibrant civil society gives the state moral depth and political vitality, even as a justly constituted state creates the conditions in which all its citizens can build a rich world of networks and associations. He emphasizes that while drawing on the rich insights of the tradition of discourse on civil society from Hobbes to Walzer, we also need to correct and go beyond them.

Craig Calhoun in his essay explains how Nationalism appeared in the post-1989 discourse on transitions to democracy and in theories of democracy as a hazard to be avoided, not as a central dimension of the subject. He emphasizes that discussions on the idea of nation and social integration need to be joined. The language of civil society has been the most prominent way in which claims to peoplehood and self-determination have been grounded in appeals to social integration. He claims that nationality is not primordial but constructed and nationalism is not easy to define. He argues that Nationalism is not an intrinsically 'bad' ideology. It has been and remains an important source of inspiration. However, in other sense nationalism has totalitarian potential. Nationalism is benign only when it does not tend towards pseudo-democracy of sameness. And this is where civil society comes in. Civil society is the locus of diverse groups and individuals and more importantly of their contact with each other. Some sources of difference may arise within civil society or be brought into it from the family or other less public realms. But in civil society, the exchange not only of goods but of ideas can take place. This essay suggests that it is impossible to pin down any single, substantive source of nationalism as its universal base. Rather, seeing nationalism as a rhetoric in which projects of large-scale collective identity are pursued and challenged, he explores how this figures in relation to democratic theory, first as central to the drawing of boundaries around polities and second as a powerful source of pressures for internal conformity and repression of contrary dimensions of identity politics.

As described by Robert Post and Nancy Rosenblum in their essay 'Introduction to Civil Society and Government,' there are vastly disparate understandings of the relationship between civil society and government. Civil society is alternatively viewed as a source of legitimacy and suitability for government and as a source of resistance against arbitrary, oppressive and overweening government. Civil society is sometimes a spontaneous growth independent of government and sometimes it is dependent on government. The concept of civil society is historically bounded and it is not an organizing concept in early tradition. The authors of this essay propose to focus primarily on the topic on the boundary between civil society and government and discuss the normative question of how this boundary should be conceived and why it matters. The history of political thought shows that the issue of the boundary between civil society and government is ceaselessly contested. Civil society is not merely plural; it is also particularist. The civil society will remain, from the perspective of the state, a domain of partial and particular identities. Particularism marks the boundary that separates civil society from the state. The legal framework is the means by which government performs its civilizing role of transforming arrant particularism into civil society. The analytic distinction between civil society and government has functional implication. As stressed in the essay, civil society cannot persist without government's interventions to maintain civil order and personal legal right. But civil society also requires government to abstain from interventions that undermine pluralism. In evaluating how government and civil society may be accommodated, therefore, the authors can place congruence and modus vivendi along a spectrum. To the extent that civil society flourishes and evidences general agreement about significant public values, greater degree of congruence can be tolerated. Modus vivendi is real achievement and a reasonable accommodation to civil society. Democratic values are relevant to the goal of securing a proper accommodation between civil society and government. The authors conclude from the analysis of relation between civil society and democracy that civil society is no guarantee of democracy, but it is necessary for democracy and can serve important democratic functions. A flourishing pluralistic civil society and strong democratic government are reciprocally supportive. The authors tried to make it clear that civil society and government are complementary constructions. Civil society cannot exist without government and democratic government cannot exist without civil society. However, there is enormous tension over the boundary between civil society and government. The resolution of this tension – the determination of which elements of civil society are salient for political resistance, democratic participation, or effective governance, or exactly how government may secure and promote civil society – is of course contingent and contestable.

In her essay, Ellen Meiksins extends the discussions of democracy to current preoccupations with civil society and politics of identity. She attempts to explain how does the concept of civil society fare in dealing with the diversity of social relation and identities? It is argued that we are living in a post-modern world, a world in which diversity and difference have dissolved all the old certainties and all the old universalities and that by all means let us have diversity, difference and pluralism; but not an undifferentiated and unstructured pluralism. What is needed is a pluralism that does indeed acknowledge diversity and difference, not merely plurality or multiplicity. This means a pluralism that recognizes the systematic unity of capitalism from other inequalities and oppressions. She also points out that current intellectual fashions of the left which emphasize post-modern fragmentation, difference and the politics of identity can barely accommodate the idea of capitalism, let alone subject the capitalist system to critique.

Baogang He explains the origin and various meanings of the term and the place of civil society in theories of democracy. He also considers whether the faith placed in civil society as a means of democratization, for example by dissident intellectuals in Eastern Europe, has led its advocates to exaggerate its importance once parliamentary regimes are established. Finally, he examines a rather different function for civil society – namely, how it can contribute to resolving disputes that cross over territorial boundaries or that require their modification. By drawing upon recent examples from international politics, He suggests that whether the nation-state is unable to resolve such conflicts, civil society organizations (national and international) can play a useful role. He argues where this occurs, democracy is not diminished but enhanced.

The essay of Marina Ottaway begins with an acknowledgement of the ambiguity of the concept of civil society and of its lack of definitional clarity. It ends on the same note, but with a normative addendum. It is possible to narrow down the definition closely. The idea of the common good and the public interest obfuscate the reality that all societies are made up of groups with different and often conflicting interests and that all groups are equally part of the society, whether their goals conform to a specific ideal of civility or not. In developing countries, civil society organizations perform a wide range of functions. It is also mentioned in the essay that many voluntary associations in developing countries try to provide services, the state is unable to deliver. If we want to understand how people come together to defend their interest or pursue their goals, we need to accept the diversity, the complexity and in many cases the flow of the associational realm that has become known as civil society. When the state is weak and incapable of delivering services, civil society organizations seek to ignore the state and avoid its control, rather than press for reforms. When the state is strong, civil society organizations are well developed, relations tend to be cooperative and constructive. This essay emphasizes that democracy requires a large, active, democratically oriented civil society, but what is found in most countries is a bifurcated situation. The concept of civil society became an important part of all discussions of democratization and developing civil society meant promoting government by the people and for the people.

Jean Cohen discusses the relation between politics of a civil society and the state or the economy. And he wants to argue that no version of two-part model whereby civil society includes everything outside the state sector is helpful today. The opposition between civil society and the state can only be a slogan, but it is certainly not adequate for serious analysis or politics within civil societies. Instead, he insists on a three-part model which differentiates between civil society, the state, and the economy. The three-part model has two advantages. First, it avoids an unpleasant ambiguity in the programme of the defence of civil society against the state, for it allows one to distinguish between the 'civil' and the 'bourgeois'. On three-part model, the autonomy of civil society is not the same as the autonomy of the market. Second, the three-part model also helps us to counter conservative conceptions of the social life. It allows us to see that the defense of civil society does not have to entail a traditionalistic hierarchy as opposed to a modern (egalitarian) life world. He defines civil society as a sphere of social interaction distinct from economy and state, composed of all associations (including family) and publics. He says that civil society is a project, a terrain and target of democratic politics. The institutions of civil society can and ought to be the target of democratization, of egalitarian projects and the institutions of political and economic society can and ought to be the targets of actors in civil society seeking to render them more receptive to their influence. In short, he can identify, on his conception, four types of politics which he calls politics of identity, influence, inclusion, and reform, which address civil, political and/or economic society, the economy, and state, respectively. All of these comprise the policies of civil society. He concludes that Utopian ideals are not on the wane, political projects are still possible. We need not indulge in resignation, for a democratic and egalitarian civil society is still a project worth fighting for.

Kai Nielsen gives an account of the Gramsci's conception of civil society and tries to forge some conceptualizing or reconceptualizing of civil society which would be useful, given, on one hand, some important political or ethical purposes or, on the other, some theoretical purposes. He asserts that a clarified form of conception of civil society is both politically and theoretically more useful than more standard conceptions. It helps us to understand what make societies tick. In addition to an adequate conception of civil society, we need to understand the politics of civil society in order to provide a corrective for characteristics failure of liberalism. In locating civil society we must look for those organizations or practices that are not directly governmental or economic but which generate opinions and goals. He emphasizes that the wheel of the world having turned, our analysis of the politics of civil society will have to be somewhat different from Gramsci's. Still, deploying the notion of civil society may continue to be useful, perhaps even more useful than before, for analyzing and critiquing the contemporary world. For proper functioning of the institutions of civil society, he prescribes preconditions. (a) the society must be a complex society with many different social functions and roles into which people are slotted and (b) the state and economic organizations cannot incorporate or even completely control the various practices and institutions of the society that are non-economic and non-governmental. He realizes that the preconditions for civil society are met in our world, but it is also true that the strength, and so far the growing strength, of economic-corporate and political-bureaucratic organizations threaten to undermine the institutions of civil society. A colonization of the life-world and the power of corporate-bureaucratic structures also threaten the very existence of civil society. A viable civil society seems to require some effective sense of community to which people are committed. The norms of a viable civil society must be justified and the conceptualized civil society must really be a civil society that could come to be in our world. After delineating civil humanism, he observes that it is as unrealistic and unworldly as the classical normative theories of democracy and the tradition of civic humanism is every bit as much an unfeasible utopian vision. It is a conception of a political culture that could have no instantiation in our complex societies, and it does not bring with it a civil society that is much of a bulwark against the economic order of a state that is anything but the realization of an ethical ideal.

Michael Edwards asserts that the goal of his essay is not consensus (something that would be impossible to achieve in the civil society debate) but greater clarity. And greater clarity, he hopes, can be the basis for a better conversation in the future. He tries to show in the essay that follows, ideas about civil society can survive and prosper in a rigorous critique. Then he reconstructs the relationships between the different schools of thought in a new and more convincing synthesis. The first school believes that voluntary associations act as gene carriers of the good society – for developing values like tolerance and cooperation, and the skills required for living a democratic life. His second school of thought – civil society as the good society – sets the contributions of voluntary associations in the proper context and guards against the tendency to privilege one part of society over the others on ideological grounds. He refers to third school of thought and considers civil society in its role as the public sphere. In its role as public sphere, civil society becomes the arena for argument, deliberation and collaboration. He concludes that civil society is simultaneously a goal to aim for, a means to achieve it and a framework for engaging with each other about ends and means. According to his assertion, the ideal of civil society is compelling because it speaks to the best in us and calls on the best in us to respond in kind.

In his essay Bruno Jobert analyses the public debates on civil society and return of civil society in India. And he shares the hypothesis exposed in the writings of Parth Chatterjee (2001) that the Indian case can only be understood by making a distinction between civil society and political society and by analyzing its inter-relationship. The political society corresponded to a model of political mediation developed in the anti-colonial struggle and in Indian democracy. The modes of action in political society were profoundly different from those of associational life. This essay analyses uncomfortable coexistence which persisted throughout the various stages of India's political evolution and begins with the emergence of tutelary model after independence, when civil society organizations were clearly subordinated to the political institutions. Sections of this essay delineate the various answers given to the ongoing expansion of political participation and their impact on civil society frames. The political consecration of civil society after emergency was followed by alternative patterns of political mediation, when Hindu nationalism and the caste appeared on the political scene. Finally, the economic reforms of the 1990s modified the stakes and fields of action for the civil society organizations, bringing the question of the civilization of the state to the fore. The author draws some conclusions from the discussion that the hypothesis that civil society becomes a point of reference whenever established politics enters into crisis is illustrated by the return of civil society after the state of emergency in the late 1970s. The framing of alternative references for relations between the state and civil society has borrowed much from the international discourse on good governance and, particularly, on the crucial role of voluntary associations in the empowerment of beneficiaries. Civil society embodies a mass of people consisting of citizens, whereas Indian political society is structured around inherited and imagined communities. The place that particularist actors have in political society puts civil society into awkward position. To be sure, greater participation by the working or poor classes in the elections is a remarkable feature of Indian democracy, yet it remains to be seen whether this 'revolution' will bring civil society and political society closer together.

Rob Jenkins examines civil society in the 'World's largest democracy'. A democratic political system of India attributed to the vibrancy of its civil society. After outlining some of the salient features of India's recent political history, this essay examines (1) controversies surrounding the size and composition of India's civil society; (2) issues relating to regional variations in the nature of associational life; (3) the question of whether states can help to spur the development of civil society; (4) problems in understanding the contribution of civil society to improved governance, including consideration of civil society's darker side.

K.N. Panikkar argues that the influence of religion in the public sphere has not declined, but in fact, has increased. It is not only that religion has emerged as a powerful influence in the public sphere all over the world. This is particularly so in India. He asserts that the formation and development of the public sphere in India during nineteenth and twentieth centuries was different from the public sphere that emerged in Europe in the eighteenth century. This was primarily because India was under colonial domination and Indian society did not have the necessary independence to shape its destiny. For a variety of reasons, the ability of the agencies which contributed to the formation of the public sphere in India – such as the media, voluntary organizations and social and religious movements – to constitute a public sphere was restricted. He concludes that the renaissance, enlightenment and scientific revolution being either borrowed or weak, the capacity of modernization in India to impact on secularization and marginalization of religion is itself not pronounced. Instead, religion remains a powerful force in civil society. Secondly, the use of religion for political ends has substantially increased during the last few decades and retrieving the secular character of the public sphere is therefore imperative; otherwise its religious character is likely to impinge upon the functions of the state.

By commenting on some definitions of civil society, G.K. Rathod seeks to outline the origin of the concept of civil society and its characteristics. He delineates the relationship between civil society and public sphere, civil society and the good society, and civil society and nationalism. He also focuses on civil society and politics and gives some idea of social order and public interest.

To understand the democracy, civil society should be the subject matter of sociology. It should be understood in particular context. The scope of its heuristic value requires to be increased to improve its quality. We need to recognize that it is possible to put in practice civil society because of empirical research of the subject matter. In sociological approach, normative value of civil society can be tested by empirical study and by way of reasoning method.

The idea of civil society as a subject required to be comprehensively debated by scholars. This book covers a diversity of discussions and arguments on the subject from several relevant perspectives. It also explores the historical and political evolution and political potential of the idea. Therefore, it will be useful as a standard work of reference to readers from various fields.

2

Putting Civil Society in Its Place

Bhikhu Parekh

There is today an almost universal consensus that civil society is a vital component of a good society, and that the stronger and more developed it is, the better governed and more stable the wider political community is likely to be. This belief underlies the widely held view that Western societies are vibrant, free and democratic because they have, and the erstwhile communist societies came to grief because they did not have, a civil society, and that if the developing world is to avoid the fate of the latter, it should foster civil society. Large and well-meaning Western foundations devote huge resources to helping the developing world do just this, and Western governments and international institutions make it a precondition of their aid. The fact that the consensus has acquired the status of an intellectual orthodoxy is a good enough reason to subject it to a critical scrutiny. The further fact that it has profound consequences for the lives of large parts of humankind, and that similar recent orthodoxies such as the Structural Adjustment Programme of the International Monetary Fund (IMF) have turned out to be deeply problematic, reinforces the need for scrutiny. In this chapter I do two things. I briefly outline the historical discourse on civil society and tease out its central features. I then analyze its explanatory and normative strengths and weaknesses, and suggest its proper place in a well-ordered political community.

WHAT IS CIVIL SOCIETY?

Although the concept of civil society (societas civilis) goes back to the Romans, who contrasted it with the 'natural society' of animals and used it to refer to the rational and law-governed society of humans, the concept did not become dominant until the seventeenth century (see, for example, Cahoone 2002; Ehrenberg 1999; Keene 1998). Hobbes was one of the first to articulate it with great clarity, followed by such other writers as Locke, Grotius, Puffendorf and Montesquieu. For them human beings were by nature free and equal and endowed with the capacities for rationality and self-determination. They could not flourish in the unregulated state of nature and needed a well-ordered society that ensured them maximum freedom to pursue their self-chosen purposes. Such a society had a public or civil authority entitled to take and enforce collectively binding decisions. The authority was derived from the consent of its members, did no more than protect the basic rights of its members' and governed according to general laws. Its subjects were free to lead such lives, pursue such purpose, and enter into such relations as they thought proper within the limits set by the laws. Hobbes, Locke and others called this 'civil society'.

Civil society referred to a group of individuals held together, and forming a single society, by virtue of subscribing to a consensually based public authority and sharing in common the practice of civility. Civil society was a human artefact, created, sustained and capable of being changed by human beings. It was not an organic expression of human sociability as Cicero and Aquinas argued, nor a teleological requirement of human nature as Aristotle maintained. It was a rational and artificial institution, growing, no doubt, out of the natural desire to live but in no way dictated or sustained by it. It called for its own distinct institutions and practices, as well as virtues and motives that it sought to cultivate in its members by educational and other means. Civil society was not separate from the state nor one of its institutions; rather it was a way, and for Hobbes, Locke and others the only proper way, of constituting the state.

Writers of the Scottish Enlightenment, who were particularly influential in popularizing the concept of civil society, shared their predecessors' view of it. Although they added minor novel touches, they did not radically depart from it. In their view human beings were inherently social, and the concept of the state of nature made neither logical nor historical sense. They contrasted civil society with 'savage', 'primitive', 'rude' or 'militaristic' society, and equated it with civilized society (Ferguson 1767). Civilized society was distinguished by increased wants, division of labour, growth of the arts and sciences, self-restraint, moderation, rationality, liberty, gentle and refined manners, and respect for the law, all of which were believed to be enabled by and closely tied up with the development of commerce. A civilized society was above all a commercial society, and was constituted as a civil society based on a civil authority governing by means of laws and maintaining the basic rights of its citizens. Only a civil society was believed to create the framework necessary for the development of a civilized and commercial society. Non-European societies had remained backward because they lacked such a civil society, and had no hope of turning the corner without developing one with or without European help.

Hegel marked an important stage in the discourse on civil society. He too shared the earlier view of civil society, and his originality consisted in giving it a new orientation and probing its philosophical foundations. For him, as for his predecessors, civil society or burgerliche Gesellschaft referred to a legally constituted association of free and equal individuals pursuing their self-chosen goals. It was characterized by subjective freedom, personal autonomy, individual rights, mutual respect and recognition, satisfaction of needs, a system of exchange, rational legal norms, abstract morality, and a minimum structure of public authority. Unlike his predecessors, Hegel argued that civil society was inherently unstable. It threw up acute contrasts of wealth and poverty, created a rootless and discontented 'rabble', and was ridden with tensions and conflicts that it could not itself regulate. It also lacked collective self-consciousness, capacity for collective self-reflection, and a sense of moral direction. For these and related reasons, civil society was incomplete, pointed beyond itself, and required the institution of the state. While nurturing civil society, the state also regulated it, gave its atomized members a sense of community, and provided a higher and fully rational level of social existence. For Hegel, the state could never be constituted as civil society as the earlier writers had maintained. It included civil society as its necessary moment, but transcended it and provided it with a rationally and morally necessary wider framework (Taylor 1975). While most earlier writers had equated civil and political society and used the two terms inter-changeably, Hegel drew a fairly sharp distinction between them.

For Hegel, civil society occupied a space between the family and the state. The former was based on love, unselfish concern for its members, overlapping selves, and so on and represented an organic unity of reason and nature. Civil society was the realm of differentiation, in which free, independent, and otherwise unrelated individuals pursued their self-interest in a spirit of mutual respect and within the limits of the laws. The state embodied individuals' dialectical unity, and represented objective rationality, rationally regulated sentiments of love and disinterested concern for the whole, pursuit of collective well-being, and a non-instrumental view of public authority.

Karl Marx represented another stage in the developing discourse on civil society. He too shared the earlier view of it, but differed from his predecessors in his analysis of the nature and dynamics of civil society and its relation to the state. As he put it, 'material conditions of life are summed up by Hegel after the fashion of the English and the French of the eighteenth century under the name 'civil society'. For Marx civil society referred to the 'whole communal and industrial life of a given stage', 'all the material relations of production possible within a definite stage of the development of productive forces' (Marx and Engels 1973: 362–3). Although Marx sometimes suggested that civil society existed in all historical epochs, his considered view was that it was unique to the modern bourgeois society, especially in respect to the autonomy and the freedom from moral and communal constraints that it had currently acquired. For Marx as for the earlier writers, civil society was characterized by individualism, rights, pursuit of self-interest, satisfaction of needs, liberty and equality.

Following Hegel but far more so than him, Marx saw civil society as the realm of conflict, indeed a state of war between organized classes. Being inherently unstable, it needed the state to sustain the prevailing economic order. Unlike Hegel, Marx argued that the liberty, equality and so on that lay at the heart of civil society were deeply distorted and rendered vacuous by the class structure of the capitalist society. Workers had no choice but to alienate their labour, and were not really free. Lacking the necessary opportunity and resources, their rights too remained largely formal and empty. This was just as true of equality and individual choice. Unlike Hegel, Marx argued that the state did not and could not transcend civil society. Being the product of and inextricably tied to the class conflict inherent in civil society, it lacked the capacity to act autonomously. The universality that it claimed to represent was nothing but the particular interest of the dominant class masquerading as that of the society as a whole.

For Marx civil society was not a moment of the state as it was for Hegel, but its basis. Once the classes were abolished and the civil society was radically reconstituted, the state forfeited its rationale. People would reclaim the power they had hitherto alienated to the socially transcendental state, and govern their collective affairs democratically. Civil society would be replaced by a planned economy based on the principle of 'from each according to his ability and to each according to his need'. Marx called such a society 'communist'. It represented the dialectical unity of civil society and the state. It was not collectivist, as it became in the hands of the Soviet communist regime, for example, and was more like a socialist version of Locke's civil society. Individuals were its basic units, but they were socially conscious and motivated, not egotistical and self-interested. They enjoyed maximum freedom, but used it to expand their human powers and enrich their being rather than to accumulate wealth or increase consumption. While the concept of civil society dominated Marx's early writings, it virtually disappeared from the later ones, where Marx preferred to talk of 'material relations', 'relations of production', the 'economic' 'structure of society' and so on in contexts where he would earlier have used the term 'civil society'.

Within the Marxist tradition, the term 'civil society' played a limited role until Gramsci reintroduced it and made it one of the central categories of his thought. Since he drew heavily not only on Marx but also on Hegel, Croce and other Italian idealists, his usage was both inconsistent and richly suggestive. For Gramsci, 'it is not the economic structure which directly determines the political action, but the interpretation of it', or what Marx had called ideology. He therefore shifted the focus of attention from the material relations of society to the 'cultural and spiritual' agencies that shaped the consciousness of its members, and called them civil society. In this broad sense, civil society was not peculiar to the bourgeois society, and existed in the middle ages, where the 'church was civil society' (Gramsci 1971: 170). Civil society referred not to the economy but to the realm of free associational activity, and included the family, universities, the press, trade unions, cultural institutions, working men's clubs and publishing houses. Unlike the state or the political society, which exercised 'direct domination', or coercion over society, the dominant class used the institutions of civil society to mobilize popular consent in favour of the prevailing economic order and to establish 'cultural and spiritual supremacy' or "hegemony" (Gramsci 1971: 12, 53, 125). Working classes and their organic intellectuals needed to contest this by carrying on the class struggle not only at the economic level but also in the civil society.

Gramsci's vision of the classless communist society was very similar to Marx's. People would reclaim the power they had hitherto abdicated to the state, and all social institutions including the family, the schools, the universities and the state would be run democratically. 'Coercive elements of the state would wither away by degrees', and individuals, now liberated from all unnecessary constraints and inequalities, would enjoy maximum freedom (Gramsci 1971: 263). Such free, equal and socially conscious individuals would spontaneously carry out the laws they had given themselves, and the external discipline of the law would be replaced by the internal pressure of morality. Since people would readily appreciate the legitimacy of the prevailing economic and political order, their consent to it would be genuine and spontaneous, and would not need to be manufactured. Gramsci called such a society an 'ethical state' or 'civil society' (1971: 263). Unlike the capitalist society in which the institutions of civil society were manipulated to generate consent for a hegemonic social order, the communist society represented the 'reabsorption of political society into civil society', and symbolized the full flowering of the latter with free and equal individuals autonomously forming their views (Gramsci 1971: 253).

In recent years the term 'civil society' has experienced a revival and found favour among people of different ideological persuasions. The current usage draws heavily not only on the European discourse but also on the American, especially the Tocquevillian, account of the vital role of voluntary associations in American life. For Tocqueville, American democracy was dominated by the idea of equality, which had its great virtues but also the tendency to isolate and atomize individuals. The only way to hold such a society together and forge bonds of solidarity was to create an extensive network of voluntary associations. Drawing on this tradition of thought, Robert Putnam (2000) has in his influential writings stressed the value of a thick associational life in building up trust, social capital and solidarity.

Michael Walzer (1994) blends the two and captures the current usage well when he say that 'the words "civil society" name the sphere of uncoerced human association and also the set of relational networks formed for the sake of family, faith, interest and ideology that fill this space'. As an area of uncoerced associative life, civil society includes such associations as the family, trade unions, universities, the press, professional bodies, churches, Non-Governmental Organizations (NGOs) and social movements. It excludes the state, which is seen as inherently and exclusively coercive institutions. Political parties are also excluded, largely because, although voluntary, their purpose is to capture the state and use its coercive resources to realize their objectives.

In the light of our brief historical sketch, the discourse on civil society displays a remarkable consistency. It refers to what I might call the area of associative freedom, that is to the freedom of individuals to enter into relations with others, pursue common purposes, and form intrinsically or instrumentally valuable associations. It refers not to freedom per se, nor to how individuals lead their personal lives, but to the active exercise of freedom in forming networks of social relations. The concern with associative freedom arises out of the belief that as free, equal, rational and self-determining individuals, human beings desire to, and should be able to, form such social relations as they please. Since coercion violates their dignity and rational nature, it is inherently undesirable, and should ideally be avoided. However, since human beings sometimes fail to act rationally, some more than others, coercion becomes necessary. However, it should be minimized, placed in the care of a legitimate public authority, and exercised according to clearly stated and rationally defensible laws. The basic idea behind civil society is to minimize all avoidable forms of coercion and to maximize the area of associative freedom.

Since different societies have different histories, the idea of civil society plays a different part and acquires a different degree of urgency in their political discourse. In the erstwhile communist countries, the state was an overpowering presence in society and stifled all areas of life. Not surprisingly, when communism collapsed, the demand for the long-suppressed associative freedom dominated popular consciousness and the concept of civil society became the central category of political discourse, especially among creative writers, trade unionists and political activists, who had suffered the most from its absence. Asian and African experiences were different. Despite its brutality, the colonial state there was not unduly oppressive, and left considerable space for associative freedom. At independence the idea of civil society did not therefore dominate their political discourse. Their primary concern was how to organize and structure their political life so that the state pursued developmental goals and remained accountable to its people. Insofar as they thought of civil society, they looked to the state to nurture it and, where necessary, to create its preconditions.

Since different societies hold different conceptions of human life, they take different views on the role of coercion in social life and what areas should or should not be subjected to it. In deeply religious societies, the economic life is regulated by moral and religious norms enforced by religious organizations and social pressure. It does not enjoy the autonomy that it does in the modern bourgeois society, and is not generally seen as part of civil society. Again, in different societies, different social institutions limit associative freedom. In some it is tribes, in some others castes, in yet others religion. In each case the struggle to create a civil society involves different targets and strategies, and the resulting structure of civil society has a different character. We should not therefore make the mistake of thinking that civil society must have the same shape and form the world over, or that an institution that forms part of civil society in one country must also form part of it in another. Rather than universalize the Western history and model of civil society and expect all others to conform to it, we need to take different views of it and appreciate its diverse forms. It is odd, even self-contradictory, to take a monistic view of the very area of life that is supposed to be the home of plurality.

CRITICAL ASSESSMENT

Civil society has much to be said for it, and the associative freedom that forms its constitutive principle is an essential part of a well-organized society. Freedom, including associative freedom, is an emblem of human dignity and sense of self-worth. By freely associating with others in pursuit of personal and common purposes, human beings also express and cultivate their sociability, discover themselves, develop civic virtues, and grow to their full stature. Economic, professional, neighbourhood, civic and other associations arrest the atomization and feeling of helplessness inherent in modern industrialized society, generate multiple centres of power, cultivate moral and social discipline, provide formal and informal spaces in which to interact with others and rise above one's subjectivity, and foster social cohesion. They also provide a vitally necessary counterweight to the state and limit its power. All states have a tendency to become remote and arrogant, and need to be checked by citizens' movements and NGOs. Furthermore, power accrues to the state through its functions. As citizens assign more and more functions to it out of inertia, apathy or indolence, it acquires more and more power and legitimacy. It cannot be controlled merely by means of an internal system of checks and balances, because that only regulates its exercise of power and does not decrease the amount of power and moral status it enjoys. We need to limit its range of functions by fostering the spirit of self-help among its citizens and encouraging them to undertake as many of them as possible through voluntary associations. A vibrant civil society ensures that citizens accept the responsibility for their shared life, and do not alienate their power to and help create an overbearing state.

While these and other virtues of a vibrant civil society are obvious, much of the discourse on it exaggerates its importance and gets it out of perspective. The discourse has a built-in bias against non-voluntary associations. As we saw, it is based on the deeply held belief that as free and self-determining agents human beings should not be subject to the authority of associations they have not themselves created and which they cannot leave at will. Associations based on traditional allegiances, ties of blood, inherited loyalties or the 'accident' of birth – such as castes, clans, tribes and ethnic and religious communities – are viewed with disfavour. They are to be discouraged, even dismantled, in order that their members can be fully free, and civil society can emerge in its purest and uncompromised form. Where they are not dismantled, for prudential reasons, their presence is regretted, and their members are seen as unfree, truncated and even inadequate human beings.

This bias against non-voluntary associations is unjustified. They do have their obvious drawbacks. They sometimes have rigid norms, oppressive practices and structures of authority, limited mutual contacts, and encourage frozen social identities and narrow loyalties. However, they also have their strengths. They are often historical communities with deep bonds based on shared collective memories of struggles, achievements and failures. They encourage a strong sense of social obligation, mutual commitment, and spirit of self-sacrifice. They provide a readily available network of support and represent a valuable resource for their members and an asset to the wider society.

Since they are not deliberately created and cannot be dissolved or left with ease, they have tenacity, are free of volatile individual impulses, tend to strike deep roots in the lives of their members, and evoke strong attachments and loyalties. They are narrow but deep, demand much but also offer much, and make up for some loss of liberty by offering a sense of existential security and rootedness. They can certainly corrupt public life by encouraging nepotism and narrow partiality, but voluntary associations are not free from these vices either. While ensuring that they do not become oppressive and deny exit to dissenting members, we should value the contribution they make to the good life. Not all voluntary associations are inherently good, nor all non-voluntary ones inherently bad.

While voluntary associations form civil society, non-voluntary associations form community. In civil society we meet as strangers, colleagues, neighbours, fellow professionals, fellow trade unionists, and citizens; in a community as friends, kin, fellow ethnics, Jews, Catholics, tribespeople, and speakers of a common language. Civil society is based on reciprocity, distance, respect for rules, loyalty to institutions, and so on; community on intimacy, affection, warmth and mutual concern. Civil society nurtures associative life, community communal life. In civil society we share common interests and hobbies and 'bowl' together, to use an evocative image of Robert Putnam's (Putnam 2000). In a community, we celebrate common festivals, grieve together, holiday together or spend Christmas together. 'Bowling alone' represents the decline of civil society; grieving or spending Christmas alone that of community.

In many Western societies, traditional communities have largely disappeared, and almost all social relations including the family are cast in the mould of civil society. This has brought both gains and losses. While individualism, the adventure of self-creation and civil society have flourished, communities have declined. The voluntarist spirit that drives civil society has a tendency to encourage expectations, attitudes and values that militate against the inherited loyalties and acceptance of non-contractual obligations and traditional bonds that lie at the heart of communal life. In many non-Western societies the opposite is the case. Communities of different kinds remain strong, but civil society is weak. While they need to foster civil society, there is no obvious reason why they must be expected to declare a war on communities. They can create a space for civil society by loosening up and restructuring rather than destroying these communities, as Indians are doing with castes, African societies with clans and tribes, and Muslim societies with their religious institutions. The Western model of civil society is culturally and historically specific and has its obvious limitations. It should not be held up as a universal norm and used to mould the rest of the world in the Western image, as is currently done by many enthusiastic governmental and non-governmental champions of civil society.

The second limitation of the discourse on civil society has to do with its failure to give an adequate account of the nature and role of the state. This is so because it considers coercion inherently evil, identifies the state with it and civil society with its absence, and aims to maximize the role of civil society at the expense of that of the state. The distinction between the coercive state and non-coercive civil society is too crude and sharp to do justice to either. The state certainly uses coercion, but it also does much more. It plays symbolic, inspirational, educative, facilitative and coordinating roles. It symbolizes the unity of society, fosters social cohesion, and gives society a sense of historical continuity and depth. It enshrines certain norms and values in its institutions and practices, and embodies a particular vision of the good life. It nurtures formal equality and encourages the ideas of fair trial and procedural justice in a society that might be wholly innocent of them. It can use its coercive power to challenge vested interests, remove unacceptable inequalities, fight pockets of coercion in different areas of social life, and increase the freedom and opportunities of its citizens.

Just as the state is not exclusively coercive, civil society is not wholly non-coercive. It does, of course, ensure associative freedom, this being true by definition, but the freedom is not and cannot be without constraints. All associations affect public order and public interest, and the state cannot be indifferent to their structures and practices. It may rightly ban associations that incite religious, ethnic or racial hatred, and require that they should not discriminate against blacks, untouchables, gays or women, or impose unacceptable cost on their dissenting or departing members. Civil society does not precede or exist outside or behind the back of the state. Instead it is made possible by the state, which both permits and protects associative freedom, and exists as a moment, a space, within it.

Although associative freedom is most valuable, or rather precisely because it is so valuable, we must avoid the mistake of dissociating it from its wider context, as Marx highlighted, the formally equal civil, political and other rights are unequally enjoyed in an unequal society and even used to legitimize and perpetuate it. This is just as true of associative freedom. Although it is in principle equally available to all in a well-ordered society, in practice its exercise is highly uneven. The poor and the marginalized are often too atomized and overwhelmed by a sense of powerlessness to have the confidence to set up vibrant associations. They also often lack the necessary skills and resources, and do not understand the complex mechanisms of the modern society well enough to target its weak spots. It is hardly surprising that civil society in almost all societies is dominated by the middle classes, and even the organizations of the oppressed and marginalized are often set up and led by the middle classes. The powerless find it difficult to organize and, since organization represents power, their failure perpetuates and intensifies their powerlessness.

Associative freedom, further, can be used to legitimize state inaction. Since the state is expected to ensure maximum space to civil society it is required to pursue minimum goals and to intervene as little as possible in economic and social life. This is how Oakeshott, Hayek, Friedman and others justify a libertarian state in the name of civil society. For these and related reasons, we should not make the mistake of idealizing civil society in the abstract. We need to ask how it is constituted, who exercises and benefits from associative freedom, and how we should restructure civil society so that all citizens and groups can exercise it equally. Since the state can play a vital emancipatory role here, we should not allow it to be undermined by an uncritical ideological commitment to the maximum autonomy of civil society.

Voluntary associations, social movements, and so on that comprise civil society lack historical continuity, and are often issue-based and unable to take a long-term and comprehensive view of society. They are not popularly elected and accountable, and sometimes they are authoritarian and remote from their members. Their decision-making procedures are not always transparent, and their decisions open to public scrutiny. It is wrong to assume that just because an association is voluntary, it is democratic or speaks for all its members, or that a protest movement against the policies of the state necessarily serves public interest or even that of those in whose name it claims to speak. We should not homogenize the civil society, which encompasses a wide variety of networks, interests and associations not all of which are equally welcome. And nor should we take the naive view that all coercion is inherently undesirable. Coercion tends to spring up subtly and stealthily in so many different areas of life and forms of social relations that the coercion of the state often becomes necessary to monitor and deal with it.

The civil society and the state are based on different principles and play a complementary role. Neither can replace nor should be privileged over the other. A varied and vibrant civil society gives the state moral depth and political vitality, even as a justly constituted state creates the conditions in which all its citizens can build a rich world of networks and associations. Rather than set up an abstract opposition between the two, a well-considered political theory should establish a partnership between them on terms that are relevant to our times. Locke's and Adam Smith's reduction of the state to civil society disables it from dealing with corporate capitalism and grave social and economic injustices. Hegel saw the importance of both the civil society and the state better than any other writer, but made the mistake of romanticizing the state, overestimating its independence, and underestimating the tensions of civil society. Marx and Gramsci avoided his mistakes, but naively thought that once the classes were abolished the state could be dissolved into a loosely coordinated structure of the voluntary associations of socialized individuals. Many contemporary writers, including Walzer, idealize civil society without fully appreciating how deeply it is implicated with the economy and the state. Cohen and Arato's (1992) work provides a stimulating account of how the discourses on civil society and democracy should be integrated. While drawing on the rich insights of the tradition of discourse on civil society from Hobbes to Walzer, we also need to correct and go beyond them.

References

Cahoone, L. (2002), *Civil Society: The Conservative Meaning of Liberal Policies*, Oxford: Blackwell.

Cohen, J. and Arato, A. (1992), *Civil Society and Political Theory*, Cambridge MA: MIT Press.

Ehrenberg, J. (1999), *Civil Society: The Critical History of an Idea*, New York: New York University Press.

Ferguson, A. (1767), 'An Essay on the History of Civil Society', Cambridge: Cambridge University Press.

Gramsci, A. (1971), 'Selections from Prison Notebooks', Edited and Translated by Q. Hoare and G. Nowell Smith, London; Lawrence and Wishart.

Keene, J. (1998), *Civil Society: Old Images, New Visions, Stanford*: Stanford University Press.

Marx, K. and Engels, F. (1973), Selected Works, Vol. 1, Moscow: Progress Publishers.

Putnam, R. (2000), *Bowling Alone; The Collapse and Revival of American Community*, New York: Simon and Schuster.

Taylor, C. (1975), *Hegel*, Cambridge; Cambridge University Press.

Walzer, M. (ed.) (1994), *Toward a Global Civil Society, Providence RI*: Berghahn Books.

3

Nationalism and Civil Society: Democracy, Diversity and Self-Determination

Craig Calhoun

In 1989, the self-declared 'free world' reveled in the collapse of communism. Capitalism and democracy seemed simply and obviously triumphant. The Cold War was over. Everyone would live happily ever after.

Of course, there would be 'transitional problems.' Word came of fighting in Nagorno-Karabak. It crossed some minds that many residents of Soviet Central Asia might find fundamentalist Islam more appealing than American capitalism. Enthusiasm for Lithuanian nationalism was occasionally dimmed by memories of Lithuanian fascism and anti-Semitism. But in an efflorescence of faith in progress not seen since the nineteenth century, most western politicians and intellectuals confidently saw 'excesses' of nationalism as at most minor detours on the road to capitalist democracy. Even thinkers on the left joined the enthusiasm and, embarrassed by seeming association with the losing side, hastened to forget the lessons of history and the need for serious analysis.

But 1989 imperceptibly gave way to 1992, and anxiety began to regain a little intellectual respectability. Still, it has taken quite dramatic events, from Ethiopia to the former Soviet Union and especially Yugoslavia, to focus attention on the possibility that nationalism might be more than a passing problem. Serbian talk of 'ethnic cleansing' brought shudders of recollection, yet many treated it – like the Nazi ideology it recalled – as a throwback to the pre-modern. It is no accident, however, that 'ethnic cleansing' is the project of academics and technicians, not of peasants, just as Nazism was rooted in scientific discourse and technological dreams as well as old hatreds. Both are fundamentally and horribly modern. And if nationalism is a central problem of post-communist transitions, this is because it is a central way of organizing collective identity throughout the modern world.

Academics have repeatedly announced the death of nationalism, but like that of Mark Twain's demise, the reports have been greatly exaggerated. In one of the most recent waves of such assertions, analysts correctly observe that states are having difficulty organizing and controlling global markets, multinational corporations, large-scale migration flows and internal 'tribalism.' Yet these analysts seldom consider the possibility that, rather than spelling the end of nationalism, all these trends and difficulties are its occasion. All encourage the renewal and continuing production of nationalism because nationalism is the rhetoric of identity and solidarity in which citizens of the modern world most readily deal with the problematic nature of state power and with problems of inclusion and exclusion. Rather than following state-building in a neat correlation, nationalism is mostly an issue where the boundaries and power of a state do not coincide neatly with the will or identity of its members or the scale of action undertaken by other collective actors.

Nationalist claims are one genre of answers to the question of what constitutes an autonomous political community capable of 'self-determination.' These claims come in two main versions: one places crucial stress on the ethnic or cultural similarity of the members of a political community; the other on their common citizenship in a specific state (with its characteristic modes of political activity). But in both versions, nationalist answers to the question of what constitutes a political community underestimate the importance of the institutions, networks, and movements that knit people together across lines of diversity internal to nations and states; they underestimate, in other words, the specifically sociological problems of social integration.

Nationalism appeared in the post-1989 discourse on transitions to democracy – and in theories of democracy generally – primarily as a hazard to be avoided, not as a central dimension of the subject. Yet nationalism is directly and fundamentally involved in questions about the social foundations for democracy. Leaving nationalism to one side theoretically – and too often anti-democratic activists in practice – the discourse on transitions did sometimes take up the question of what social foundations enable a collectivity of people to organize their institutions through popular political participation. It did so most prominently under the rubric of 'civil society.' This concept was invoked to account for the various resources outside direct state control that offered alternatives to the state organization of collective life. In many invocations, thus, the role of more or less self-regulating markets or processes of capital accumulation was not distinguished from the roles of networks of interpersonal relations, social movements and public discourse.

The significance of this became apparent when the economic challenges of post-communist transition began to compete with efforts to increase democratic participation. Various different programmes for the rapid creation of 'free-market' economies, thus, were all claimed by their proponents to strengthen civil society, whether or not they increased the capacity of ordinary people to join together in associations and movements or otherwise to create a public sphere capable of shaping social and political decisions on the basis of rational-critical discourse. Many of these programmes of economic privatization, in fact, did relatively little to increase the extent of popular participation in decisions regarding investment and economic structure. While some did seek to increase opportunities for entrepreneurship and the development of new small businesses, others focused more on transferring large-scale state enterprises to 'private' owners. The link between the two was faith in the importance of subjecting as much as possible of the formerly 'administered' economies to the discipline of the market. The market, however, was understood as an abstract, impersonal and self-regulating force, and moreover one that either did or should transcend national and state boundaries.

A tension was created, in short, between the pursuit of democratization and the pursuit of economic development. The former was seen as essentially a matter of domestic institutions and actions while the latter involved participation in an increasingly global economy. The constraints and demands imposed by the effort to compete in this global economy were and are frequently cited as reasons for limiting or postponing the project of increasing democratic participation. Indeed, perhaps paradoxically, voters in the new electoral democracies have even been persuaded on several occasions that voting their pocketbooks meant voting against democratization. The prestige of the cadres of international economic consultants brought in to replace the cadres of communist central planners has often been placed behind such conclusions. The result often has been to replace the imperatives of party and state bureaucracies with the imperatives of impersonal market forces as interpreted by technical experts and politicians.

In confronting so dramatically the tension between economic globalization and the pursuit of democracy through domestic institutions, the ex-communist and newly independent states of Eastern Europe highlight an issue faced much more generally in the contemporary world. A broad range of commentators and pundits have pointed to globalization and suggested that the era of the nation-state is at an end.[1] The mobility of capital and impossibility of containing economic activity within the bounds of state control allegedly suggest that states are no longer crucial units of organization and power. This misrepresents, however, the nature and significance of economically driven globalization. First, this is not an entirely new trend, but a continuation of the historical pattern of the whole modern era. Second, this economic globalization may reduce certain of the capacities of states, but it does not make them less important or imply that in general they are likely either to break up or amalgamate. Modern states have always existed and derived much of their significance from their contraposition to other states in a 'world system' that has always been too large for any single state to control. States have existed in part to manage economic – and also military – relations that cross their boundaries. What is most distinctive about the current globalization is not that it creates a level of global integration that states cannot readily manage, but that it brings close to completion the process of continuously incorporating more and more parts of the world into the capitalist world system.[2]

The travails of Eastern Europe reveal that incorporation into the global economy does not stop states from being crucial arenas of struggle. States remain the organizations of power through which democratic movements have the greatest capacity to affect economic organization. Given the current organization of the United Nations, states remain the highest level of institutional structure at which programmes of democratization themselves can consistently be advanced. And states remain the most crucial objects and vehicles of efforts to achieve 'self-determination' or autonomy as a political community. As states remain of crucial importance, so too does the ideology of nationalism. Characteristic of the whole modern era, this reflects the constitution of the modern world system as a system of states. The primacy of national identity is implicit in both sides of the Eastern European transition. It is what gives force to the notion of using domestic institutions to attempt to position a people in the global economy. It is also what constitutes the most basic notion of a people capable of claiming rights over and against a government. This is equally the case whether the claims are those of secession or more simply of self-governance without change of borders. The definition of boundaries and constitution of a collective identity are crucial components of the constitution of a political community in the modern world system of states.

The problems of collective identity formation are commonly ignored by democratic theory. They are, however, endemic to modern political life. Nationalism, as the most potent discourse of collective identity, appears alike in projects of unity and division. It may be an irony of history, thus, but it is not a sociological contradiction that Western Europe is pursuing the path of unification at the same time that Eastern European countries are being rent by nationalist splits. By the same token, however, this reveals that nationalism is not itself an adequate explanation of such processes of integration or disintegration so much as it is a political rhetoric in which many of them are pursued.

Discussions of the idea of nation and of social integration need therefore to be joined. The theory of democracy needs to deal with both of the two senses in which they raise the question of how political communities are constituted. The first is the bounded nature of all political communities, and the embeddedness of all claims to constitute a distinct and autonomous political community in relationships of contraposition to other such communities or claimants. The second is the web of relationships that constitutes a people (or nation) as a social collectivity existing independently of common subjection to the rule of a particular state.

CIVIL SOCIETY

It is not mere coincidence that the opposition to totalitarian role and the transition to democracy have brought ideas about civil society to the foreground. The language of civil society – though often sociologically underdeveloped – has been the most prominent way in which claims to peoplehood and self-determination have been grounded in appeals to social integration. The events of 1989 catapulted this concern from academic circles to the broader public discourse. The phrase is now on the lips of foundation executives, business leaders, and politicians; it seems as though every university has set up a study group on civil society, and the phrase finds its way into half the dissertations in political sociology. Too often, the phrase is invoked without sorting out whether civil society means Milton Friedman's capitalist market policies or social movements like Solidarity or the sort of 'political society' or 'public sphere' beloved of thinkers from Montesquieu to Tocqueville and Habermas, and once thought to exist mainly in cafes and coffee houses.[3]

Two basic questions are raised in discussions of civil society. First, what counts as or defines a political community? Second, what knits society together, providing for social integration? There are several contenders in each case: state, market economy, cultural similarity (e.g., nationality), social networks, political participation by autonomous agents. The idea of civil society entered political philosophy and social theory as a way of describing the capacity of self-organization on the part of a political community, in other words the capacity of a society to organize itself without being organized by a state. If society had such capacity, then 'the people' integrated in that society could better be seen as the source of political legitimacy rather than merely the object of rule. In some early uses – notably the Scottish moralists including Ferguson and Smith – the notion of civil society referred to all such non-state capacities for social organization. The economy was not only included, it provided a key example. To these early capitalist thinkers, the self-regulating character of markets demonstrated the possibility for social organization without the direction of the state.

As Charles Taylor has argued, however, it is crucial to distinguish two different branches of the discourse of civil society.[4] While one followed Ferguson and Smith in stressing the economic-systemic character of civil society, the other followed Montesquieu, Rousseau and Tocqueville in stressing social relations entered into by autonomous agents. The Eastern European discourse of the 1980s and much of the recent usage blurs important distinctions between the two.[5]

The issue is not solved by declaring that civil society must be kept conceptually distinct from capitalist economic organization. On the contrary, capitalism itself appears in both voluntary and systemic guises. On the one hand, capitalist ideology typically asserts that capitalist economic life is precisely the realm of free social relations. It offers a model of capitalist life as quintessentially the activity and relationships of owner-operators of small businesses and individual consumers. One might object that these are relations only among buyers and sellers, but one cannot deny that capitalism offers certain genuine freedoms. At the same time, capitalist ideology itself negates its proffered freedom by reference to the immutable 'laws' of the market. It claims that the systemic character of markets dictates that interference from states or other collective actors (unions, social movements, etc.) must be kept to a minimum so that the capitalist system can organize itself. This kind of limit on free collective action is asserted by capitalist ideology itself, even when it refuses to recognize the salient distinctions between giant corporations and human individuals, or the inevitable dependence and mutuality between capitalist economics and certain forms of state support.

Nonetheless, capitalism did historically and can still play a special and crucial role in the growth of a civil society. The early growth of capitalist business relations provided essential support to the development of a sphere of political discourse outside the realm of state control. This is not to say that businessmen were the primary protagonists of the bourgeois public sphere. On the contrary, various state employees from ministerial clerks through university professors, and dependents of aristocratic sponsors played far more central roles in the eighteenth-century 'golden age' of the public sphere. But the development of a public discourse in which private persons addressed public issues was made possible, in part, by both the policy issues posed by the growth of the non-state-dominated market activity, and the creation of settings for such discourse in coffee houses, journals, and other forums operated as businesses.[6]

It is crucial not to accept capitalist ideology uncritically, and therefore to imagine that capitalism is somehow by itself an adequate support for democracy or a viable alternative to state power. It is equally crucial not to ignore the role of certain kinds of at least quasi-autonomous business institutions in facilitating the development of a sphere of public discourse and capacity for social organization outside the immediate control of the state. Above all, we must look beyond capitalism (and more generally beyond the narrow realm of the economy as a putatively self-sufficient and self-regulating system) to seek (1) the extent to which societal integration can be accomplished through webs of interpersonal relations, and (2) the extent to which both these social relations and the more abstract ones of the economy can be organized voluntarily through public discourse. Only when these possibilities are addressed do we have a conception of societal integration that can serve as foundation to a theory of democracy.

In other words, from the point of view of democracy, it is essential to retain in the notion of civil society some idea of a social realm which is neither dominated by state power nor simply responsive to the systemic features of capitalism. The public sphere of civil society cannot be simply a realm in which representatives of state authority vie for attention with economists claiming to predict the economy like the weather on the basis of its reified laws. It must include an institutionally organized and substantial capacity for people to enter as citizens into public discourse about the nature and course of their life together. This capacity depends not just on formal institutions, but on civil society as a realm of sociability.

In this conceptualization, civil society must also be a realm of intermediate associations. Communities, movements, and organizations (from churches to political parties and mutual aid societies) are all potentially important. Though the nationalist impulse is sometimes to condemn these as intrinsically 'partial,' this needs to be affirmed as one of their major virtues. For it is precisely in such partial social units that people find both the capacity for collective voice and the possibility of differentiated, directly interpersonal relations. Such intermediate associations are also the crucial defenses both of distinctive identities imperiled by the normalization of the mass, and of democracy against oligarchy.[7]

Hidden in this discourse – in two centuries of public discourse as well as in the last few paragraphs – is the problem of identifying 'the people' who may be members of a discursive public or a civil society. From its earliest instantiations, from classical Athens through revolutionary America or Enlightenment Europe, the democratic public sphere has been marred by exclusionary tendencies. Not just slaves, but non-natives, aboriginals, propertyless men and all women have been excluded at various points from both direct political participation (e.g., voting) and from participation in the discourse of the public sphere. Some other exclusions seem more justifiable, though the theoretical status of the justifications is complex: the participation of children, criminals, and the mentally incompetent is almost universally restricted. In short, 'the people' have not all been citizens.

That democracy has always been restrictive has certainly been noticed. But there is an equally basic version of the question 'who are the people?' which is less often posed. When we say, for example in relation to the breakup of Yugoslavia that we believe in the right of 'self-determination,' just what self is involved? The notion of self-determination is basic to democracy, and yet both neglected by democratic theory and shrouded in illusions of primordiality. The problem of self-determination is that for every socially relevant self we can see internal divisions and vital links to others. There is no single, definite, and fixed 'peoplehood' which can be assumed in advance of political discussion.

Moreover, as 'no man is an island unto himself,' no nation exists alone.[8] Each is defined in relation to others and exists within a web of social relationships that traverse its boundaries. Supposed historical autarky was never complete, and modern attempts to close borders have had only partial and temporary success.[9] Conversely, claims to indivisibility are always at least partially tendentious and often (as in the United States pledge of allegiance) recognitions of the successful application of force to preserve unity. In short, do we speak of Macedonians, Croats and Serbs, of Yugoslavians, of Slavs, of Christians and Muslims, or of Europeans? The answers are obvious only from particular and partisan vantage points. Too often it is only forcible repression which makes us sure we see a true national identity. We lack a theory of the constitution of social selves which will give descriptive foundation to the prescriptive notion of self-determination. We are poorly prepared to talk about national identity or nationalism.[10]

NATIONALITY AND NATIONALISM

Ideologists of nationality almost always claim it as an inheritance rather than a contemporary construct. This is true whether the inheritance is conceived as a 'primordial' identity, rooted deep in the mists of ancient history, or as deriving from a more recent founding moment like the French Revolution.[11] The notion of inheritance is not by any means simply false, for national identity is something that shapes individuals – a Durkheimian social fact, external, enduring, and coercive – not a matter of completely free individual choice. Claims to ancient origins and especially primordiality are, however, problematic. At the very least, they nearly always radically oversimplify the complexities of national identity and history. The issue is not just whether people are members of one or another nation, or whether a particular claimed nation has the right to self-determination, but what it means to be a member of that nation, how it is to be understood, and how it relates to the other identities its members may also claim or be ascribed.[12]

Such notions of primordial inheritance are among of the bases for the widespread illusion that somehow earlier traditions and identities can just be picked up and the communist era treated as an inconsequential interregnum. Among some groups in Russia, for example – and in a good deal of western discussion of Russia – the idea is current that the 'real' Russia is that of the czars. To some this means an ancient spiritual identity, preserved through long travails and waiting to flower again as beacon to all Slavs. To others, this means a political and cultural development, moving forward rapidly in the late nineteenth and early twentieth centuries, when Russia could aspire to European leadership. Protagonists of each interpretation imagine that somehow when the pall of communism is lifted, the Russians of the late twentieth century will begin to write like Tolstoy and pick up the torch of an interrupted political development. In this remembered history, the struggles against Orthodox religion, against czarist rule and rural landlords, and between narodniki, bourgeois democrats, and various stripes of socialists are somehow submerged, and communism becomes something both alien and accidental, not an outgrowth of national history.

In Hungary, it is easier to make the case that communism was something imposed from outside, but it is still not obvious that the nation can simply go forward in 1992 as a direct extension of that of 1945's imposed communism or 1921's repression of revolution. Is national identity simply ancient and timeless? Or has it been forged and remade in centuries of struggle? What is the relationship between the Hungary which struggled against Habsburg rule – and flowered under it, the Hungary which struggled to maintain independence and build a modern state in the early twentieth century, that of Nazi rule and resistance to it, that of communism, both domestic and imported, that of the Georg Lukacs who lived in Budapest and the one who lived in Moscow, that of 1919 (just after collapse of the Austro-Hungarian empire), 1956 (rebellion against communism and its crushing), and 1989 (communism's collapse)? Different answers to these questions flow from different visions of what it means to be Hungarian. There are similar questions in every country's history, and they are central to the reasons why nationalism is always caught in an intimate but ambiguous relationship with history. Nationalist movements always revere martyrs and cherish sacred dates; they always give nations a history. But as Ernest Renan wrote in perhaps the most famous essay ever written on the subject, 'Forgetting, I would even go so far as to say historical error, is a crucial factor in the creation of a nation, which is why progress in historical studies often constitutes a danger for [the principle of] nationality. Indeed, historical enquiry brings to light deeds of violence which took place at the origin of all political formations, even those whose consequences have been altogether beneficial. Unity is always effected by means of brutality ...'[13]

The issue goes further. History is problematic for nationalism and the tacit assumption of national identity because it always shows nationality to be constructed, not primordial. The history which nationalism would write of itself begins with the existence of national identity, continues through acts of heroism and sometimes struggles against oppression, and unites all living members of the nation with the great cultural accomplishments of its past. It is usually not a sociological history, of diversity forged into unity, of oppression of some members of the nation by others, of migration and immigration, and so forth. Precisely because it is not a sociological history, it allows all present-day Russians to identify with nineteenth-century novelists, and for the westernizing efforts of Peter the Great to make him now a nationalist hero. And even in cosmopolitan Budapest it encourages some Hungarian patriots to identify with Magyar horsemen, accept centuries of international influences, and yet think of Hungarian Jews as members of an alien nation.

So nationality is not primordial but constructed. It is, moreover, a construction specific to the modern era and to the emergence of a modern world system in which claims to statehood became crucial bases for standing in world affairs, and potentially for autonomy, and in which claims to statehood can be justified most readily by professions of nationhood. This does not make nationality or the sentiments of nationhood any less real. But by the same token, nationality is not more real than many other identities which people may 'claim, or feel, or reproduce in their social relations. The nationalist claim is that national identity is categorical and fixed, and that somehow it trumps all other sorts of identities, from gender to region, class to political preference, occupation to artistic taste. This is a very problematic claim.

It is not easy to define nationalism. There are important variations where different cultures are at issue, where conquest has subordinated one group of people to another, where older ethnic groupings are being recast in terms of the idea of nation, and where an attempt is being made to forge a new unity out of previous diversity. It seems better to see nationalisms in terms of family resemblances (following Wittgenstein) rather than to search for an essentialist definition of nationalism. When we speak of nationalism, thus, we speak of a somewhat arbitrary subset of claims to identity and autonomy on the part of populations claiming the size and capacity to be self-sustaining. For the purpose of any specific analysis we may want to include, say, the religious and political struggles in Northern Ireland or keep them distinct; there is no perfect boundary, no criterion of selecting nationalisms which includes all the familiar cases we are sure we want to consider without also including a variety of dubious outliers.

With more confidence, we can address the underlying factors which gave rise to nationalism and made it a major genus of identity claim and source of political mobilization in the modern era. Indeed, by noting these underlying factors we can see why in a strong sense only the modern era has produced nationalism. People have always been joined in groups. These groups have derived their solidarity from kinship and other forms of social (including economic) interconnection, from a common structure of political power, from shared language and culture. But in the modern era, cultural and social structural factors have converged to create and disseminate the notion of national identity and make it central.

Culturally, the most decisive idea behind nationalism (or national identity) is the modern notion of the individual. The idea that human beings can be understood in themselves as at least potentially self-sufficient, self-contained, and self-moving is vital. It is no accident that Fichte is crucial to the histories of both individualism and nationalism. For Fichte's notion of self-recognition, of the person who seemingly confronts himself (or herself) in a mirror and says 'I am I' is inextricably tied to the notion of the nation as itself an individual. Just as persons are understood as unitary in prototypical modern thought, so are nations held to be integral. As Benedict Anderson has indicated, this involves a special sense of time as the history through which the nation as perduring and unitary being passes rather than as a differentiable internal history of the nation.[14] The process of individuation is important not just metaphorically, but as the basis for the central notion that individuals are directly members of the nation, that it marks each of them as an intrinsic identity and they commune with it immediately and as a whole. In ideology, at least, the individual does not require the mediations of family, community, region, or class to be a member of the nation. This is a profound reversal of the weight of competing loyalties from the pre-modern era (and much of the rest of the world). In this we see the sharp difference of nationalism from the ideology of honour of the lineage, and the chilling potential for children to inform on their parents' infractions against the nation.[15]

Nineteenth-century ideologists of nationalism emphasized a world-historical (or evolutionary) process of individuation in which the world's peoples took on their distinctive characters, missions, and destinies. Or at least the world's 'historical nations' did so; others lacked sufficient vigour or national character; they were destined to be failures and consigned to the backwaters of history. Not surprisingly, this is typically how dominant or majority populations thought of minorities and others subordinated within their dominions. This was another conceptualization, in effect, of the Springtime of Nations. It was the period when France took on its 'mission civilisatrice,' Germany found its historical destiny, and Poles crystallized their Romantic conception of the martyr-nation.[16] Each nation had a distinct experience and character, something special to offer the world and something special to express for itself. 'Nations are individualities with particular talents and the possibilities of exploiting those talents.'[17]

It is no accident, thus, that philosophers like Fichte emphasized simultaneously the individuation of the person and of the nation. The two notions remain inextricably linked.[18] This very linkage, however, could create tensions. The great cultural geniuses of a nation's history were widely celebrated in the nineteenth century; the proliferation of individual geniuses was proof, especially for the Romantics, of the greatness of the nation. Though Norway had but recently gained an independent cultural status (and was not yet independent politically) her production of geniuses in the late nineteenth century, from Munch to Grieg to Ibsen, was proof enough of her standing even for the German intellectuals of the period. But being cast as the bearer of national identity was not always entirely comfortable for geniuses (or others) with their own individual identities. Writing to Ibsen on his 70th birthday in 1898, the Norwegian poet Nils Kjoer tried to recover something of the autonomy of the, person from the demand for representation of national character: "But a people's individuality is manysided, sufficient to explain any peculiarity of the mind and therefore it explains nothing."[19] If recognized geniuses could feel a tension with the demand that they serve as icons of the nation, pressures of a much more troubling nature were (and are) brought to bear on cultural deviants and minorities.[20] Though nations are ideologically composed of individuals, they are not generally promoters of individual distinctiveness. In the formative phases of nationalism, heroic individuals – cultural as well as military and political heroes – figure prominently, but often in the established nation, conformity to the common culture becomes a central value. The character of nationalism is changed as it shifts from insurgent movement to dominant ideology, though even insurgents can be sharply intolerant of diversity. It is easier to admire heroes from afar, and easiest to claim them when they are dead.

The key structural change which makes it possible to conceive of the nation as unitary is the rise of the modern state. Previous political forms neither demarcated clear boundaries nor fostered internal integration and homogenization. Cities dominated hinterlands; sometimes particularly powerful cities dominated networks of others together with their hinterlands. The various kinds of military (and sometimes religious) elites we call 'feudal' controlled substantial territories but with a minimum of centralization of power and limited ability to remake everyday life. Though empires could call on subject peoples for tribute and sometimes foster substantial interaction among diverse subjects, they posed few demands for cultural homogenization. Yet the rise of the modern state involved remarkable administrative integration of previously quasi-autonomous regions and localities. This was true both for purposes of military contest with other states and for internal economic activity and political rule.[21] Eventually, state power could be exercised at the farthest point of a realm as effectively as in the capital. Not only could taxes be collected, but roads could be built, schools run, and mass communications systems created. Linguistic standardization is a common measure of national integration, and historical research reminds us how recent such standardization was in most European countries. Most Frenchmen did not speak French before the second half of the nineteenth century.[22] Even demographic behaviour – fertility rates, for example – which once varied from locality to locality, become strikingly uniform within nineteenth and twentieth century European nation-states.[23]

The capacity of states to administer distant territories with growing intensity was largely due to improvements in transportation and communications infrastructure, on the one hand, and bureaucracy and related information management on the other. It was part of a general growth in large-scale social relations. More and more of social life took place through forms of mediation – markets, communications technologies, bureaucracies – which removed relationships from the realm of direct, face-to-face interaction. 'In addition to facilitating state power, this growth in 'indirect' and large-scale relationships directly facilitated nationalism. It encouraged, for example, increasing reliance on categorical identities rather than webs of relational identities.[24] This transformation was closely related to the growth of capitalism. In the first place, a growing division of labour and intensification of trade relations knit localities and regions together in relations of mutual dependence. Capitalism continually drove its agents out beyond local markets, established competitive pressures around the globe, and demanded coordination of ever-growing supplies of labour and raw materials – even before the generation of increasing consumer demand became an obsession. Capitalism thus both depended on and continually increased the capacity for large-scale and indirect social relations. Because more and more of the activity on which lives and livelihoods depended was taking place at a distance from immediate locales, attempts to conceptualize the commonalities and connections among locales were increasingly important. Beyond this, connections established only through markets and the commodity form were especially prone to reification and representation in categorical terms. The nation became the domestic market, other nations international competitors or clients.[25]

Partly (though not entirely) under pressure of capitalist expansion, the entire world was divided into bounded territories. Every inch of land was declared the province of one state or another. No longer were there hinterlands in which people could follow their ways of life relatively undisturbed by pressures to conform to one or another state's dominant culture. Attempts to preserve local tradition now required active resistance. Where empires demanded mainly political loyalty, states imposed pressures for multifarious forms of cultural loyalty and participation. The opportunity for a people to be self-organizing was increasingly limited to those who could mount a successful claim to state sovereignty. Whatever the actual form of government claimants anticipated, from the moment that sovereignty came to be a claim from below, by the people, rather than from the rulers above, the modern ideal of the nation-state was born. Even Hobbes, in justifying the absolute sovereignty of kings, required first a body of citizens – a nation – capable of granting the right to rule in explicit or implicit social contract. And these citizens were, perforce, basically interchangeable as members of the nation.

This is a crucial contrast between the empire and the nation-state, or, as Weintraub has shrewdly noted, between the cosmopolitan city and the polis. The creation of a political community called for a new kind of interrelationships, and something more than a 'live and let live' urbanity. In the cosmopolis or empire, since 'heterogeneous multitudes were not called upon to be citizens, they could remain in apolitical coexistence, and each could do as he wished without the occasion to deliberate with his neighbours.'[26] In both the polis and the modern nation-state, membership in a common polity requires more than tolerance and common subjection to an external sovereign. It requires mutual communication. This poses an impetus for erasure of differences among the citizens. One of the crucial questions of the modern era is whether meaningful, politically efficacious public discourse can be achieved without this erasure.

The claim to be a nation was a claim to be entitled to a state (or at the very least, to special recognition in the constitution of a state). Though the reciprocal claim was not logically entailed, it was common. By the nineteenth century it was thought not only that every nation deserved a state, but that each state should represent one nation. Nationalism, as Ernest Gellner writes, held that nations and states 'were destined for each other; that either without the other is incomplete, and constitutes a tragedy.'[27] One of the features of this new way of conceptualizing sovereignty was that it treated all nation-states as formally equivalent, whatever their size or power. It was no longer possible to conceive of derogated levels of partial or subordinate sovereignty – kings and dukes below emperors, autonomous cities under the protection of princes, etc. Either Burgundy was part of France or it was an alien state; if part of France, it was merely part and not nation in itself. In the mid-nineteenth-century United States, extreme claims to 'states' rights' in a weak confederacy of strong subsidiary parts were not so much the claims of one or more alternative nationalisms as claims against nationalism itself. The 'country' to which Confederate soldiers owed a duty was conceived from the immediate family and local community outward (and largely through a hierarchy of aristocratic connections, not laterally). It was not conceived primarily as a categorical identity, coterminous with a single polity and culture.[28]

Just as the spread of capitalism created a world system in which only capitalist competition could be effective, so the division of the world into states created a continuing pressure for the production of nationalisms. Claims for greater autonomy or greater unity could gain legitimacy primarily as claims to create a nation-state, that is, to create a new state to match a pre-existing nation. This is why the single term nationalism encompasses both fissiparous or secessionist movements and unificationist or 'pan-'nationalist movements. Croatian or Ukrainian nationalism and pan-Slavic nationalism are dimensions of the same process. Programmes for the unification of Europe draw on new histories which emphasize the commonality of the European experience and identity; the specificity of Europe is counterposed to the rest of the world, rather than the specificity of France being counterposed to Britain or the Netherlands. At the same time, fringe nationalist movements (and claims for regional autonomy) flourish within the European Community, while on its eastern border, the former Yugoslavia and perhaps other countries seem set to splinter into tiny nation-states. Indeed, nationalist struggles in Eastern Europe reveal the continuing relevance of nationalism in a Western Europe whose publicists had claimed it had moved beyond it. Divergent visions of the European Community and divergent interests have been brought out not just by German unification, but by fighting in former Yugoslavia and appeals from Poland, Czechoslovakia, and Hungary for community membership. Not least of all, east-to-west migration both results from nationalist strife (and nationalist protectionism which creates economic strife) and contributes to xenophobic nationalist responses.

Contrary to some over-glib journalism, there is no global reason for nationalism to be more integrating or disintegrating. The same rhetoric can as readily be deployed to claim unity across separate states (all Slavs or all Arabs) as to demand autonomy for a region of one (e.g., Slovakia or Ruthenia). But there are global reasons why nationalism remains the central form of identity in which people pose their claims to sovereignty. The most important of these is simply the creation of the world system as a system of states. Though some analysts predict the dissolution of such states in a postmodern welter of local identities and global corporations, the states do not yet seem to have given up the ghost. Nationalism remains important in part because claims to state sovereignty do matter – not least of all because states remain the central organizational frameworks within which democracy can be pursued.

Of course, as state administrative power was growing, and the world was divided into bounded territories, not all potential nationalisms thrived.[29] A variety of factors helped. One was simply the history and development of nationalist discourse itself. As Anderson points out, nationalist discourse was not simply a product of simultaneous invention around the globe. It was, at least in part, diffused; in his view it originated in certain colonial experiences and was exported to Western Europe and thence re-exported.[30] The nationalist discourse has grown during the last 300 or so years; more is available as resource to latecomers. Within any putative nation as well, there may be greater or lesser history of nationalist discourse. There may be richer and more evocative discourses on national history and culture to provide particular content to nationalist aspirations. Specific experiences of external challenge or oppression may help to promote national consciousness, providing a clear and significant other for self-identification by contrast. It may be more or less possible to frame other discontents within the nationalist idiom. And other organizing bases, class above all, but also religious organizations, may be either absent or congruent and supportive rather than competitive.

By the same token, not all nationalisms take the same form. They are shaped in different international contexts and from different domestic experiences. Some grow in response to histories of direct colonialism, others in response to present weakness in the world system without any specific colonial antagonist to shape them.[31] Some are elite, others democratic. Some seem to absorb an entire culture, claiming everything from language and literature through political practices and agricultural methods as specific to the nation. Others are more narrowly political movements, recognizing common participation in a broader culture. And last but not least, nationalist movements are shaped by the periods of their flowering: it was easier to believe in a happy fellowship of nations in the 1840s than it is today.

NATIONALISM AS SUCCESSOR IDEOLOGY

As recently as the early Gorbachev years of the mid-1980s, the leadership of the Soviet Union was still propounding a modified vision of the happy fellowship of nations. The condition of this fellowship was the elimination of the social antagonisms which set capitalist nations against each other and made nationalist conflicts an attractive distraction from class struggle. As a book in Novosti's series on 'the Soviet Experience' put it, 'as social antagonisms disappeared under socialism, so did national strife and racial inequality and oppression in every form. The socialist multinational culture has been enriched through an intensive exchange of cultural and intellectual values. The socialist nations that have emerged in the USSR have formed a new historical community of people – the Soviet people. ... Today it would be no exaggeration to say that a feeling of being members of one family prevails among Soviet people.'[32] On the one hand, such lines from a work entitled 'How the Soviet Union Solved the Nationalities Question' seems laughably divorced from reality. On the other hand, a moment's reflection on the rapid return of nationalist conflict to what was once the Soviet sphere of influence reminds us why for so long Soviet ideology claimed the resolution of 'the nationalities question' as one of the central accomplishments of communism.

Nationalism enters contemporary politics most strikingly in the wake of communist crisis and retreat. As obviously in Ethiopia as in Eastern Europe, this has much to do with conditions which preceded (and sometimes coincided with) communism. Contemporary nationalism is, in part, a direct continuation of old struggles for autonomy from neighbours and stature among nations. This is accentuated in much of Eastern Europe (and western or central Asia) by the extent to which communism appeared in the guise of Russian domination. But Russian nationalism is also resurgent, so this cannot be the whole story. Similarly, communism was in many cases imposed on people who had not made a commitment to it through struggles of their own. This too has probably made nationalism more likely as a successor ideology, but its effects should not be exaggerated, for the countries in which communism had most indigenous strength before becoming a Soviet – supported state ideology do not seem markedly less prone to nationalism than those for which communism was more clearly an external imposition.

Communist regimes were perfectly prepared to try to mobilize nationalist sentiments to bolster their legitimacy. The Romanian state made a massive enterprise of reproducing folklore in ways it could both claim and control.[33] The reconstruction of historical buildings was a major part of post-war rebuilding in both Poland and Hungary. Enormous resources and prestige were invested in production of international athletic successes. At the same time, communist states acted in ways which highlighted national identities in arena where they officially denied or minimized their significance. Thus, Stalin sought to build 'socialism in one country,' and his Chinese counterparts still pursue 'communism with Chinese characteristics.'[34] Russia imposed its language as primary in the Soviet Union and secondary throughout the Warsaw pact. In Yugoslavia, the very stratagem of holding the country together by balancing national groups (and even making sure each nationally defined state contained regions with substantial members of other nationalities) reaffirmed infra-Yugoslavian national identities at the same time that it temporarily held nationalist rivalries in check.[35] Not least of all, the Soviet Army's occupation of much of Eastern Europe could hardly fail to stir some nationalist resentment, especially when coupled with political interference.

Indeed, the most basic reasons for nationalism to flourish in the wake of communism have to do with political repression, not socialist – or statist – economics. Communist states repressed most forms of subsidiary identities and discourses on alternative political arrangements. Faced with pressures or opportunities for collective action, people were thrown back on preexisting bases for identification and collective action. This worked in two ways. First, when people chafed under centralized misrule their national identities were the most readily available ways to understand and respond to abuse. Second, when communism collapsed, nationalism was available to take its place. The latter was true especially where communism collapsed without the development of strong indigenous movements of resistance and counterculture. In Poland, solidarity offered an alternative arena of cultural production and discourse – though of course solidarity had a strong nationalist current of its own. In varying degrees other Eastern European countries had both opportunities for cultural creativity and public discourse, and movements which both challenged the existing order and offered an alternative cultural discourse. In much of the Soviet Union, by contrast, repression was more severe, and insurgency from below less developed. One result was that in many settings – the Transcaucasus, for example – nationalism could emerge as the primary form of identity and the basic medium through which people expressed their aspirations for a better life.[36]

Communist states did not encourage the cultural creativity and free flow of discourse which could have both knit them together and opened a variety of bases of identity. This had several effects. It meant that in large and heterogeneous countries like the Soviet Union, only state-sponsored cultural productivity could work to unify the country as a whole. When the state lost its credibility, so did much of the cultural basis for unity at the largest level. Behind this suggestion is the general postulate that for populations to achieve some unity as citizenries, they need to be knit together by a common discourse. This does not mean that they are knit together simply by similarity of ideology. On the contrary, mere ideological similarity is a fairly brittle and easily fractured form of cultural unity, particularly when confronted with problems outside its familiar range. A shared .discourse of problem solving provides a stronger foundation for confronting new challenges. More generally, culture is a stronger source of unity when it is open to rich and varied forms of creation and discussion. When discussion and creativity are foreclosed in order to maintain ideological conformity, it becomes difficult to achieve the manifold continuous cultural adjustments which are essential to both legitimation processes and sense of common membership in a political community. So, ironically, the very attempt to maintain complete conformity undermined identification with the whole left it superficial and easily forgotten.[37]

At the same time, the absence of an open cultural sphere or political discourse meant that the development of multiple bases for individual identity was impeded. Outside the range of authoritarian rule and strong nationalism, it is common for people to gain their identities from a range of cross-cutting group affiliations (as Simmel suggested), and from membership in a variety of different salient cultural categories. Thus a woman in the United States may feel a strong sense of identity stemming from her occupation, her gender, her family, her community, her political activity, and her religion as well as and partially in competition with her nation. Though national identity may be a source of inspiration or pride, or of a sense of obligation to help others by pursuing the common good of the United States ahead of the general good of humanity, it is unlikely to be an identity which 'trumps' all others. Of course, it is an open question how long this would last if the US ever came under severe external pressure, or wars were again fought on American soil. Nationalism comes to the fore under a variety of historically specific circumstances – like war – as well as perhaps being comparatively stronger in some cultural traditions than others.[38]

In the face of such pressure – and its immediate memory, as in Eastern Europe – liberalism may seem a fairly thin ideology. Liberal capitalism is, however, the main ideological option offered by the West today. There is of course the Catholic Church, with its resurgent conservatism on the one hand (abetted by a Polish pope) and the remnants of liberation theology on the other. The Left remains relevant mainly by pursuing a variety of ameliorative reforms within the framework of welfare state capitalism, and defending various special interests of subordinated groups. But it is in disarray overall and no longer seems to offer a very compelling positive vision to complement its critique of liberal capitalism. Indeed, the Western Left's failure of vision is directly related to the resurgence of nationalism in Eastern Europe, as the Left has not been able to make much significant connection with advocates of a 'third way' or a more robust notion of civil society. Westerners 'on the Left' found East Germany's 'New Forum' group appealing, thus, but were unable to connect with it in very deep or sustaining ways which would help to provide a viable electoral alternative to the vision of unity promoted by the Christian Democrats (largely because their own social democratic vision had been narrowed to a series of ameliorations of capitalist ills). The weakness of the Western Left (not least its defensive posture in the US) helped to open the way to a discourse in which liberal capitalism and versions of nationalism are the main contenders for succession to communism. These contenders, as the German example reveals, are not as antithetical as has sometimes been thought. Many forms of nationalism can thrive quite happily on a capitalist foundation and put forward their claims in the rhetoric of liberalism. Indeed, liberalism's strengths run to the enunciation and preservation of certain liberties, not to the constitution of strong social or cultural identities. Nationalism can be its complement – rooted in the same individualism – as readily as it can be dissolved by liberalism's advocacy of the individual as the basic unit of analysis.

NATIONALISM AND DEMOCRACY

Nationalism is not an intrinsically 'bad' ideology. It has been and remains an important source of inspiration. Any account of the political problems attendant on nationalism which does not recognize the achievements of poets, painters and composers who were moved by nationalist sentiments misses an important part of the story.[39] Any accounts which imagines that citizens or human beings could be rational actors unmoved by cultural commitments and pre-rational identities loses touch with reality. In the political realm itself, nationalism is not intrinsically pernicious or antidemocratic. In the first place, there needs to be some culturally constructed identity behind the word 'self' in the idea of self-determination. It is worth recalling too that in the 1840s nationalism often appeared as a progressive, liberal ideology in which a domestic push for democratic expression was coupled with a respect for other nations. Even more than respect, Romantics of the early nineteenth century were sufficiently inspired by heroic nationalist struggles to offer their own lives on behalf of alien nations. Yet even this phrase reveals a tension. To the strong Romantic humanist – to Byron, say – there were no alien nations, only many expressions of a common humanity striving for freedom and creative voice. Yet in extremes Romanticism (like its current postmodernist successors) had as much trouble making sense of difference as Enlightenment rationalism; neither grappled well with the problem of incommensurable practices, with the reasons why differences become hostilities.[40] And the exclusivity implied by the word 'alien' is more common in the rhetoric of nationalism. Nationalism is all too often the enemy of democracy rooted in civil society.

In the first place, nationalism in power is very different from nationalist resistance to alien rule. Not unlike authoritarian regimes as I described them above, nationalists too often tend to promote the pseudo-democracy of sameness instead of the recognition and respect of difference. Ironically like communism, nationalism often stifles cultural discourse – not in the name of the state or even necessarily by the imposition of state power; it can work by a closure of the mind. Nationalism in power is often a repressive ideology demanding strict adherence to the authority of the official embodiments of national tradition – and very unlike nationalism in opposition, which is generally a strong stimulus to cultural productivity. The problems arise with the assertion that there is only one right way for any individual to be a Pole or a Russian, an Azeri or an American.

Repression is wielded not just against diversity of cultural expression but against the variety of alternative bases for personal identity which might compete with the nation. Thus the common antagonism of nationalists to autonomy and equality for women is not just a continuation of sexist traditions. Nationalism encourages this sexism by internal (and I think non-essential) cultural traditions – e.g., valuing the family as the source of the nation's continuity in time, and seeing men as future martyrs, women as mothers. Beyond this, however, nationalists resist women's movements because accepting the domination of male interests and perceptions merely perpetuates a taken-for-granted, monolithic view of the nation, while encouraging women to identify their distinctive interests and views opens claims that gender has autonomous status as a basis for personal identity which does not pale into insignificance before the commonalities of (male-dominated) nationhood.

In this sense, nationalism has totalitarian potential. It can be treated as a categorical identity more fundamental than other personal identities, even able to override them, and as fixed in both biographical and historical time. This is what I mean by saying that nationalism is used to 'trump' other identities or values.[41] Nationalists often want the sentiment or sense of national identity to go beyond the feeling of being more at home in one place than another, beyond placing a special value on the traditions with which one grew up, beyond focusing one's attention more on one subset of humanity than on the whole. In its extreme forms, nationalism, like religious fundamentalism, often involves claims to monopolize the sources of legitimate identity. As Hannah Arendt wrote, we are apt since Tocqueville to blame conformism on the principle of equality, but 'whether a nation consists of equals or non-equals is of no great importance in this respect, for society always demands that its members act as though they were members of one enormous family which has only one opinion and one interest.'[42]

The decisive question about nationalism, therefore, is whether it can thrive with the nation open to competing conceptualizations, diverse identities, and a rich public discourse about controversial issues. These issues were faced in France in the late nineteenth century; in the Dreyfus affair, victory went to the forces of openness and heterogeneous civil society as the basis for democracy. There have been attempts to revoke the victory, notably by Second World War era collaborationists and the contemporary radical right, under the leadership of nationalists like Jean-Marie Le Pen. But in central and Eastern Europe there have been few such signal victories, and, as Adam Michnik has suggested, the issue is a very current one: 'In both France and Poland the question was whether the nation was to be open and the state tolerant and multicultural, or whether the state was to be based on authoritarian principles and nationalistic doctrine. And I think this has been the central question ever since. Whenever the shadow of anti-semitism arose in polish public life, it was an unmistakable signal that people with antidemocratic, intolerant views were on the political offensive.'[43]

It would be good, but not enough to say that tolerance should reign within states. Even multinational, multicultural states require more than simply tolerance among subsidiary peoples. They require public discourse. Citizens from different nationalities, as from different regions, religions or occupations, need to be able and willing to engage each other in discourse about the social arrangements which hold them together and order their lives – in brief, about the common good. Moreover, the same is crucial within nationalities. There is no reason to accept monolithic conformity within any one nation or people (insurgent or in power). Not only may states be multinational or multicultural, nations themselves must – if they are to be allies of liberty – admit and encourage internal diversity whether they are coterminous with states or exist as subsidiary identities within states. It is necessary, in other words, that the nation be open to democracy and diversity, whether or not the close link between nation and state is severed. In power, extreme nationalists do not just repress other peoples, they repress the diversity and creativity of people within the very nation they cherish.

Without diversity, democracy is hardly distinct from a dictatorship of the mass. Indeed, it is hard to imagine how such a monolithic mass could be sustained beyond an ephemeral uprising except by means of centralized totalitarian power. Nationalism is benign only when it does not tend towards this pseudo-democracy of sameness. And this is where civil society comes in. Civil society is the locus of diverse groups and individuals and more importantly of their contact with each other. Division of labour and other sources of difference may arise within civil society or be brought into it from the family or other less public realms. But in civil society, the exchange not only of goods but of ideas can take place. Advocates of democracy in the late twentieth century are called upon to discover whether the virtues of diversity, sociability, and tolerance associated with the ideal of the cosmopolis can be combined with the self-governing political community of the polis. Can political arguments be considered on their merits, at least partially autonomous from the identities of the arguers? [44]

The locus classicus of such public life lay in European cities of the eighteenth century. It may be that current trends in Europe – especially the integration of the European Community but also perhaps the creation of small states in the east – may actually restore some of the early modern prominence of cities in public life and social organization. Links among cities and/or regions may partially replace those among states. But major improvements in the nature of modern public discourse cannot come about simply through direct interpersonal relationships in cities. They must happen also through television and newspapers. They must happen on the scale of millions of people in powerful states. Political parties with their patronage, bureaucracies, and public relations staffs will mediate the relations between groups as much as cafes with their intellectual arguments.[45] These parties must remain open to diversity for they are crucial means of achieving not consensus so much as reasonable compromises where consensus is impossible. If democracy is to flourish, nationalism must not become the enemy of difference.

The events of 1989 showed the power of mass media to further an internationalization of culture and politics. I was in Beijing that spring, and watched with amazement. Chinese students deliberately echoed Poland's Solidarity movement, and within days protesting students in Eastern Europe marched with headbands and placards proclaiming their sympathy with the Chinese. And today Chinese democrats – and nationalists – look to Eastern Europe for inspiration. The nationalism which figured centrally in these movements is an international phenomenon – as nationalism was in 1848. Not only is it shared through mass communication, it is driven by global processes that value and priviledge nations as categories of identity between the immediately interpersonal and the local. It is often repeated that the twin tendencies of the present era are towards globalization and localization. This has an element of truth, but it is an overused mantra. It neglects the importance of states as arenas for democratic struggles, and as agents for contesting an economic power which has not ceased to be concentrated as it has become global. And it suggests that the division of the world into ever smaller units of putative internal sameness is the only way to achieve happiness in our immediate lifeworlds. It is as though someone decided that Durkheim's mechanical solidarity is the only kind that works.

Nationalism encourages the identification of individuals not with locality per se, not with the webs of their specific interpersonal relationships, but with an abstract category. This category of nation may be a helpful mediation between the local and the global. Indeed, I think this is one crucial reason why nationalism is unlikely to disappear any time soon. Globalization, where it occurs, is likely to call forth new and different nationalisms and more generally politics of identity. Far from producing a cosmopolitanism somehow antithetical to nationalism, the massive international migrations currently under way are apt to accentuate in both predictable and unpredictable ways the salience of cultural divides and identities in many people's everyday lives. Simply getting rid of nationalism is thus not a viable response to its disagreeable features.

Contrary to much received wisdom, I have argued that both states on the one hand, and nationalism and the discourse of national identity on the other, are likely to remain of central importance in an increasingly globalized world. Much of the question of how this will affect human life turns on the extent to which and manner in which institutions of civil society provide social foundations for democracy. Whether claims to national identity will be used to override other identities, either within or across national boundaries will be determined not just by the cultural content of nationalist ideologies or the choices of nationalist ideologies. It will be determined also by the presence or absence of cross-cutting social ties and mediating institutions.

Is it possible to build states and even confederations of states in which cohesion and self-rule are established through public discourse across lines of difference? Can we conceive the growth of a cultural unity within such states or confederations that does not devalue or demand the obliteration of other sources of personal and political identity? Or must we fall back on nationalism alone as our shelter in a world grown too frightening, or as the one immediately satisfying identity with which to confront the globalization of capital?

References

1. This has been one of the themes of postmodernism as well as of more conventional political economy. See the sympathetic but critical survey in David Harvey: *The Postmodern Condition* (Oxford: Blackwell, 1990).

2. Of course the related end to the political-military rivalry between the capitalist world system and communist countries is also significant. It is possible, but remains to be seen, that global integration is sufficient to prevent the emergence of a new state-capitalist military block that, like the Axis of the 1930s, seeks to carve an alternative world system to that built around capital accumulation through multilateral trade.
3. See the contrasting reviews and theorizations in Adam Seligman, *Civil Society* (New York: Free Press, 1992); Jean Cohen and Andrew Arato, *The Political Theory of Civil Society* (Cambridge, MA: MIT Press, 1992).
4. Charles Taylor, *Modes of Civil Society*, Public Culture, Vol. 3, No. 1 (1991): pp. 95–118.
5. This point is also made in a very different way by Jean Cohen and Andrew Arato, *Political Theory*. Cohen and Arato want to get away from a simple opposition of state to all other social organization (the sort of usage that resulted in a discourse of 'society versus the state' in Eastern Europe). They place an important stress on the role of social movements in democratic process and on 'resources of solidarity' that enable individuals to join together in collective action to limit the power of state or economy (see Ch. 9, esp. p. 472). Yet, drawing primarily on readings of Hegel and Habermas, they neglect both the Scottish moralists and the French tradition, treating social organization primarily in terms of notions of system integration developed by Talcott Parsons and Niklas Luhmann. Rather than calling attention to the reified and therefore anti-democratic nature of the description of social life as impersonally steered 'system,' they simply accept as given that much social life is so organized. Crucially, they accept without challenge the idea that power is a steering medium in the same sense as money. They also accept the Parsons-Luhmann understanding of economic life as simply a self-regulating functional system steered impersonally by money. They thus either neglect or reject the Marxian notion of the way in which capitalism structures not only the economy but the categories of economic understanding (1) so that money appears as the primary element in the economic system, (2) so that the centrality of capital accumulation is obscured, and (3) so that the system appears as necessary rather than transcendable. Such

a view is elaborated in Moishe Postone, *Marx's Critique of Money, Labor and Time* (Cambridge: Cambridge University Press, 1993). Their sociological theory thus marginalizes the role of direct social relations – the kinds of structures studied, for example, under the rubric of social networks, and the basis of the communities, intermediate associations, and mediating institutions vital to democratic life – and thereby underestimates the capacities of actors to create and modify social institutions.

6. See Jurgen Habermas, *The Structural Transformation of the Public Sphere* (Cambridge, MA: MIT Press, 1989) and the various qualifications, extensions, and refinements suggested by the essays in *Craig Calhoun, Habermas and the Public Sphere* (Cambridge, MA: MIT Press, 1992).
7. This is a theme associated especially with Alexis de Tocqueville, *Democracy in America* (New York: Schocken, 1840–4) but also important to Durkheim, e.g., in the preface to the second edition of *The Division of Labor in Society* (New York: Free Press 1933) and a range of other thinkers since Montesquieu. See also Craig Calhoun, 'Democracy, Autocracy and Intermediate Associations in Organizations: Flexibility or Unrestrained Change?' Sociology, Vol. 4, No. 3: pp. 345–61.
8. Even if one could point to completely self-contained island cultures somewhere in the South Pacific (and my reading of the anthropological evidence is that one cannot), these would not be nations in anything like the modern sense of the term, for that implies the definition of one by contraposition to others (as, indeed, do a variety of other forms of identity from lineage segment to clan to locality). Key to nationalist discourse is its rejection of any notion that identity is essentially fluid and shifting from one situation to another. National identity is commonly claimed to trump all others.
9. See especially R. Brubaker, *Citizenship and Nationhood in France and Germany* (Cambridge, MA: Harvard University Press, 1992) and *G. Noiriel, Le Creuset Francois* (Paris: Seuil, 1988).
10. Perhaps the greatest single weakness of Habermas's *Structural Transformation of the Public Sphere* is his treatment of identity formation as essentially private and prior to participation in the

idealized public sphere of rational critical discourse. A "politics of identity," therefore, could appear only as a degenerate intrusion into the public sphere, owing first to growing democratic inclusiveness and second to public relations manipulation. One result is that nationalism, a prototypical form of the politics of identity, and one broached crucially in the public sphere, did not figure significantly in Habermas's account.

11. It is common that a bit of each sort of claim is made. In France, histories trace French character back to the Gauls as well as anchoring national identity crucially in the Revolution and the distinctive notion of citizenship it brought forward. In China, national identity (a notion deriving in part from contact with the West) is at once seen as something extraordinarily ancient (and this with better claim than most of the world's other peoples) and as something given special purpose by the unification under the Qin dynasty.
12. Anthony Smith, esp. in *The Ethnic Origins of Nations* (Oxford: Blackwell, 1986), is the most articulate modern voice for the importance of ethnicity to nationalism, but see also the review and critique in Craig Calhoun, 'Nationalism and Ethnicity,' Annual Review of Sociology (1993).
13. 'What is a Nation,' Tr. M. Thorn, in H.K. Bhabha, Ed., *Nation and Narration* (London: Routledge, 1990), pp. 8–22, quotation from p. 11.
14. Benedict Anderson, *Imagined Communities* (New York: Verso, 1983; Rev. Edn. 1991).
15. National identity, thus, in its main western ideological form, is precisely the opposite of the reckoning of identity and loyalty outward from the family. Where the segmentary lineage system suggests 'I against my brothers, I and my brothers against my cousins, I, my brothers and my cousins against the world,' nationalism suggests that membership in the category of the whole nation is prior to, more basic than any such web of relationships. This suggests also a different notion of moral commitment from previous modes of understanding existence. The prototypical discourse of nationalism carries the form even into non-western settings where kinship and communal bonds may figure more prominently or be claimed specifically against western individualism. See Partha

Chatterjee: Nationalist *Thought and the Colonial World: A Derivative Discourse*, Rev. Edn. (Minneapolis: University of Minnesota Press, 1993) and *The Nation and Its Fragments: Studies in Colonial and Post-Colonial Histories* (Princeton, NJ: Princeton University Press, forthcoming).

16. Hans Kohn: *The Idea of Nationalism* (New York: Macmillan, 1944); Andrzej Walicki: *Philosophy and Romantic Nationalism: The Case of Poland* (Oxford: Oxford University Press, 1982); Joan S. Skurnowicz: *Romantic Nationalism and Liberalism: Joachim Lelewel and the Polish National Idea* (New York: Columbia University Press, 1981); Friedrich Meinecke: *Cosmopolitanism and the National State*, Tr. R.B. Kilmer (Princeton: Princeton University Press, 1970).
17. Fichte, quoted in Meinecke, 'Cosmopolitanism and the National State, p. 89.'
18. William Bloom: *Personal Identity, National Identity and International Relations* (Cambridge: Cambridge University Press, 1990).
19. Nils Kjoer to Ibsen on the celebration of his 70th birthday (1898), quoted p. 7 of *Henryk Ibsen – Our Contemporary*, the 1991 Ibsen Stage Festival in Norway, ed. Margrethe Aaby (Oslo, 1991).
20. See George L. Mosse, *Nationalism and Sexuality: Middle-Class Morality and Sexual Norms in Modem Europe* (Madison: University of Wisconsin Press, 1985).
21. See, among many general treatments, Anthony Giddens, *The Nation-State and Violence* (Berkeley: University of California Press, 1984); *Charles Tilly, Coercion, Capitol and European States* AD 990–1990 (Oxford: Blackwell, 1990); Michael Mann, *The Sources of Social Power*, Vol. 2 (Cambridge: Cambridge University Press, 1992).
22. E. Weber: *Peasants into Frenchmen* (Stanford, CA: Stanford University Press, 1976).
23 Susan Cott Watkins: *From Provinces into Nations: Demographic Integration in Western Europe*, 1870–1960 (Princeton: Princeton University Press, 1991).
24. See C. Calhoun, 'Imagined Communities and Indirect Relationships,' in P. Bourdieu and J. Coleman, eds, *Social Theory for a Changing Society* (Boulder, CO: Westview Press, 1991).

25. A relatively benign though potentially problematic aspect of nationalism in Eastern Europe and the former USSR is the intentional deintegration of markets and division of labour. Rather than enhancing their cross-border relations, most formerly communist countries seem bent on developing their own individual relations with the West, and their own autonomous development plans. Economic integration seems to be experienced as a lack of national freedom, but this both forfeits comparative advantages in economic exchange and makes future conflicts more likely.
26. Jeff Weintraub, 'The Theory and Politics of the Public/Private Distinction,' paper presented to the American Political Science Association, 1990, p. 16; see Weintraub and K. Kumar, eds, Public and Private in Thought and Practice (Chicago: University of Chicago Press, forthcoming).
27. Ernest Gellner, *Nations and Nationalism* (Oxford: Blackwell, 1983), p. 6.
28. As Hobsbawm writes, 'we cannot assume that for most people national identification – when it exists – excludes or is always or ever superior to, the remainder of the set of identifications which constitute the social being' (Notions and Nationalism since 1780 [Cambridge: Cambridge University Press, 1990, p. 11]). But part of nationalist ideology is precisely the notion that national identity does 'trump' other identities.
29. This point is made with some force by Eric Hobsbawm in *Nations and Nationalism since 1780* and Ernest Gellner in *Nations and Nationalism*. Both authors stress that this is not accidental, for 'a world of nations cannot exist, only a world where some potentially national groups, in claiming this status, exclude others from making similar claims, which, as it happens, not many of them do' (Hobsbawm, Nations and Nationalism since 1780, p. 78).
30. Anderson's notion of 'modular' nationalism may overstate the case to the point of denying creativity and indigenous roots to later nationalist discourses. See Partha Chatterjee, *Nationalist Thought and the Colonial World: A Derivative Discourse*? (London: Zed Press, 1986).
31. Resentments seem especially central to some nationalisms of central and Eastern Europe. Some domestic religious traditions,

like Russian and other 'eastern' Orthodoxies, seem to encourage xenophobia beyond any influence of historical wrongs or current international threats. See Liah Greenfeld, 'The Formation of the Russian National Identity; The Role of Status Insecurity and Resentment,' *Comparative Studies in Society and History*, Vol. 32, No. 3 (1990): 549–91.

32. Albert Nenarokov and Alexander Proskurin: *How the Soviet Union Solved the Nationalities Question* (Moscow: Novosti Press Agency Publishing House, 1983).

33. See Gall Kligman Calus: *Symbolic Transformation in Romanian Ritual* (Chicago: University of Chicago Press, 1984); Katherine Verdery: *National Ideology Under Socialism: Identity and Cultural Politics in Ceausescu 's Romania* (Berkeley: University of California Press, 1991).

34. Communism has always been linked to nationalism in China, though the label 'nationalism' was appropriated by its competitor, the Guomindang. In general, a kind of modernizing nationalism has often been part of communism's appeal, and it is no accident that communism has flourished especially in settings where people have felt cheated of their due stature by the capitalist world system (not in the advanced centers of capitalism as Marx predicted). As the case of largely ethnically homogeneous China illustrates, nationalist aspirations are not limited to the constitution of states or the alteration of their boundaries, but include pursuit of a range of goals including regeneration, liberation, modernization, and power.

35. Ivo Banac: *The National Question in Yugoslavia: Origin, History, Politics* (Ithaca: Cornell University Press, 1984); Walker Connor: *The National Question in Marxist-Leninist Theory and Strategy* (Princeton: Princeton University Press, 1984).

36. It was, of course, this same nationalism and this same weakness of other cultural and movement forms which rendered the Transcaucasus unable to sustain its federation after 1917, and unable to mount significant resistance to the Red Army's imposition of Soviet rule.

37. This is congruent with the suggestion of N. Abercrombie *et al.*, The Dominant Ideology Thesis (London: Allen and Unwin, 1984) that

dominant ideologies are more effective in establishing cohesion among elites than in enabling elites to 'delude' or persuade the 'masses'.

38. On the connection to war, See Bryan Turner, *Citizenship and Capitalism: The Debate over Reformism* (London: Allen and Unwin,1986).

39. Similarly, it is analytically untenable to try to treat 'nationalism' and 'Patriotism' (or other labels amounting to 'good' and 'bad' nationalism) as though they were fundamentally different ideological species. Artistic inspiration, needed identity, will to power, and politics of repression can be and often are bound inseparably together. The differences among nationalisms come as much from the nature of international contexts as from differences in internal form or content.

40. Practices are incommensurable when they are not only different but impossible to combine within the same framework of understanding and action – as for example one cannot play American football and soccer at the same time. While some differences can be resolved by translation, incommensurability cannot. Where they exist in important and competitive practices (like Chinese v Western medicine) they remain sources of tension unless overall frameworks of practice are transformed. See Charles Taylor, *Philosophy and the Human Sciences* (Cambridge: Cambridge University Press, 1985); Craig Calhoun, 'Culture, History and the Problem of Specificity in Social Theory,' in S. Seidman and D. Wagner, eds, Post-modernism and General Social Theory (New York: Blackwell, 1991), pp. 244–88.

41. Charles Taylor has argued that identity and moral commitment are intimately intertwined, so that it is almost redundant to say 'identities or values'. See Sources of the Self (Cambridge, MA: Harvard University Press, 1989).

42. Hannah Arendt, *The Human Condition* (Chicago: University of Chicago Press,1958), p. 39.

43. 'Poland and the Jews,' New York Review of Books, May, 30, 1991, pp. 11–12, quote from p. 11.

44. This is, of course, a core theme to Habermas's work from the Structural Transformation of the Public Sphere to the present. One may accept the centrality of the question without accepting quite the extreme of abstraction from issues of personal identity which is characteristic of Habermas's work.
45. See Craig Calhoun, 'Populist Politics, Communications Media, and Large Scale Social Integration,' *Sociological Theory*, Vol. 6, No. 2 (1988): pp. 219–41.

4

Introduction to Civil Society and Government

Robert C. Post and Nancy L. Rosenblum

Civil Society is so often invoked in so many contexts that it has acquired a strikingly plastic moral and political valence. The recent renaissance of the term began with anticommunist dissent in Eastern Europe, which gave civil society its association with opposition movements and a 'parallel polis' to the state. But the term has been endlessly invoked since that time. In the United States, where 'civil society' has become a staple of both academic and political discourse, its ideological orientation runs the entire partisan spectrum; we can identify social democrats, grass-rooters, neo-Tocquevilleans, centrists, conservatives of many stripes, libertarians, multiculturalists, and civic republicans.

There are also vastly disparate understandings of the relationship between civil society and government. Civil society is alternately viewed as a source of legitimacy and stability for government and as a source of resistance against arbitrary, oppressive, and overweening government. Civil society is sometimes conceived as a spontaneous growth, prior to and independent of government, and sometimes as dependent on government for legal structure, robust recognition, or outright fiscal support. Civil society is described both as developing in partnership with government and as substituting for the failings of government. Prescriptions for privatization, devolution, and 'subsidiarity' can arise from faith in communalism or in voluntarism, or from a loss of faith in the justice or efficacy of government.

This volume[@] portrays the relation between civil society and government as seen from a variety of perspectives in political theory. Our compass is not exhaustive, but it is unusually inclusive. These essays[#] discuss civil society and government from the point of view of classical liberalism, egalitarian liberalism, critical theory, feminism, natural law theory, Judaism, Catholicism and Protestantism, Islam and Confucianism. Our goal is comparative; we wish to provide the materials for assessing how theorists from diverse political and religious traditions understand the relationship between civil society and government.

The concept of civil society is historically bounded, and it is not an organizing concept in every tradition. Where the concept is alien, we have instead inquired into the functional equivalents, if any, to oppositions like those between state and society, citizenship and membership. The essays have been organized topically, according to six basic inquiries:

BOUNDARIES: In terms of function and consequences, does it matter where the line is drawn between civil society and the state?

NEEDS: Do civil society and the state need each other? If so, what does civil society need from the state? What does the state need from civil society? What are the particular values they impart to one another?

LIABILITIES: Do civil society and the state pose liabilities for each other? If so, what liabilities does civil society pose for the state? What liabilities does the state pose for civil society? How are these liabilities to be contained?

GROUPS AND INDIVIDUALS: In what contexts and/or under what conditions, should government interact with individuals (a) directly? (b) indirectly through communal associations? In general, what factors should determine the appropriate arrangements?

CITIZENSHIP: In moral rather than strictly legal terms, what are the prerogatives of citizenship? What are its duties? What, if anything, is the role of civil society in forming good citizens?

@ This means *Civil Society and Government edited by Nancy L. Rosenblum and Robert C. Post* (Princeton University Press-2002), 1–25.

This means essays included in volume *Civil Society and Government edited by Nancy L. Rosenblum and Robert C. Post* (Princeton University Press-2002), 26–396.

CONFLICT: How are conflicting demands of citizenship and membership in the non-governmental associations of civil society to be handled?

By organizing each essay topically, we have tried to make comparisons among cultures and traditions accessible. Mindful that theoretical perspectives are not internally uniform, we have included critical responses to each account.

In this introduction we propose to focus primarily on the first topic, on the boundary between civil society and government. We will not address the descriptive question of how state entities may be empirically distinguished from their private counterparts. We will instead discuss the normative question of how this boundary should be conceived and why it matters.

To say that the boundary between civil society and government is located differently in diverse political regimes and that its purposes are justified differently by various political, moral, and religious theories is just the beginning. Within any given state, the boundary is shifting in practice; it responds to the ongoing contingencies of political experience. The history of political thought shows that it is ceaselessly contested. We have only to think of the varying kinds and degrees of separation of church and state, or of the range of feminist challenges to articulations of a public/private divide, to get a sense of this.

Nonetheless, contemporary political theories distinguish between government and civil society, and they identify a boundary between them, even if it is not fixed. What resources do we have for understanding the constant postulation of some boundary between civil society and government, on the one hand, and the variability of its location, purpose, and justification, on the other?

We propose a general theoretical proposition about the boundary between civil society and government. To employ the usual spatial metaphor, civil society is the realm of social life which, when viewed from the perspective of government, is characterized by plural and particularist identities. Government, by contrast, is an inclusive sphere, which, when viewed from the perspective of civil society, is characterized by overarching public norms made and enforced by official institutions. Civil society is a zone of freedom for individuals to associate with others and for groups to shape their norms, articulate their purposes, and determine for themselves the internal structure of group authority and identity. Government is a domain of common purpose and identity.

In the remainder of this introduction, we shall explore the many implications that follow from this seemingly simple theoretical proposition, and we shall indicate how they may be used to frame the questions discussed in the essays collected in this volume.

CIVIL SOCIETY

The elements of civil society range from groups based on religion and ethnicity to more fluid voluntary associations organized around ideology, professionalism, social activities or the pursuit of money, status, interest, or power. They range from circles of friends, which Humboldt described as the condition for cultivating 'beautiful individuality,' to single-purpose political advocacy groups. Civil society also includes communities, like formally organized religious settlements, with their implication of primary socialization, strong attachment, and common history and expectations. Civil society harbors cultural institutions of all kinds, from the deep, constitutive practices of a cultural group with a common language and history, to the wildly eclectic popular culture of self-help groups in the United States. From many perspectives, the family counts as an element of civil society; it is the premier mediating, moralizing institution. These essays demonstrate that the purposes of association and their personal meanings for members are as various as human needs and imagination. The value of association is as encompassing as the value of liberty.

In saying that civil society is the realm of pluralism, we are endorsing Isaiah Berlin's observation of the historicity of human nature, his notion that human identities cannot be other than local and particular, and his belief that this diversity is not transitory. Civil society is not a residue on the way to a unified state in which citizenship eclipses other aspects of belonging, or on the way to a cosmopolitan order in which universality is our essence. Pluralism has a normative as well as a descriptive dimension.

The substantive content of group purposes and the internal organization of associational life are as various and malleable as human creativity. From any given perspective, the groups that are singled out as shaping the nature of civil society will depend on theoretical commitments. There is sharp dispute, for example, on the question of whether market institutions should be included in the concept of civil society. From our perspective, however, this dispute can be framed as turning on the degree to which market institutions are seen as contributing to the formation of the identities of their participants or, by contrast, as primarily engaged in instrumental or strategic action that objectifies or alienates these participants.[1]

With respect to those aspects of associational life that are pertinent to identity formation, we would stress that a key variable is the degree and manner in which the diverse groups that make up civil society are open and permeable. The structure of pluralism is of great significance. We can in fact range pluralist societies along a spectrum from fluid to rigidly segmented.

From a number of perspectives, the 'ideal type' of civil society is identified with voluntary association, meaning that membership is consensual and exit possible without loss of status or public rights and benefits. Escape from hereditary and ascriptive attachments (or their willing affirmation) and the ceaseless formation of new associations for every conceivable purpose mark this type of civil society. There are few obstacles to the proliferation of groups through creation or schism.

A defining characteristic of civil society in this view is the capacity of individuals to move freely among groups and to shift involvement among them. So long as this capacity realistically obtains, even traditionalist or 'functionally traditionalist' associations serve to underscore individualism, voluntarism, self-construction, and self-expression.

Another crucial aspect of a fluid civil society is that men and women typically join more than one group; membership is plural. Group identifications overlap and conflict. Beyond having a pluralist structure, then, a fluid civil society affords individuals the experience of pluralism.

The significance of civil society is not exhausted by its meaning for individuals. Self-expression and self-development are not the only justifications for groups. Even in fluid civil societies, some associations are not voluntary or chosen. As a matter of moral psychology, belonging is often a matter of assent rather than consent. This is sometimes true, although not always, with religion; it is truer for race, or indeed for any ascriptive trait that a given society singles out as especially valued or despised. One of the principal purposes of association is pursuit of 'recognition' by minority groups. The aim is to get symbolic and distributive signs of the group's status, exhibitions of public respect for the group's unique differences.[2]

Many perspectives challenge individualist, voluntarist accounts of civil society that give priority to personal autonomy. They substitute accounts of civil society in which the openness of groups and shifting involvements among them is less important than the capacity of groups to endow persons with stable and enduring identities. In such circumstances, civil society is not fluid, but segmented. It is comprised of deeply embedded spheres or orders, classes, or cultural groups, or corporations that are closed and that restrict membership – whether by ascriptive traits or status. Membership is not a matter of contribution, merit, or active joining, but of a person's general characteristics. Groups may claim individuals as their own and attribute obligations to them regardless of subjective identification or participation in a cultural 'way of life.' From these perspectives, identification with a group is not psychological – and not (or not only) a matter of subjective affiliation expressed through affirmative membership – but objective. Indeed, presumptive identity trumps personal identification, and presumptive identity is oriented to the collective identity of presumably integral groups and communities.

In segmented societies, groups are more inclined to see membership as mutually exclusive and to be hostile to the idea of plural identities and multiple, overlapping memberships. Groups and communities inevitably experience internal divisions over authority and over the interpretation of norms and purposes, but those who value a segmented vision of civil society believe that conflicts should be resolved internally, insulated from government intervention and from the influence of other powerful and intrusive socially dominant groups.

Some civil societies verge toward the segmented because of the power and authority of tradition and because of the relative weakness of social forces encouraging to social mobility and voluntary association. But the character of legal regulation is also important for the fluidity of civil society. The law can range from ascribing to people group identity to actively suppressing all forms of group rights, with a myriad of intermediate positions. Those who wish to use the law to maintain social segmentation employ a 'politics of recognition' whose goal goes beyond public respect, and beyond the degree of self-government afforded voluntary associations in relatively liberal societies. Rather, the goal is to secure a group's legal and political authority over members and over the distribution of public goods. The associations of civil society claim authority over personal status law and even criminal law as it pertains to group members.

Within civil society, then, there are inequalities of rights and responsibilities and resources. These differentials subsist between groups and within groups. In segmented civil societies with codified membership and authority that controls the distribution of important rights and benefits, these inequalities are entrenched. We have only to think of the status and opportunities of women in hierarchic religious communities governed by religious laws and courts. Where civil society is segmented and association ascriptive or closed, the critical questions are whether government codifies communal identities and deals directly with group authorities and corporate communities rather than directly with individuals on the basis of universal norms, and for what purposes.

Political theory has continuously shifted between envisioning civil society as fluid and as segmented. It oscillates between imagining persons within civil society as possessing identities circumscribed by singular cultures, religions, and autonomous communities, and imagining persons as autonomous individuals who are members of diverse arrays of primarily voluntary associations.

In practice, however, fluid and segmented civil societies exist on a continuum. Voluntary and ascriptive associations, open and closed groups, coexist in any given civil society in different proportions. The identities constituted by and affirmed in groups develop out of history and available norms and social forms; we all come from somewhere, and we begin making decisions within the options we know. But identity is not exhausted by history; individuals are not 'radically situated.' If our points of origin provide us personally and collectively with an initial source of meaning, they are not the sum or stopping place for meaningfulness in our lives. Ascriptive identity is not the whole of identity, either phenomenologically or morally, if for no other reason than that recognized contributions to associations, not objective belonging, are an essential part of self-respect.

Within civil society, individual well-being is tied to, and understood to be tied to, the well-being and independence of groups. But this means that it is also connected to the self-government of associations, with struggles for control over the group's authority, membership, internal rules, and purposes. Thus if associations are constitutive, they are not wholly constitutive. Every component of civil society, even hermetic separatist communities, are permeable to the influence of other groups, to overarching public culture, to influences from abroad, and to the ceaseless invention of novel values and social forms.

This suggests that segmentation within civil society must have limits. The freedom that produces pluralist associations must be prized and enforced. Some allowance for multiplicity of memberships and some possibility of shifting participation by individuals among at least some social and political groups is always a defining characteristic of civil society. When that sphere of freedom is too constricted, the capacity to shape and sustain associations that provide the structure of personal and collective life is choked off. It is one thing to give precedence to affirmation of the group over members' freedom to join and leave; it is another thing to erect very costly obstacles to exit that make membership effectively inalienable. Where freedom of association is truncated, civil society fragments into an aggregate of unalterable ascriptive attachments defined by heredity, tribal identity, race, ethnicity, or caste. A pluralist society that affords autonomy only to particularist groups and not to individuals loses its normative standing as a civil society.

Civil society is not merely plural; it is also particularist. Within civil society identity is always specific. Identity springs from contingencies of socialization and from choice; it is not the product of a single and unified design. It comes from participation in particular groups and associations, and is not imposed uniformly upon all by the state.

Every form of civil society recognizes that groups and associations are not coterminous with the state. Groups and associations need not be sovereign to flourish. They are jurisgenerative, and their members are subject to authoritative norms and practices. But their goods and services – from burial societies to education – are distributed only to members. They are 'partial publics' that acknowledge the distinction between member and citizen. Within civil society, therefore, membership is diverse and particular.

It is not necessary, however, that each such group or association understand itself as particularist. Sometimes groups and associations within civil society conceive themselves as the bearers of universal truths, which all ought to acknowledge. Groups and associations may seek to use the state to impose their truths. If they were to succeed, however, and if the conformity required by their vision were extensive enough, the viability of civil society would be mortally threatened. The grip of the state can impose a uniformity fatal to pluralism.

The persistence of civil society, therefore, depends upon a complex equilibrium among diverse groups and associations. The power to deploy the state in the service of group identity must be reasonably diffused among competing associations. Or groups and associations must implicitly agree, however grudgingly, to compete for adherents through persuasion rather than through legal compulsion. Or there must be implicit understandings about the limits of the state's ability to impose uniformity. However this equilibrium is maintained, the upshot will be that civil society will remain, from the perspective of the state, a domain of partial and particular identities. Particularism marks the boundary that separates civil society from the state.

GOVERNMENT

Associations proliferate and assume their structures in part in response to law, to the various provisions of corporate, tax, tort, or constitutional law that create the framework within which associations define their purposes and carry out their activities. Groups and the experiences groups make possible are partially shaped by these forms.

The legal framework is the means by which government performs its civilizing role of transforming arrant pluralism into civil society. The 'civil' in civil society is not exhausted by civility. Most fundamentally, society is civil when it is not subject to militarism, violence, and the will to domination on the part of particularist groups. Government is the agency responsible for controlling private armies and private oppression. It sets limits to the authority of associations over their members and outsiders, and protects against at least the worst oppression by private authorities. It enforces rules for settling disputes and looks for ways of diminishing hostility and enabling coordination and alliances among groups. Without government, the result is anarchy, private oppression, or the private engrossment of collective resources.[3] Neither individual rights nor the rights of collectivities are meaningful without the enforcement of law. This implies that limited government must be distinguished from weak government.

It is the responsibility of government to provide groups and associations with sufficient public goods and entitlements to commit them to publicly imposed order and cooperation.[4] At a minimum these benefits must include civil peace and the distribution of certain rights. At a maximum they might include public funding for parochial education and cultural reproduction, support for services to group members, and public recognition of group identity.

Government must also establish an appropriate legal framework for formalizing and securing associations.[5] Often this is done through the concept of legal personhood. Government assigns individuals and corporations enforceable civil and political rights; legal status as a person signifies the capacity to enter contracts, form agreements, own property, and to form associations for these and other purposes. Civil society is inconceivable absent a reasonably stable structure of civil law, which is a vehicle for particularism.

Government, finally, is a collective agent whose identity and purpose transcends the instrumental. In contrast to the pluralism and particularism of civil society, government may be defined as standing for inclusive public norms and common identity. Through an overarching public political culture embodied in institutions and perpetuated through many forms of public education, direct and indirect, government articulates and sustains shared ground. It claims authoritatively to represent common interests. The substance of common political identity is variable, as is its capacity to attract the commitment of groups and the identification of citizens. It may consist of democratic norms of individual autonomy and equal and universal civil and political rights, or of public norms identified with a national culture ('American' or 'French'), or of established religion and the secular norms that complement it. But in every case, government claims to embody the fundamental nature of a polity.

Common political identity is made manifest not only in formal institutions, but also in public rituals and monuments.[6] It is cultivated through public education and proselytizing of various kinds. It is made effective by strategies of inclusion. All governments claiming to represent common interests must serve, if not every interest, then every group and association capable of challenging its stability and legitimacy, every element of civil society whose cooperation is needed. Common identity requires that these benefits be palpable and appreciated, that cooperation be general. And this demands a minimal degree of fairness--of public justification for the distribution of rights and benefits and costs. In this sense, Michael Walzer contends, every state is to some degree a welfare state.

The claim of government to represent the common good and the common identity is of course entirely putative. It is the everyday stuff of politics to expose this kind of claim as merely masking the particular interests of specific groups or associations. Under the conditions of diversity characteristic of civil societies, it is most improbable that there is any single common identity, and of course any vision of the common good is always somebody's vision.

What is at issue with respect to this kind of claim, therefore, is the right to speak in the name of a common good and identity. The right is authorized by whatever structures of legitimacy sustain the state. But it is from the perspective of the particularism of civil society that this right acquires meaning, for the common good is that which purports to transcend particularism. This contrast between the common good and the particular is expressed in the distinction between citizen and member.

If membership expresses particular commitments of discrete groups and associations, citizenship reflects the overarching norms of a government. For the pluralism of civil society to persist, these norms must be limited. They must not radically preempt or displace the possibilities of membership. It follows that the scope of citizenship must have intrinsic limitations.[7]

In fact citizenship in a modern state, even in a liberal democracy with its positive norms of public respect and avenues of effective participation, is often circumscribed. In the absence of external threats, citizenship is typically invoked only with respect to a restricted number of political occasions, instrumental and ritualistic, open to citizens regardless of merit, like voting, jury duty, or military service. Often participation in these occasions is not mandatory. Citizens are presumptively equal, and for this reason birthright citizenship has nothing to do with individual merit or ability. While in many contexts citizenship can be a source of pride and identity, citizenship does not ordinarily serve within quotidian domestic politics as a principal source of self-respect.

Exclusion from citizenship is demeaning, of course, an injurious mark of public disrespect, but inclusion per se does not have the opposite, positive significance. Although citizenship can call up the disposition to participate through one's own acts and energy, industry and skill, in the same ways that membership in private associations can summon these dispositions, it normally does not. Most frequently these dispositions are instead cultivated, exhibited, and appreciated through the associations of civil society, where contributions are suitably fitted to individuals' capacities and wants.

The development of a full and rich personality thus ordinarily draws upon participation in civil society. The philosopher Hegel, for whom 'the creation of civil society [is] the achievement of the modern world,' explained this best. The Philosophy of Right teaches that civil society must be seen against the historical background of alienation and a falling off from original social unity. But at the same time as civil society disconnects individuals from traditionalist moorings, it is the 'tremendous power' that draws individuals into itself, provides them with a 'second family,' and reorients them. 'The sanctity of marriage and the dignity of Corporation membership are the two fixed points round which the unorganized atoms of civil society revolve.' What Hegel called the corporation – meaning economic organizations, religious bodies, learned societies, and so on – is the principal 'ethical entity' that provides members rank and dignity, and 'work of a public character over and above their private business . . . which the modern state does not always provide.'[8]

CONCEPTUALIZING THE BOUNDARY BETWEEN GOVERNMENT AND CIVIL SOCIETY

Against this background, how, then, are we to conceive the boundary between government and civil society? The boundary functions to set civil society and government in productive tension. It defines the pluralism and particularism of civil society in opposition to the inclusive and overarching norms of government. Push the boundary too far in the direction of government, and civil society can wither away. Push the boundary too far in the direction of civil society, and government can collapse into anarchic disorder. Yet civil society requires government to survive, and government, at least democratic government, draws deeply from the strengths of civil society. The location of the boundary is a matter of judgment, which means that it is subject to perennial dispute and contestation. It has no single correct or fixed position, but moves with contingencies of history, tradition, culture, and politics.

Wherever the distinction between civil society and government is marked, however, there must always exist a boundary between them, because each is defined in opposition to the other. Government fails if it embodies merely particularist values. A police officer betrays his office if he does not treat citizens equally, but gives favour to members of his own group. Government must have reasonably independent police and courts, as well as an impartial administrative apparatus. If religious authorities establish theocratic rule; if ethnic or religious groups hold sway and deny civil and political rights to members of other groups; if government is captured by (or is itself) a dominant economic interest; if the common good is conflated with, and understood to be conflated with, particularist goods, government ceases to sustain civil society.

Without independence from civil society, government cannot protect basic rights or well-being. The associations of civil society mirror, reinforce, and actively create social inequalities of all kinds, with the accompanying enmity and rivalry. Government must be able to intervene to set bounds, to enforce basic requirements of peace, order, civil equality, and so forth. Government cannot perform even these minimal tasks if we assume that government 'independence' is, like 'impartial government,' a ruse or an impossibility. Government's claim that it is not simply the mirror and agent of the most powerful forces in society must be credible.[9]

Conversely, civil society must be independent of government. The divide between civil society and government sets off civil society as nongovernmental: that is, as distinct from the official, coercive, political apparatus. In this limited sense the distinction between civil society and government corresponds to the split between private and public, where the term 'public' is understood to signify 'official' government entities. Associations in civil society must speak in their own name;

they do not have the authority 'officially' to speak in the name of the common good.

In contrast to government, civil society must remain particular and plural. Whether or not membership in the associations of civil society is wholly voluntarist and best conceived as unfettered individual choice rather than inherited or ascriptive, it is not, with the important exception of the family, mandated by public law. To the extent that groups and associations are authorized by government to exercise coercive legal authority over their own members or outsiders, the domain of civil society begins to lose its character. The internal laws of groups may be powerful, command obedience, and regulate members' lives in minute ways, but members must be able to exit from associations. There are frequently material and psychological costs to disassociation, of course, but the promise is that membership status does not determine civil standing or vital civil and political rights. A background of general civil laws of contract, property, marriage, and so on, allows people, particularly women, to disassociate from the authority and restrictive personal laws of specific religious and ethnic groups.[10]

The analytic distinction between civil society and government has functional implications. As we have stressed, civil society cannot persist if government does not actively intervene to maintain civil order and personal legal rights. But civil society also requires government to abstain from interventions that undermine pluralism. The very origin of civil society is inseparable from the theory and practice of limited government. Totalitarianism is its antithesis; so is authoritarian repression of self-organized groups and any form of paternalistic regime that does not provide space for autonomous associational life.

Members of groups within civil society must experience themselves as normally free from official repression and from regulation that conscripts their identities, membership, and self-government. Civil society is unintelligible without defined limits both to the means government can legitimately use to regulate groups and to the justifications that count in such regulation. Associations must be free from intervention that undermines their singular purposes and activities, inhibits self-definition, chills expression, or threatens viability. To the extent these limits are transgressed, civil society is endangered.

ACCOMMODATING CIVIL SOCIETY AND GOVERNMENT: FROM CONGRUENCE TO MODUS VIVENDI

There is an obvious tension, however, between a government that aspires to speak in the accents of a common good and identity and a civil society that encourages pluralism and particularism. Unless citizens actually have common values and beliefs, how can government possibly function? This question has led theorists from a variety of perspectives to argue that the internal lives of groups should be closely regulated to conform to public values and common principles of justice. They advocate what Rosenblum has called the 'logic of congruence.'

Advocates of congruence fear that the multiplication of intermediate institutions does not mediate but balkanizes public life. They are apprehensive that plural associations and groups amplify self-interest, encourage arrant interest-group politics, exaggerate cultural egocentrism, and defy government. What is needed, in their view, is a strong assertion of public values and policies designed to loosen the hold of particular affiliations, so that members will be empowered to look beyond their groups and to identify themselves as members of the larger political community. The 'logic of congruence' envisions civil society as reflecting common values and practices 'all the way down.'

Congruence is often advocated with regard to the egalitarian norms of liberal democracy. The claim is that the internal lives of associations should mirror public norms of equality, nondiscrimination, due process, and so on. In the United States, for example, norms of equality and due process have been imposed on vast areas of social life, even on small, informal associations. Antidiscrimination law, for instance, requires most groups to admit unwanted members. By this means the government compels association.

Until recently, the principal rationale for such law was equality of opportunity. Regulation of groups was deemed necessary to redress past discrimination and to underwrite necessary economic advancement. But such regulation is now also defended on the grounds of moral education. Antidiscrimination law is seen by some as a means by which a tutelary government teaches egalitarian values. Such instruction is necessary because groups that discriminate in 'private' will cultivate dispositions in their members that are antagonistic to public egalitarian commitments. If government depends upon the dispositions formed through membership in groups, then 'a crucial task of educational statecraft is to foster a healthy structure of group life.'[11]

Taken too far, however, this logic of moral education potentially trespasses across the boundary that separates civil society from government. It invites state institutions to colonize social life in the name of progressive public ideals. It follows the same logic as contemporary proposals to democratize the family by enacting statutes requiring partners to share domestic chores and income, or to democratize religion by requiring churches to ordain women or gay priests as a condition of receiving the tax status of a charitable organization.

Advocates of congruence properly note that the boundary between government and civil society should not be overdrawn or mechanically interpreted. Every government uses law to define and educate its citizens. When a state creates rights to sue for defamation or invasion of privacy, for example, it uses law to protect common values and to safeguard a certain common ideal of personality.[12] The riotous plurality of democratic civil society subsists upon a substrate of common values and identity that is legally fostered and enforced.

The question of congruence is therefore one of degree. To the extent that the common values established by law are too thick, to the extent that the common identity protected by law is too pervasive, civil society will suffer. The degree of appropriate uniformity will depend upon many factors, including the antecedent cultural homogeneity within a society and the particular domain of civil society that is subject to regulation. The aspiration for thick and pervasive congruence will be more damaging to a truly heterogeneous society than to a culturally homogeneous one; and we are far more tolerant of intrusive moral regulation of the marketplace than of religious institutions.

The question of congruence is also one of kind. Government has many means by which to create congruence. It can do so by direct legal regulation, by asserting its rights as a coercive sovereign. But it can also exercise its capacities as educator, patron, sponsor, employer, and owner. There are important differences between legally mandating churches to ordain women and refusing to extend tax benefits to churches that acknowledge only male priests. The latter alters the 'terms, conditions, and public status' of groups, thus enabling groups to choose the terms of their accommodation to public values.[13] On the other hand, the powerful inducements of governmental largesse can be exceedingly seductive; it can exemplify aggressive state 'capture' of independent groups and create a climate of passive clientelism.[14] The impact of government action on the particularism and plurality of civil society must always be kept in mind.

Congruence represents only one possible form of the accommodation between civil society and government. Advocates of civil society may care more for the conditions of independent associational life than they do for the conditions that reinforce overarching norms and that incline groups to contribute to governmental efforts to maintain political stability. They may be content if vigorous independent associations exhibit only a minimal commitment to public order. Recognizing that common norms impose costs on the purposes and internal culture of many groups, they may lobby for exceptions to general laws and special accommodations for group autonomy.

If advocates of congruence desire that common norms be inculcated all the way down, those partial to civil society argue that public life can be sustained by a modus vivendi among competitive groups, or by an 'overlapping consensus' in which elements of civil society bring their own distinct principled reasons for cooperation to bear in justifying government. The hope is that individuals as group members can wear their citizenship lightly and avoid testing whether their primary loyalty is to their particular group or to a common public life. This does not necessarily indicate that government is weak; within limits, it may prove a justifiable compromise between civil society and strong government.

In evaluating how government and civil society may be accommodated, therefore, we can place congruence and modus vivendi along a spectrum. To the extent that civil society flourishes and evidences general agreement about significant public values, greater degrees of congruence can be tolerated. But to the extent that civil society is less open and more segmented, with deep social divisions based on class or status, modus vivendi may as a practical matter be all that is attainable. If a genuinely inclusive public identity is fragile and government resources limited, modus vivendi is a real achievement and a reasonable accommodation to civil society.

CIVIL SOCIETY AND DEMOCRACY

Democratic values are relevant to the goal of securing a proper accommodation between civil society and government. This is because democracy turns on the value of self-government, of a people ruling themselves. Implicit in this value is the distinction between a people and the state that represents them. This distinction is lost if a state merely programs persons in its own image, as, for example, in Aldous Huxley's Brave New World. Implicit in democracy, therefore, is a boundary between state and persons that is analogous to the boundary between state and civil society.

Although all states, including democratic states, contribute in multiple ways to the identity of their citizens, the independence of persons within democracies is typically marked sociologically and politically by the independent institutions and associations of civil society. This implies that the logic of congruence is bounded by democratic values, as well as by those of civil society. Even the most stalwart advocates of strong democracy would acknowledge that values and identity derive significantly from sources that reach beyond public norms like democracy or social justice. Most persons care intensely about matters that are the exclusive business of groups in civil society. Our interests, convictions, cultural, religious and sexual identities, status, salvation, exhibition of competence, exhilarating rivalries may have nothing to do with citizenship or the state. Democratic accountability is importantly measured by a state's responsiveness to these independent concerns.

Consider, for example, Hannah Arendt's analysis of the Nazi and the Stalinist regimes. The origins of totalitarianism, Arendt argued, lay in the weakening of secondary groups and associations. The defining characteristic of totalitarianism is the combination of 'atomistic individualism' with techniques of terror. The absence of social buffers between individuals and the state makes persons vulnerable to ferocious mobilization and extinction. Totalitarianism can be understood as the end point of unremitting congruence.

For close to half a century this view of civil society has been exploited by political theorists who describe what they perceive as conditions of growing atomism and privatism and raise the specter (not always apt) of totalitarianism. Theorists like Francois Furet pronounce the continuity between the Jacobin heritage of the Revolution and French 'statism,' and warn of the 'matrix of totalitarianism.'[15] American theorists portray the 'megastructures' of American government as hostile to healthy pluralism. They claim that government erodes the independent life of groups and associations directly by official regulation, subsidy, and control, and indirectly by monopolizing social functions and displacing secondary institutions. It is said that overbearing government has transformed the United States into a 'mass society' and that the revival of civil society is necessary to transfer 'meaning and value to the mega-structures of public order.'[16] Recapturing the density of association life has been deemed a necessary protection against atomism and its invitation to an antidemocratic totalitarianism.

Whatever the accuracy of these various diagnoses, they have in common the assumption that democracy depends on the activities of particularist, self-determining associations of civil society, where independent commitments, interests, and voices are developed. They express the insight that civil society is the precondition for democratic decision making, whether democracy is conceived as deliberation or as interest group pluralism, and that this is true even if the goal of democracy is to transcend particularism and arrive at uncoerced agreement or a common will. They stress that democratic values will be imperiled if congruence is pursued too comprehensively or too vigorously.

Political theory since World War II has also stressed the complementary insight, however, that democracy presupposes citizens who come genuinely to identify with the state as 'their' representative. This perspective has important implications for pursuing modus vivendi as an acceptable model of the relationship between civil society and government within democracies. To the extent that democracy presupposes the forging of a genuine common will, a mere modus vivendi must be ruled out as an option for accommodating civil society and government.

This perspective is implicit in the work of many theorists who stress that civil society is vital to the efforts of a democratic government to achieve consensus by building structures of 'interpenetration' between government and interest groups for making and implementing public policy. Associations are crucial to governance, particularly to the delivery of public services, even where they have no formal role and are best described as social or civic rather than political groups. In the United States, churches and neighbourhood groups, ethnic associations and civic charities, as well as for-profit organizations, share responsibility for addressing social needs with local, state, and federal governments in everything from housing to crime control.

This should not be conceived as pure voluntarism; groups may be neither an alternative to public provision nor unsupported by the state. Catholic Charities, the Boys and Girls Clubs, tenants' advocates, literacy centers, immigrant support services, after-school youth centers, family planning clinics, and innumerable others have been publicly subsidized. Lester Salamon calls this partnership between government and civil society 'third party government.'[17] At its essence, such interpenetration forges genuinely common commitments that underwrite a democratic allegiance and legitimacy far removed from a modus vivendi.

This analysis suggests that democratic states must pursue a logic that avoids the extremes of congruence and modus vivendi. A legitimate democratic state neither mechanically reproduces its citizens nor rules merely by default. Whatever compromise between these extremes is ultimately reached, political theory since World War II has stressed that the independent groups and associations of civil society will perform at least three functions that have special importance for democracies.

The first is to serve as a centre of collective political resistance against capricious and oppressive government. This aspect of civil society received particular emphasis in the struggle against Soviet imperialism. 'Civil society' entered the political lexicon of Central and Eastern Europe as an oppositional idea. Because it was imperative to break free from party dictatorship and because overt political opposition was ineffective, even suicidal, the principal resistance to centralized authority became associated with intellectual and cultural circles. Civil society signaled the ability to eke out some portion of negative liberty: 'Let me be, leave me alone, don't try to tell me how to live.'[18] Civil Society referred initially to an underground 'parallel polis' of groups attending to ostensibly non-political affairs.

Poland's Solidarity came to epitomize civil society as a seedbed of more active human rights claims and dissident movements.[19] As communist regimes collapsed, trade unions, professional organizations, churches, and political parties were prized as 'a living society in which public life and activities originating 'from below' are possible.' 'The social self-organization of society' became an ideal.[20] In the enthusiasm of the moment, however, it was forgotten that civil society and government are complementary and that they require each other, so that some actually proposed civil society as a substitute for government. For our purposes, however, it is sufficient to stress the ways in which civil society functioned to counterbalance oppressive and antidemocratic state actions.

A second function civil society performs for democracy is to organize people for democratic participation. There is nothing mysterious or organicist about this. Experience tells us quite a bit about the unpredictable origin and course of political participation. Groups that engage in political advocacy and agenda setting are not always formed initially for political purposes; their politicization is contingent and unpredictable. Group life is transformative. Thus when American jeremiahs interpret low voter turnout as a crisis of democracy, they see association as a resource for revivifying participation. They search for substitutes for groups like trade unions that were once strong, often looking to 'new social movements' to counterbalance entrenched interests and alter political agendas. Government initiatives are propelled by the mobilization of feminists and environmentalists, taxpayers and consumers, student groups and the politically organized elderly. Political parties are of course a key association, but all kinds of groups expose political arbitrariness and corruption and hold officials accountable by agitating outside of formal political arenas.

It would be a mistake, however, to imagine that civil society is a guarantee for successful democratic mobilization. Freedom of association may be a necessary condition for responsive and accountable democratic institutions, but it is not a sufficient condition. Not all 'interests' find their way into 'interest groups' and effective political representation. Groups may be too dispersed and trivial to set agendas and effectively energize democratic politics.[21] Individuals and groups may lack the resources for organization. The very pluralism of civil society can be politically intimidating. Jurgen Habermas observes that instead of creating strong new public identities, pluralization can produce a sense of 'impotence in the face of an impenetrable systemic complexity.'[22] Others caution that if politicized groups are too many and too strong, a 'hyperpluralist' crush can create crises of ungovernability.[23]

A third function civil society performs for democracy concerns socialization into the political values necessary for self-government. Many political theorists conceive civil society as the 'seedbed of virtue.' The governing assumption is that associations inculcate civic virtues and constructive dispositions like sociability and trust. They understand this socialization to spill over into public life. The phrase 'mediating institutions' is meant to capture this idea. The thought is that the sense of cooperation and shared responsibility generated by associations produce 'social networks' and 'virtuous cycles' of trust on an ever-expanding scale. Civil society is said to provide participatory, egalitarian experiences that foster the disposition to care for others. The moral dispositions and 'social capital' generated within groups are deemed invaluable for the conduct of democracy.

This point, however, can easily be overstated. Not all associations provide exemplary education. Certain groups cater to dark emotional needs and amplify selfish interests. They may even inculcate in members antisocial dispositions like snobbery or ethnic hatred, dispositions that Madison's 'mischiefs of faction' do not begin to encompass. In the face of such patently uncivil associations, theorists either define civil society in terms of benign formative associations, omitting vicious and incongruent groups from the start, or they assign government a stern tutorial and regulative role, invoking the logic of congruence.

We can conclude from this analysis that civil society is no guarantee of democracy, but it is necessary for democracy and can serve important democratic functions. A flourishing pluralistic civil society and strong democratic government are reciprocally supportive.

PERSPECTIVE ON CIVIL SOCIETY

The conception of civil society that we have sought to develop in this introduction is unmistakably a product of Western culture and institutions. It not only presupposes characteristically occidental social and governmental structures, but it draws upon a long intellectual history of attempting to comprehend the normative implications of these structures.

This history is most vividly displayed in the essays in this volume discussing natural law and Christianity. Both natural law perspectives and Christianity have over the millenniums sought to endow evolving occidental social structures with normative political significance. Within the natural law tradition, as Fred D. Miller[a] demonstrates, this significance can vary from imagining society as 'an organism with government as its head' to envisioning individuals as endowed with inalienable rights. All natural law theories are committed to explicating the social implications of human nature, and this commitment creates a certain strain when confronted by the particularism of modern civil society. Indeed, as William M. Sullivan[b] observes, influential Stoic contributions to natural law stressed the universalism of transcendent values 'available through 'right reason,'' which they contrasted to the particularism, the *ius gentium*, of specific states.

This attribution of universal value to extragovernmental sources heavily influenced early Christian thinking. John A. Coleman's essay[c] traces the efforts of modern Catholic thought to reconcile the transcendent truth of the church to the particularism of contemporary civil society. The principle of subsidiarity does yeoman's service in this context. Unresolved tensions about how Christianity can accommodate the pluralism and particularism of civil society are at the root of Max L. Stackhouse's[d] advocacy of 'the 'federal-covenantal' view, most fully articulated by the Reform tradition,' as distinct from 'the 'hierarchical-subsidiarity' view, most fully articulated by the Roman Catholic tradition.'

From the vantage of these historical traditions, the various contemporary perspectives on the relationship of government to civil society that are represented in this volume – classical liberalism, liberal egalitarianism, critical theory, and feminism – all seem remarkably similar. All accept the basic notion that the state speaks for the common good, while participants in civil society engage in enterprises that are

---

a. See essay 'Natural Law, Civil Society and Government' Fred D. Miller Jr. in *Civil Society and Government* ed. Nancy Rosenblum and Post, pp.187–215.

b. See essay 'Natural Law: A Response' William Sullivan in *Civil Society and Government* ed. Nancy Rosenblum and Post, pp. 216–222.

c. See essay 'A Limited State and a Vibrant Society: Christianity and Civil society' John A. Coleman in *Civil Society and Government* ed. Nancy Rosenblum and Post, pp. 223–254.

d. See essay 'Christianity, Civil Society and the State: A Protestant Response' Max L. Stackhouse in *Civil Society and Government* ed. Nancy Rosenblum and Post, pp. 255–264.

plural and particular. All accept the interdependence of civil society and the state, while at the same time recognizing the potential danger that each holds for the other. These contemporary perspectives differ from each other largely in matters of emphasis and focus.

It is 'almost definitive' of classical liberalism, as Steven Scalet and David Schmidtz[e] characterize it, to be simultaneously driven by a fear of the potential abuse of state power and a complementary passion for voluntarism. These very practical apprehensions profoundly influence the ways in which classical liberalism conceives the appropriate relationship between government and civil society, as the comments of Tom G. Palmer[f] illustrate.

Liberal egalitarianism, by contrast, seems to be guided as much by a profound commitment to certain ideals, like justice and equality, as by practical concerns. Will Kymlicka's essay[g] exemplifies how liberal egalitarians reason backward from the attainment of these ideals to conclusions about how the state ought to relate to civil society. Kymlicka concludes that equality requires the state to reach deeply into the socialization processes of civil society. William A. Galston[h], however, cautions that such intervention may come only at the price of undermining the independent and equally important value of liberty.

Critical theory, as explained by Kenneth Baynes[i] is less concerned with the achievement of specific values than with the complex dialectical processes by which values can be clarified and legitimized in modern society. Critical theory explores the preconditions for such legitimation.

---

e. See essay 'State, Civil Society; and Classical Liberalism' Steven Scalet and David Schmidtz in *Civil Society and Government* ed. by Nancy Rosenblum and Robert Post, pp. 26–47.

f. See essay 'Classical Liberalism and Civil Society: Definition, History and Relations' Tom G. Palmer in *Civil Society and Government* ed. by Nancy Rosenblum and Robert Post, pp. 48–78.

g. See essay Civil Society and Government: A Liberal-Egalitarian Perspective' Will Kymlicka in *Civil Society and Government* ed. by Nancy Rosenblum and Robert Post, pp. 79–110.

h. See essay 'Liberal Egalitarianism: A Family of Theories, Not a Single View' William A. Galston in *Civil Society and Government* ed. by Nancy Rosenblum and Robert Post, pp. 111–122.

i. See essay 'A Critical Theory Perspective on Civil Society and the State' Kenneth Baynes in *Civil Society and Government* ed. by Nancy Rosenblum and Robert Post, pp. 123–145.

It especially focuses on the question of how the particularities of civil society can be transmuted into the common values necessary to sustain state action, and how state action can in turn sustain civil society's capacity to create undistorted and legitimate values. Stephen K[j]. White's comment emphasizes that historically critical theory was not always satisfied with such abstract structural analysis, but focused also on the 'lived experience of suffering on the part of the disadvantaged segments of the population.'

Feminism is quite attentive to such experience. More than any of the other contemporary perspectives, feminism purports to speak for a substantive political perspective – its paramount concern is gender equality. As Rosenblum[k] notes, feminists may differ on a myriad of strategic and tactical questions, but they all embrace the task of 'patrolling the civil society/government boundary' so as to nourish and support the lives of women. Susan Okin's commentary[l] confirms the deep ways in which this substantive orientation informs and illuminates feminism's understanding of the relationship between government and civil society. Like other essays in this section, Rosenblum's looks ahead to perspectives marked by more profound disjunctures between equal citizenship and the laws of groups, between bounded government and civil society.

The differences between classical liberalism, liberal egalitarianism, critical theory, and feminism, which loom so large in the contemporary theoretical landscape, dwindle almost to insignificance when these perspectives are compared to the Confucian tradition explored by Peter Nasco.[m] If modern conceptions of civil society presuppose that persons move between distinct and inconsistent roles, the Confucian

---

j. See essay 'Skeptics at the Celebration: Civil Society and Early Frankfurt School' Stephen K. White in *Civil Society and Government* ed. by Nancy Rosenblum and Robert Post, pp. 146–150.

k. See 'Feminist Perspectives on Civil Society and Government' Nancy L. Rosenblum in *Civil Society and Government* ed. by Nancy Rosenblum and Robert Post, pp. 151–178.

l. See 'Comment on Nancy Rosenblum's Feminist Perspectives on Civil Society and Government' Susan Moller Okin in *Civil Society and Government* ed. by Nancy Rosenblum and Robert Post, pp. 179–186.

m. See 'Confucian Perspectives on Civil Society and Government' Peter Nasco in *Civil Society and Government* ed. by Nancy Rosenblum and Robert Post, pp. 334–359.

imagination pictures society as an 'organic' whole. This unitary order rules out any vision of the social world as resting agonistically on an endless opposition between the particularism of a civil society and the universalism of the state. Henry Rosemont thus concludes that 'the question of drawing boundaries between civil society and the state is not a meaningful one for classical Confucians.'

A similar point can be made about Jewish perspectives on civil society, as developed by Noam J. Zohar.[n] Questions of particularity and pluralism simply have no internal traction within the biblical and medieval Jewish tradition, where Torah is supreme law and the state is an alien threat to the covenental community. Zohar describes the minority Jewish community in larger states as analogous to elements of civil society. This history of semi-autonomous communities in exile, recognized as minorities but not as full citizens, has had a formative effect on the modern state of Israel, Zohar argues, where there is an uneasy equipose between the public system of justice for all citizens and private law, which requires individuals to be legal subjects of a particular religious group and assigns rights and duties on the basis of membership. But the question, as David Biale[o] points out, is whether such categories can 'work' in the context of a contemporary state with a fully modernized economy.

As John Kelsay[p] explains, the analogue to civil society/government in classical and modern Islam is the idea of 'complementarity' between religious and government authorities, the ulama/khilafat relation. From Islamic perspectives, the tie between Muslim status and citizenship is pervasive. The elements of civil society recognized as legitimate and autonomous are more constrained than in any Lockean or Hegelian account. Although religious authority is loosely structured so that there is a plurality of Muslim 'groups,' professional and business classes do not yet have secure liberties, and there is, for example, little freedom for voluntary association in Iran. The boundaries between government

n. See 'Civil Society and Government: Seeking Justice Insights' Noam J. Zohar in *Civil Society and Government* ed. by Nancy Rosenblum and Robert Post, pp. 265–279.

o. See 'Response to Noam Zohar' David Biale in *Civil Society and Government* ed. by Nancy Rosenblum and Robert Post, pp. 280–283.

p. See 'Civil Society and Government in Islam' John Kelsay in *Civil Society and Government* ed. by Nancy Rosenblum and Robert Post, pp. 284–316.

and social groups are defended principally in terms set by the `ulama as guardians of Islamic law and by governors worried about the sectarian potential of religion. While arguing for the importance of the distinction between society and state, Farhad Kazemi[q] underscores ongoing contention over the applicability of 'civil society' to Islamic societies. He sets it in the context of questions of state authority and exclusionary norms with regard to religious minorities and women – part of a larger debate about the congruence of Islam, civil society, and democracy.

The conceptual dissonance underlined by these essays is of obvious political importance. As globalization spreads Western institutions throughout the world, the question of how these institutions will be received assumes increased significance. The essays in this volume on classical liberalism, liberal egalitarianism, critical theory, feminism, natural law, and Christianity illustrate the family of meanings that civil society has received in the West. But the essays addressing Confucianism, Judaism, and Islam query whether and how these meanings can be transposed to radically different traditions. David Biale, for example, points to the anomaly of ultrareligious groups in Israel seeking to participate in a modern state using a conceptual framework derived from a biblical and medieval past. John Kelsay observes that moves to impose gender equality by government from above are depicted as anti-Islam and as a threat to the traditional role of religious leaders. He predicts that changes will come mainly from within religious institutions. Globalization can only magnify the extent and reach of such anomalies. The essays in this volume[%] are intended to provide a framework within which the diffusion, adoption, or imposition of Western concepts and social structures can be analyzed and understood.

The volume concludes with a comprehensive overview by Richard B. Miller.[r] Miller explores how distinct perspectives on civil society and government conceive the question of human flourishing. He asks

---

q. See 'Perspective on Islam and Civil Society' Farhad Kazemi in *Civil Society and Government* ed. by Nancy Rosenblum and Robert Post, pp. 317–333.

% Essays in this volume means essays included in volume *Civil Society and Government* edited by Nancy L Rosenblum and Robert C. Post (Princeton University Press-2002), 26–396.

r. See 'Overview: The Virtues and Vices of Civil Society' Richard B. Miller in *Civil Society and Government* ed. by Nancy Rosenblum and Robert Post, pp. 370–396.

'whether the attitudes and practices that materialize in civil society are civil and civilizing, and how we are to distinguish civilizing attitudes and practices from those that are not.' He usefully summarizes how different perspectives understand the proper role of the state in promoting human flourishing.

CONCLUSION

Our own view of these questions, which we have tried to defend in this introduction, is that freedom of association is an independent good, whose value can be realized only within a flourishing civil society. Perhaps that is why the concept of 'civil society' is almost always used with positive import. Civil society is the 'chicken soup' of the social sciences.[24] The valence is invariably positive, despite the enduring array of manifestly uncivil societies, hateful associations, and private despotisms. It is not too much to say that 'civil society' is the locus of what there is of utopianism in contemporary political thought.

In the flush of this utopianism, it is sometimes assumed that civil society can substitute for government. But, as we have tried to make clear, civil society and government are complementary constructions. Civil society cannot exist without government, and democratic governments cannot exist without civil society. The difficulty, however, is that government and civil society represent discrete values that are conceptually exclusive. There is thus enormous tension over the boundary between civil society and government. The resolution of this tension – the determination of which elements of civil society are salient for political resistance, democratic participation, or effective governance, or exactly how government may secure and promote civil society – is of course contingent and contestable.

That is why nothing is more important than comparative political theory and a keen historical sensibility in getting right the dangers and the opportunities. The diverse normative and historical perspectives offered in this volume are meant to be an informative and useful means of sharpening our judgement in these matters.

REFERENCES

1. This is not the way that the participants in this dispute would characterize the questions, but compare the moral understanding of the market in Adam Smith. See too Albert O. Hirschman, 'The Passions and the Interests: Political Arguments for Capitalism before Its Triumph' (Princeton: Princeton University Press, 1977).
2. We note, however, that ascriptive belonging to an inchoate ethnic or racial group - better described as an objectively identifiable population - does not entail membership in an organized association, and undifferentiated populations are not properly speaking components of civil society except insofar as they are organized into actual groups. This is the theme of Nancy L. Rosenblum, 'Repairing the Empty Politics of Recognition,' in *Membership and Morals: The Personal Uses of Pluralism in America* (Princeton: Princeton University Press, 1998).
3. See Stephen Holmes, *Passions and Constraint* (Chicago: University of Chicago Press,1995)
4. See Stephen Holmes, and Cass R. Sunstein, *The Cost of Rights* (New York: W.W.Norton Co., 1999).
5. On the relationship between civil society and law, see Martin Krygier, 'Virtuous Circles: Antipodean Reflections on Power, Institutions, and Civil Society', East European Politics and Societies 11, no. 1 (Winter 1997): 36–88.
6. See Sanford Levinson, Written in Stone: *Public Monuments in Changing Societies* (Durham, N>C: Duke University Press, 1998).
7. See Robert Post, 'Between Democracy and Community: The Legal Constitution of Social Forum,' NOMOS 35 ("Democratic Community") (1993): 175–77.
8. G.W.F. Hegel, *Philosophy of Right* (Oxford: Oxford University Press, 1952), p. 266 addition to 182; p. 148 238; p, 276 238; p. 452; p. 133 207; p. 133 207; p. 278 255.
9. See for example Iris Marion Young, 'Impartiality and the Civic Public,' in *Feminism as Critique: On the Politics of Gender*, ed. Seyla Benhabib and Drucilla Cornell (Minneapolis: University of Minnesota Press, 1947). This parallels the argument in moral

philosophy that moral reasoning cannot transcend particularist perspectives. Cf. Seyla Benhabib's revision of Jurgen Habermas in 'The Generalized and the Concrete Other,' in Benhabib, Situating the Self (New York: Routledge, 1992), 148–77.

10. Importance of this fact is brought out by comparative studies of leal systems and the civil standing of women. See essays by Martha Nussbaum and Carol Weisbrod in Nancy L. Rosenblum, ed., Obligations of Citizenship and Demands of Faith: Religious Accommodation in *Pluralist Democracies* (Princeton: Princeton University Press, 2000).
11. Steven Macedo 'Community, Diversity, and Civil Education: Toward a Liberal Political Science of Group Life'. Social Philosophy and Policy Foundation 13, No. 1 (1996); 264, 250.
12. See, e.g., Robert Post, *Constitutional Domains: Democracy, Community, Management* (Cambridge: Harvard University Press, 1995).
13. Joshua Cohen and Joel Rogers, 'Secondary Associations and Democratic Governance,' Politics and Society 20 (1992); 393–472.
14. John Gray, 'Totalitarianism, Reform and Civil Society,' in *Post Liberalism: Studies in Political Thought* (New York: Routledge, 1993), 157.
15. Francois Furet, *Interpreting the French Revolution*, trans. E. Forster (Cambridge: Cambridge University Press, 1981), 180.
16. Peter Berger and Richard Neuhaus, To Empower People: The Role of Mediating Structure in Public Policy (Washington, D.C: American Enterprise Institute, 1977), 6.3.41.
17. Lester Salamon, Partners in Public Service: Government Nonprofit Relations in the Modern Welfare State (Baltimore: Johns Hopkins University Press, 1995). There is ample confirmation that in the United States the growth of government has been a spur to the growth of the voluntary sector.
18. Cited in John Keane, ed., Civil Society and the State: New European Perspectives (London: Verso, 1988), 5.

19. For theorist of Latin American politics, too, civil society is commonly said to habour pockets of resistance to party and military dictatorship.
20. Jan Simsa in H. Gordon Skilling, 'Parallel Polis, or an Independent Society in Central and Eastern Europe: An Inquiry,' Social Research 55, No. 1-2 (1988): 245; Valcav Benda, cited in ibid., 218.
21. Michael Walzer, 'Constitutional Rights and the Shape of Civil Society,' in *The Constitution of the People*, ed. Robert E. Calvert) Lawrence: University Press of Kansas, 1991), 123–25.
22. Jurgen Habermas, 'Further Reflections on the Public Sphere,' in *Habermas and the Public Sphere*, ed. Craig Calhoun (Cambridge: MIT Press, 1992), 453–56.
23. Claude Lefort, to take a recent example, argues that the recent French sympathy for fluid groups will overwhelm the capacity of government and administrative experts to respond in an orderly fashion as arbiter of the social contract in Ecrire: A p'epreuve du politique (Paris: Calmann Levy, 1992), 71, cited in Cheryl Welch, 'Tocqueville and the New Europe' (manuscript).
24. As Eric Uslaner say of trust, it is the 'chicken soup' of the social sciences. See *The Moral Foundations of Trust* (Cambridge: Cambridge University Press, 2002), 1. The exception is Marxist thought and early critical theorists.

5

Civil Society and the Politics of Identity

Ellen Meiksins Wood

At a time when a critique of capitalism is more urgent than ever, the dominant theoretical trends on the left are busy conceptualizing away the very idea of capitalism. The 'post-modern' world, we are told, is a pastiche of fragments and 'difference'. The systemic unity of capitalism, its 'objective structures' and totalizing imperatives, have given way (if they ever existed) to a bricolage of multiple social realities, a pluralistic structure so diverse and flexible that it can be rearranged by discursive construction. The traditional capitalist economy has been replaced by a 'post-Fordist' fragmentation, where every fragment opens up a space for emancipatory struggles. The constitutive class relations of capitalism represent only one personal 'identity' among many others, no longer 'privileged' by its historic centrality. And so on.

However diverse the methods of conceptually dissolving capitalism – including everything from the theory of post-Fordism to post-modern 'cultural studies' and the 'politics of identity' – they often share one especially serviceable concept: 'civil society'. After a long and somewhat tortuous history, after a series of milestones in the works of Hegel, Marx and Gramsci, this versatile idea has become an all-purpose catchword for the left, embracing a wide range of emancipatory aspirations, as well – it must be said – as a whole set of excuses for political retreat. However constructive this idea may be in defending human liberties against state oppression, or in marking out a terrain of social practices, institutions and relations neglected by the 'old' Marxist left, 'civil society' is now in danger of becoming an alibi for capitalism.

THE IDEA OF CIVIL SOCIETY: A BRIEF HISTORICAL SKETCH

There has been a long intellectual tradition in the West, even reaching back to classical antiquity, which has in various ways delineated a terrain of human association, some notion of society, distinct from the body politic and with moral claims independent of, and sometimes opposed to, the state's authority. Whatever other factors have been at work in producing such concepts, their evolution has been from the beginning bound up with the development of private property as a distinct and autonomous locus of social power. For example, although the ancient Romans, like the Greeks, still tended to identify the state with the community of citizens, the 'Roman people', they did produce some major advances in the conceptual separation of state and 'society', especially in the Roman Law which distinguished between public and private spheres and gave private property a legal status and clarity it had never enjoyed before.[1]

In that sense, although the modern concept of 'civil society' is associated with the specific property relations of capitalism, it is a variation on an old theme. Nevertheless, the variation is a critical one; and any attempt to dilute the specificity of this 'civil society', to obscure its differentiation from earlier conceptions of 'society', risks disguising the particularity of capitalism itself as a distinct social form with its own characteristic social relations, its own modes of appropriation and exploitation, its own rules of reproduction, its own systemic imperatives.[2]

The very particular modern conception of 'civil society' – a conception that appeared systematically for the first time in the eighteenth century – is something quite distinct from earlier notions of 'society': civil society represents a separate sphere of human relations and activity, differentiated from the state but neither public nor private or perhaps both at once, embodying not only a whole range of social interactions apart from the private sphere of the household and the public sphere of the state, but more specifically a network of distinctively economic relations, the sphere of the market place, the arena of production, distribution and exchange. A necessary but not sufficient pre-condition for this conception of civil society was the modern idea of the state as an abstract entity with its own corporate identity, which evolved with the rise of European absolutism; but the full conceptual differentiation of 'civil society' required the emergence of an autonomous 'economy', separated out from the unity of the 'political' and 'economic' which still characterized the absolutist state.

Paradoxically – or perhaps not so paradoxically – the early usages of the term 'civil society' in the birthplace of capitalism, in early modern England, far from establishing an opposition between civil society and the state, conflated the two. In sixteenth and seventeenth century English political thought, 'civil society' was typically synonymous with the 'commonwealth' or 'political society'. This conflation of state and 'society' represented the subordination of the state to the community of private-property holders (as against both monarch and 'multitude') which constituted the political nation. It reflected a unique political dispensation, in which the dominant class depended for its wealth and power increasingly on purely 'economic' modes of appropriation, instead of on directly coercive 'extra-economic' modes of accumulation by political and military means, like feudal rent taking or absolutist taxation and office holding as primary instruments of private appropriation.

But if English usage tended to blur the distinction between state and civil society, it was English conditions – the very same system of property relations and capitalist appropriation, but now more advanced and with a more highly developed market mechanism – that made possible the modern conceptual opposition between the two. When Hegel constructed his conceptual dichotomy, Napoleon was his inspiration for the 'modern' state; but it was primarily the capitalist economy of England – through the medium of classical political economists like Smith and Steuart – that provided the model of 'civil society' (with certain distinctively Hegelian corrections and improvements).

Hegel's identification of 'civil' with 'bourgeois' society was more than just a fluke of the German language. The phenomenon which he designated by the term *burgerliche Gesellschaft* was a historically specific social form. Although this 'civil society' did not refer exclusively to purely 'economic' institutions (it was, for example, supplemented by Hegel's modern adaptation of medieval corporate principles), the modern 'economy' was its essential condition. For Hegel, the possibility of preserving both individual freedom and the 'universality' of the state, instead of subordinating one to the other as earlier societies had done, rested on the emergence of a new class and a whole new sphere of social existence: a distinct and autonomous 'economy'. It was in. this new sphere that private and public, particular and universal, could meet through the interaction of private interests, on a terrain that was neither household nor state but a mediation between the two.

Marx, of course, transformed Hegel's distinction between the state and civil society by denying the universality of the state and insisting that the state expressed the particularities of 'civil society' and its class relations, a discovery that compelled him to devote his life's work to exploring the anatomy of' 'civil society' in the form of a critique of political economy. The conceptual differentiation of state and civil society was thus a pre-condition to Marx's analysis of capitalism, but the effect of that analysis was to deprive the Hegelian distinction of its rationale. The state-civil society dualism more or less disappeared from the mainstream of political discourse.

It required Gramsci's reformulation to revive the concept of civil society as a central organizing principle of socialist theory. The object of this new formulation was to acknowledge both the complexity of political power in the parliamentary or constitutional states of the West, in contrast to more openly coercive autocracies, and the difficulty of supplanting a system of class domination in which class power has no clearly visible point of concentration in the state but is diffused throughout society and its cultural practices. Gramsci thus appropriated the concept of civil society to mark out the terrain of a new kind of struggle which would take the battle against capitalism not only to its economic foundations but to its cultural and ideological roots in everyday life.

THE NEW CULT OF CIVIL SOCIETY

Gramsci's conception of 'civil society' was unambiguously intended as a weapon against capitalism, not an accommodation to it. Despite the appeal to his authority which has become a staple of contemporary social theories of the left, the concept in its current usage no longer has this unequivocally anti-capitalist intent. It has now acquired a whole new set of meanings and consequences, some very positive for the emancipatory projects of the left, others far less so. The two contrary impulses can be summed up in this way: the new concept of 'civil society' signals that the left has learned the lessons of liberalism about the dangers of state oppression, but we seem to be forgetting the lessons we once learned from the socialist tradition about the oppressions of civil society. On the one hand, the advocates of civil society are strengthening our defence of non-state institutions and relations against the power of the state; on the other hand, they are tending to weaken our resistance to the coercions of capitalism.

The concept of 'civil society' is being mobilized to serve so many varied purposes that it is impossible to isolate a single school of thought associated with it; but some common themes have emerged. 'Civil society' is generally intended to identify an arena of (at least potential) freedom outside the state, a space for autonomy, voluntary association and plurality or even conflict, guaranteed by the kind of 'formal democracy' that has evolved in the West. The concept is also meant to reduce the capitalist system (or the 'economy') to one of many spheres in the plural and heterogeneous complexity of modern society. The concept of 'civil society' can achieve this effect in one of two principal ways. It can be made to designate that multiplicity itself as against the coercions of both state and capitalist economy; or, more commonly, it can encompass the 'economy' within a larger sphere of multiple non-state institutions and relations.[3] In either case, the emphasis is on the plurality of social relations and practices among which the capitalist economy takes its place as one of many.

The principal current usages proceed from the distinction between civil society and state, 'Civil society' is defined by the advocates of this distinction in terms of a few simple oppositions: for example, 'the state (and its military, policing, legal, administrative, productive, and cultural organs) and the non-state (market-regulated, privately controlled or voluntarily organized) realm of civil society';[4] or 'political' versus 'social' power, 'public' versus 'private' law, 'state-sanctioned (dis)information and propaganda' versus 'freely circulated public opinion'.[5] In this definition, 'civil society' encompasses a very wide range of institutions and relations, from households, trade unions, voluntary associations, hospitals, churches, to the market, capitalist enterprises, indeed the whole capitalist economy. The significant antitheses are simply state and non-state, or perhaps political and social.

This dichotomy apparently corresponds to the opposition between coercion, as embodied in the state, and freedom or voluntary action, which belongs in principle, if not necessarily in practice, to civil society. Civil society may be in various ways and degrees submerged or eclipsed by the state, and different political systems or whole 'historical regions' may vary according to the degree of 'autonomy' which they accord to the non-state sphere. It is a special characteristic of the West, for example, that it has given rise to a uniquely well-developed separation of state and civil society, and hence a particularly advanced form of political freedom.

The advocates of this state-civil society distinction generally ascribe to it two principal benefits. First, it focuses our attention on the dangers of state oppression and on the need to set proper limits on the actions of the state, by organizing and reinforcing the pressures against it within society. In other words, it revives the liberal concern with the limitation and legitimation of political power, and especially the control of such power by freedom of association and autonomous organization within society, too often neglected by the left in theory and practice. Second, the concept of civil society recognizes and celebrates difference and diversity. Its advocates make pluralism a primary good, in contrast, it is claimed, to Marxism, which is, they say, essentially monistic, reductionist, economistic.[6] This new pluralism invites us to appreciate a whole range of institutions and relations neglected by traditional socialism in its preoccupation with the economy and class.

The impetus to the revival of this conceptual dichotomy has come from several directions. The strongest impulse undoubtedly came from Eastern Europe, where 'civil society' was a major weapon in the ideological arsenal of opposition forces against state oppression. Here, the issues were fairly clear: the state – including both its political and economic apparatuses of domination – could be more or less unambiguously set against a (potentially) free space outside the state. The civil society/state antithesis could, for example, be said to correspond neatly to the opposition of Solidarity to Party and State.[7]

The crisis of the Communist states has, needless to say, also left a deep impression on the Western left, converging with other influences: the limitations of social democracy, with its unbounded faith in the state as the agent of social improvement, as well as the emergence of emancipatory struggles by social movements not based on class, with a sensitivity to dimensions of human experience all too often neglected by the traditional socialist left. These heightened sensitivities to the dangers posed by the state and to the complexities of human experience have been associated with a wide range of activisms, taking in everything from feminism, ecology and peace, to constitutional reform. Each of these projects has often drawn upon the concept of civil society.

No socialist can doubt the value of these new sensitivities, but there must be serious misgivings about this particular method of focusing our attention on them. We are being asked to pay a heavy price for the all-embracing concept of 'civil society'. This conceptual portmanteau, which indiscriminately lumps together everything from households and voluntary associations to the economic system of capitalism, confuses and disguises as much as it reveals. In Eastern Europe, it can be made to apprehend everything from the defence of political rights and cultural freedoms to the marketization of post-Communist economies and the restoration of capitalism. 'Civil society' can serve as a code word or cover for capitalism, and the market can be lumped together with other less ambiguous goods, like political and intellectual liberties, as an unequivocally desirable goal.

But if the dangers of this conceptual strategy and of assigning the market to the free space of 'civil society' appear to pale before the enormity of Stalinist oppression in the East, problems of an altogether different order arise in the West, where a fully developed capitalism does actually exist and where state oppression is not an immediate and massive evil which overwhelms all other social ills. Since in this case 'civil society' is made to encompass a whole layer of social reality that did not exist in Communist societies, the implications of its usage are in some important respects even more problematic.

Here, the danger lies in the fact that the totalizing logic and the coercive power of capitalism become invisible, when the whole social system of capitalism is reduced to one set of institutions and relations among many others, on a conceptual par with households or voluntary associations. Such a reduction is, in fact, the principal distinctive feature of 'civil society' in its new incarnation. Its effect is to conceptualize away the problem of capitalism by disaggregating society into fragments, with no overarching power structure, no totalizing unity, no systemic coercions – in other words, no capitalist system, with its expansionary drive and its capacity to penetrate every aspect of social life.

It is a typical strategy of the 'civil society' argument – indeed, its *raison d'etre* – to attack Marxist 'reductionism' or 'economism'. Marxism, it is said, reduces civil society to the 'mode of production', the capitalist economy. 'The importance of other institutions of civil society – such as households, churches, scientific and literary associations, prisons and hospitals – is devalued'.[8]

Whether or not Marxists have habitually paid too little attention to these 'other' institutions, the weakness of this juxtaposition (the capitalist economy and 'other institutions' like hospitals?) should be immediately apparent. It must surely be possible even for non-Marxists to acknowledge, for example, the very simple truth that in the West hospitals are situated within a capitalist economy which has profoundly affected the organization of health care and the nature of medical institutions. But is it possible to conceive of an analogous proposition about the effects of hospitals on capitalism? Does this observation about 'other institutions' mean that Marx did not value households and hospitals, or is it rather that he did not attribute to them the same historically determinative force? Is there no basis for distinguishing among these various 'institutions' on all sorts of quantitative and qualitative grounds, from size and scope to social power and historical efficacy? Typically, the current usage of 'civil society' evades questions like this. It also has the effect of confusing the moral claims of other institutions with their determinative power, or rather of dismissing altogether the essentially empirical question of historical and social determinations.

There is another version of the argument which, instead of simply evading the systemic totality of capitalism, explicitly denies it. The very existence of other modes of domination than class relations, other principles of stratification than class inequality, other social struggles than class struggle, is taken to demonstrate that capitalism, whose constitutive relation is class, is not a totalizing system. The Marxist preoccupation with 'economic' relations and class at the expense of other social relations and identities is understood to demonstrate that the attempt to 'totalize all society from the standpoint of one sphere, the economy or the mode of production', is misconceived for the simple reason that other 'spheres' self-evidently exist.[9]

This argument is circular and question begging. To deny the totalizing logic of capitalism, it is not enough merely to indicate the plurality of social identities and relations. The class relation that constitutes capitalism is not, after all, just a personal identity, nor even just a principle of 'stratification' or inequality. It is not only a specific system of power relations but also the constitutive relation of a distinctive social process, the dynamic of accumulation and the self-expansion of capital. Of course it can be easily – self-evidently -shown that class is not the only principle of 'stratification' the only form of inequality and domination. But this tells us virtually nothing about the totalizing logic of capitalism.

To deny the totalizing logic of capitalism, it would have to be convincingly demonstrated that these other spheres and identities do not come – or not in any significant way – within the determinative force of capitalism, its system of social property relations, its expansionary imperatives, its drive for accumulation, its commodification of all social life, its creation of the market as a necessity, a compulsive mechanism of competition and self-sustaining 'growth', and so on. But 'civil society' arguments (or, indeed, 'post-Marxist' arguments in general) do not typically take the form of historically and empirically refuting the determinative effects of capitalist relations. Instead (when they do not take the simple circular form: capitalism is not a totalizing system because spheres other than the economy exist) they tend to proceed as abstract philosophical arguments, as internal critiques of Marxist theory, or, most commonly, as moral prescriptions about the dangers of devaluing 'other' spheres of human experience.

In one form or another, capitalism is cut down to the size and weight of 'other' singular and specific institutions and disappears into a conceptual night where all cats are grey. The strategy of dissolving capitalism into an unstructured and undifferentiated plurality of social institutions and relations cannot help but weaken both the analytic and the normative force of 'civil society', its capacity to deal with the limitation and legitimation, of power, as well as its usefulness in guiding emancipatory projects. The current theories occlude 'civil society' in its distinctive sense as a social form specific to capitalism, a systemic totality within which all 'other' institutions are situated and all social forces must find their way, a specific and unprecedented sphere of social power, which poses wholly new problems of legitimation and control, problems not addressed by traditional theories of the state nor by contemporary liberalism.

CAPITALISM, 'FORMAL DEMOCRACY' AND THE SPECIFICITY OF THE WEST

One of the principal charges levelled against Marxism by the advocates of 'civil society' is that it endangers democratic freedoms by identifying Western 'formal democracy' – the legal and political forms that guarantee a free space for 'civil society' – with capitalism: 'civil' equals 'bourgeois' society. The danger, they claim, is that we might be tempted to throw out the baby with the bath water, to reject liberal democracy together with capitalism.[10] We should instead, they argue, acknowledge the benefits of formal democracy, while expanding its principles of individual freedom and equality by dissociating them from capitalism in order to deny that capitalism is the sole or best means of advancing these principles.

It must be said that criticism of contemporary Western Marxism on these grounds must disregard the bulk of Marxist political theory since the sixties, and especially since the theory of the state was revived by the 'Miliband-Poulantzas' debate. Certainly civil liberties were a major preoccupation of both the principals in that controversy, and of many others who have followed in their train. Even the contention that – classical' Marxism – in the person of Marx or Engels – was too indifferent to civil liberties is open to question. But without reducing this discussion to a merely textual debate about the Marxist ('classical or contemporary) attitude to 'bourgeois' liberties, let us accept that all socialists, Marxist or otherwise, must uphold civil liberties (now commonly, if somewhat vaguely, called 'human rights'), principles of legality, freedom of speech and association, and the protection of a 'non-state' sphere against incursions by the state. We must acknowledge that some institutional protections of this kind are necessary conditions of any democracy, even though we may not accept the identification of democracy with, or its confinement to, the formal safeguards of 'liberalism', and even if we may believe that 'liberal' protections will have to take a different institutional form in socialist democracy than under capitalism.[11]

Difficulties nevertheless remain in the 'civil society' argument. There are other ways (indeed the principal ways in Marxist theory) of associating 'formal democracy' with capitalism than by rejecting the one with the other. We can recognize the historical and structural connections without denying the value of civil liberties. An understanding of these connections does not compel us to devalue civil liberties, but nor does it oblige us to accept capitalism as the sole or best means of maintaining individual autonomy; and it leaves us perfectly free also to acknowledge that capitalism, while in certain historical conditions conducive to 'formal democracy', can easily do without it – as it has done more than once in recent history. At any rate, not to see the connections, or to mistake their character, limits our understanding of both democracy and capitalism.

The historical and structural connection between formal democracy and capitalism can certainly be formulated with reference to the separation of the state from civil society. Much depends, however, on how we interpret that separation and the historical process that brought it about. There is a view of history, and a concomitant interpretation of the state-civil society separation, which cannot see the evolution of capitalism as anything but progressive. It is a view of history commonly associated with liberalism or 'bourgeois' ideology, but one that seems increasingly to underlie conceptions of democracy on the left.

The historical presuppositions underlying the advocacy of 'civil society' are seldom explicitly spelled out. There is, however, a particularly useful and sophisticated account by a Hungarian scholar, published in English translation in a volume devoted to reviving 'civil society' (East and West), which may serve as a model of the relevant historical interpretation. In an attempt to characterize three different 'historical regions of Europe' – Western and Eastern Europe and something in between – Jeno Szucs (following Istvan Bibo) offers the following account of the 'Western' model, in 'a search for the deepest roots of a 'democratic way of organizing society'.[12] The most distinctive 'characteristic of the West is the structural – and theoretical – separation of 'society' from the 'state', a unique development which lies at the heart of Western democracy, while its corresponding absence in the East accounts for an evolution from autocracy to totalitarianism.[13] The roots of this development, according to Szucs, lie in Western feudalism.

The uniqueness of Western history lay, according to this argument, in 'an entirely unusual 'take-off' in the rise of civilizations. This take-off took place amidst disintegration instead of integration, and amidst declining civilization, re-agrarianization and mounting political anarchy'.[14] This fragmentation and disintegration were the preconditions of the separation of 'society' and 'state'. In the high civilizations of the East, where no such separation took place, the political function continued to be exercised 'downwards from above'.

In the process of feudal 'fragmentation' in the West, the old political relations of states and subjects were replaced by new social ties, of a contractual nature, between lords and vassals. This substitution of social-contractual relations for political relations had among its major consequences a new principle of human dignity, freedom and the 'honour' of the individual. And the territorial disintegration into small units each with its own customary law produced a decentralization of law which could resist 'descending' mechanisms of exercising power'.[15] When sovereignty was later reconstructed by the Western monarchies, the new state was essentially constituted 'vertically from below'.[16] It was a 'unity in plurality' that made 'freedoms' the 'internal organizing principles' of Western social structure 'and led to something which drew the line so sharply between the medieval West and many other civilizations: the birth of 'society' as an autonomous entity'.[17]

There is much in this argument that is truly illuminating, but equally instructive is the bias in its angle of vision. Here, in fact, are all the staples of liberal history: the progress of civilization (at least in the West) as an unambiguous ascent of individual 'freedom' and 'dignity' (if there is a critical difference between Szucs's account and the traditional liberal view, it is that the latter is more frank about the identification of individuality with private property); the prime focus on the tension between individual or 'society' and the state as the moving force of history; even – and perhaps especially – the tendency to associate the advance of civilization, and democracy itself, with milestones in the ascent of the propertied classes. Although there was nothing democratic about the medieval West, Szucs concedes, this is where the 'deepest roots' of democracy are to be found. Although Szucs does not say it in so many words, it appears that the 'constitutive idea' of modern democracy was lordship.

Suppose we look at the same sequence of events from a different angle. Seen from another vantage point, the same 'fragmentation', the same replacement of political relations by social and contractual bonds, the same 'parcellization' of sovereignty, the same 'autonomy of society', even while their uniqueness and importance in the trajectory of Western development are acknowledged, can have very different consequences for our appreciation of 'civil society' and the development of Western democracy.

The divergence of the 'West' from the 'Eastern' pattern of state formation began, of course, much earlier than medieval feudalism. It could be traced as far back as early Greek antiquity, but for our purposes a critical benchmark can be identified in ancient Rome. This divergence, it needs to be stressed, had to do not only with political forms – but above all with modes of appropriation – and here developments in the Roman system of private property were decisive. (It is a curious but 'symptomatic' feature of Szucs's argument that modes of appropriation and exploitation do not figure centrally, if at all, in his differentiation of the three historical regions of Europe – which may also explain his insistence on a radical break between antiquity and feudalism. At the very least, the survival of Roman law, the quintessential symbol of the Roman property regime, should have signalled to Szucs some fundamental continuity between the Western 'autonomy' of civil society and the Roman system of appropriation.)

Rome represents a striking contrast to other 'high' civilizations – both in the ancient world and centuries later – where access to great wealth, to the surplus labour of others on a large scale, was typically achieved through the medium of the state (for example, late Imperial China, which had a highly developed system of private property but where great wealth and power resided not in land so much as in the state, in the bureaucratic hierarchy whose pinnacle was the court and imperial officialdom). Rome was distinctive in its emphasis on private property, on the acquisition of massive land holdings, as a means of appropriation. The Roman aristocracy had an insatiable appetite for land which created unprecedented concentrations of wealth and a predatory imperial power unrivalled by any other ancient empire in its hunger not simply for tribute but for territory. And it was Rome which extended its regime of private property throughout a vast and diverse empire, governed without a massive bureaucracy but instead through a 'municipal' system which effectively constituted a federation of local aristocracies. The result was a very specific combination of a strong imperial state and a dominant propertied class autonomous from it, a strong state which at the same time encouraged, instead of impeding, the autonomous development of private property. It was Rome, in short, that firmly and self-consciously established private property as an autonomous locus of social power, detached from, while supported by, the state.

The 'fragmentation' of feudalism must be seen in this light, as rooted in the privatization of power already inherent in the Roman property system and in the Empire's fragmented 'municipal' administration. When the tensions between the Roman imperial state and the autonomous power of private property were finally resolved by the disintegration of the central state, the autonomous power of property remained. The old political relations of rulers and subjects were gradually dissolved into the 'social' relations between lords and vassals, and more particularly, lords and peasants. In the institution of lordship, political and economic powers were united as they had been where the state was a major source of private wealth; but this time, that unity existed in a fragmented and privatized form.

Seen from this perspective, the development of the West can hardly be viewed as simply the rise of individuality, the rule of law, the progress of freedom or power from 'below'; and the autonomy of 'civil society' acquires a different meaning. The very developments described by Szucs in these terms are also, and at the same time, the evolution of new forms of exploitation and domination (the constitutive 'power from below' is, after all, the power of lordship), new relations of personal dependence and bondage, the privatization of surplus extraction and the transfer of ancient oppressions from the state to 'society' – that is, a transfer of power relations and domination from the state to private property. This new division of labour between state and 'society' also laid a foundation (as a necessary though not sufficient condition) for the increasing separation of private appropriation from public responsibilities which came to fruition in capitalism.

Capitalism then represents the culmination of a long development, but it also constitutes a qualitative break (which occurred 'spontaneously' only in the particular historical conditions of England). Not only is it characterized by a transformation of social power, a new division of labour between state and private property or class, but it also marks the creation of a completely new form of coercion, the market – the market not simply as a sphere of opportunity, freedom and choice, but as a compulsion, a necessity, a social discipline, capable of subjecting all human activities and relationships to its requirements.

CIVIL SOCIETY AND THE DEVALUATION OF DEMOCRACY

It is not, then, enough to say that democracy can be expanded by detaching the principles of 'formal democracy' from any association with capitalism. Nor is it enough to say that capitalist democracy is incomplete, one stage in an unambiguously progressive development which must be perfected by socialism and advanced beyond the limitations of 'formal democracy'. The point is rather that the association of capitalism with 'formal democracy' represents a contradictory unity of advance and retreat, both an enhancement and a devaluation of democracy. 'Formal democracy' certainly is an improvement on political forms lacking civil liberties, the rule of law and the principle of representation. But it is also, equally and at the same time, a subtraction from the substance of the democratic idea, and one which is historically and structurally associated with capitalism.[18]

I have already elaborated on some of these themes in chapters of my book *Democracy against Capitalism* 2007. Here, it is enough to note a certain paradox in the insistence that we should not allow our conception of human emancipation to be constrained by the identification of 'formal democracy' with capitalism. If we think of human emancipation as little more than an extension of liberal democracy, then we may in the end be persuaded to believe that capitalism is after all its surest guarantee.

The separation of the state and civil society in the West has certainly given rise to new forms of freedom and equality, but it has also created new modes of domination and coercion. One way of characterizing the specificity of 'civil society' as a particular social form unique to the modern world – the particular historical conditions that made possible the modern distinction between state and civil society – is to say that it constituted a new form of social power, in which many coercive functions that once belonged to the state were relocated in the 'private' sphere, in private property, class exploitation, and market imperatives.

It is, in a sense, this 'privatization' of public power that has created the historically novel realm of 'civil society'.

'Civil society' constitutes not only a wholly new relation between 'public' and 'private' but more precisely a wholly new 'private' realm, with a distinctive 'public' presence and oppressions of its own, a unique structure of power and domination, and a ruthless systemic logic. It represents a particular network of social relations which does not simply stand in opposition to the coercive, 'policing' and 'administrative' functions of the state but represents the *relocation* of these functions, or at least some significant part of them. It entails a new division of labour between the 'public' sphere of the state and the 'private' sphere of capitalist property and the imperatives of the market, in which appropriation, exploitation and domination are detached from public authority and social responsibility – while these new private powers rely on the state to sustain them, by means of a more thoroughly concentrated power of enforcement than has ever existed before.

'Civil society' has given private property and its possessors a command over people and their daily lives, a power enforced by the state but accountable to no one, which many an old tyrannical state would have envied. Even those activities and experiences that fall outside the immediate command structure of the capitalist enterprise, or outside the very great political power of capital, are regulated by the dictates of the market, the necessities of competition and profitability. Even when the market is not, as it commonly is in advanced capitalist "societies, merely an instrument of power for giant conglomerates and multi-national corporations, it is still a coercive force, capable of subjecting all human values, activities and relationships to its imperatives. No ancient despot could have hoped to penetrate the personal lives of his subjects – their life chances, choices, preferences, opinions and relationships – in the same comprehensive and minute detail, not only in the workplace but in every corner of their lives. And the market has created new instruments of power to be manipulated not only by multi-national capital but by advanced capitalist states, which can act to impose draconian 'market disciplines' on other economies while often sheltering their own domestic capital. Coercion, in other words, has been not just a disorder of 'civil society' but one of its constitutive principles. For that matter, the coercive functions of the state have in large part been occupied with the enforcement of domination in civil society.

This historical reality tends to undermine the neat distinctions required by current theories which ask us to treat civil society as, at least in principle, the sphere of freedom and voluntary action, the antithesis of the irreducibly coercive principle which intrinsically belongs to the state. It is certainly true that in capitalist society, with its separation of 'political' and 'economic' spheres, or the state and civil society, coercive public power is centralized and concentrated to a greater degree than ever before, but this simply means that one of the principal functions of 'public' coercion by the state is to sustain 'private' power in civil society.

One of the most obvious examples of the distorted vision produced by the simple dichotomy between the state as the site of coercion and 'civil society' as a free space is the extent to which civil liberties like freedom of expression of the press in capitalist societies are measured not by the breadth of opinion and debate available in the media but the extent to which the media are private property and capital is free to profit from them. The press is 'free' when it is private, however much it may 'manufacture consent'.

The current theories of civil society do, of course, acknowledge that civil society is not a realm of perfect freedom or democracy. It is, for example, marred by oppression in the family, in gender relations, in the workplace, by racist attitudes, homophobia, and so on. In fact, at least in advanced capitalist societies, such oppressions have become the main focus of struggle, as 'politics' in the old-fashioned sense, having to do with state power, parties and opposition to them, has become increasingly unfashionable. Yet these oppressions are treated not as constitutive of civil society but as dysfunctions in it. In principle, coercion belongs to the state while civil society is where freedom is rooted; and human emancipation, according to these arguments, consists in the autonomy of civil society, its expansion and enrichment, its liberation from the state, and its protection by formal democracy. What tends to disappear from view, again, is the relations of exploitation and domination which irreducibly constitute civil society, not just as some alien and correctible disorder but as its very essence, the particular structure of domination and coercion that is specific to capitalism as a systemic totality and which also determines the coercive functions of the state.

THE NEW PLURALISM AND THE POLITICS OF IDENTITY

The rediscovery of liberalism in the revival of civil society thus has two sides. It is admirable in its intention of making the left more sensitive to civil liberties and the dangers of the state operation. But the cult of civil society also tends to reproduce the mystifications of liberalism, disguising the coercions of civil society and obscuring the ways in which state operation itself is rooted in the exploitative and coercive relations of civil society. What, then, of its dedication to pluralism? How does a concept of civil society fare in dealing with the diversity of social relations and 'identities'?

It is here that the cult of civil society, its representation of civil society as the sphere of difference and diversity, speaks most directly to the dominant preoccupations of the new left. If anything unites the various 'new revisionism – from the most abstruse 'post-marxist' and 'post-modernist' theories to the activisms of the 'new social movements' – it is an emphasis on diversity, 'difference', pluralism. The new pluralism goes beyond the traditional liberal recognition of diverse interests and the toleration (in principle) of diverse opinions in three major ways: 1) its conception of diversity probes beneath the externalities of 'interest' to the psychic depths of 'subjectivity' or 'identity' and extends beyond political 'behaviour' of 'opinion' to the totality of 'life style'; 2) it not longer assumes that some universal and undifferentiated principles of right can accommodate all diverse identities and life styles (women, for example, require different rights from men in order to be free and equal); 3) the new pluralism rests on a view that essential characteristic, the historical differentia specifica, of the contemporary world – or, more specifically, the contemporary capitalist world – is not the totalizing, homogenizing drive of capatilism but the unique heterogeneity of 'post-modern' society, its unprecedented degree of diversity, even fragmentation, requiring new, more complex pluralistic principles.

The arguments run something like this: contemporary society is characterized by an increasing fragmentation, a diversification of social relations and experiences, a plurality of life styles, a multiplication of personal identities. In other words, we are living in a 'post-modern' world, a world in which diversity and difference have dissolved all the old certainties and all the old universalities. (Here, some post-Marxist theories offer an alternative to the concept of civil society by insisting that it is no longer possible to speak of society at all, because that concept suggests a closed and unified totality.[19]) Old solidarities – and this, of course, means especially class solidarities – have broken down, and social movements based on other identities and against other oppressions have proliferated, having to do with gender, race, ethnicity, sexuality, and so on. At the same time, these developments have vastly extended the scope of individual choice, in consumption patterns and life styles. This is what some people have called a tremendous expansion of 'civil society'.[20] The left, the argument goes, needs to acknowledge these developments and build on them. It needs to construct a politics based on this diversity and difference. It needs both to celebrate difference and to recognize the plurality of oppressions or forms of domination, the multiplicity of emancipatory struggles. The left needs to respond to this multiplicity of social relations with complex concepts of equality, which acknowledge people's different needs and experiences.[21]

There are variations on these themes, but, in broad outline, this is a fair summary of what has become a substantial current on the left. The general direction in which it is pushing us is to give up the idea of socialism and replace it with – or at least subsume it under – what is supposed to be a more inclusive category, democracy, a concept that does not 'privilege' class, as traditional socialism does, but treats all oppressions equally. Now as a very general statement of principle, there are – some admirable things here. No socialist can doubt the importance of diversity, or the multiplicity of oppressions that need to be abolished. And democracy is – or ought to be what socialism is about. But it is not at all clear that the new pluralism – or what has come to be called the 'politics of identity' – gets us much beyond a statement of general principles and good intentions.

The limits of the new pluralism can be tested by exploring the implications of its constitutive principle, the concept of 'identity'. This concept claims the virtue that, unlike 'reductionist' or 'essentialist' notions such as class, it can encompass – equally and without prejudice or privilege – everything from gender to class, from ethnicity or race to sexual preference. The 'politics of identity', then, purports to be both more fine – tuned in its sensitivity to the complexity of human experience and more inclusive in its emancipatory sweep than the old politics of socialism.

What, then, if anything, is lost by seeing the world through the prism of this all – embracing concept (or any analogous one)? The new pluralism aspires to a democratic community which acknowledges all kinds of difference, of gender, culture, sexuality, which encourages and celebrates these differences, but without allowing them to become relations of domination and oppression. Its ideal democratic community unites diverse human beings, all free and equal, without suppressing their differences or denying their special needs. But the 'politics of identity' reveals its limitations, both theoretical and political, the moment we try to situate *class* differences within its democratic vision.

Is it possible to imagine class differences without exploitation and domination? The 'difference' that constitutes class as an 'identity' is, by definition, a relationship of inequality and power, in a way that sexual or cultural 'difference' need not be. A truly democratic society can celebrate diversities of life styles, culture, or sexual preference; but in what sense would it be 'democratic' to celebrate *class* differences? If a conception of freedom or equality adapted to sexual or cultural differences is intended to extend the reach of human liberation, can the same be said of a conception of freedom or equality that accommodates *class* differences? There are no doubt many serious weaknesses in the concept of 'identity' as applied to social *relations,* and this applies not only to class; but if emancipation and democracy require celebration of 'identity' in one case and suppression in another, that is surely enough to suggest that some important differences are being concealed in a catch – all category.

Which is meant to cover very diverse social phenomena like class, gender, sexuality or ethnicity. At the very least, class equality means something different and requires – different conditions from sexual or racial equality. In particular, the abolition of class inequality would by definition mean the end of capitalism. But is the same necessarily true about the abolition of sexual or racial inequality? Sexual and racial equality, as I shall argue, are not in principle incompatible with capitalism. The disappearance of class inequalities, on the other hand, is by definition incompatible with capitalism. At the same time, although class exploitation is constitutive of capitalism as sexual or racial inequality are not, capitalism subjects all social relations to its requirements. It can co-opt and reinforce inequalities and oppressions that it did not create and adapt them to the interests of class exploitation.

The old liberal concept of formal legal and political equality, or some notion of so-called 'equality of opportunity', is, of course, capable of accommodating class inequalities – and for that reason, it presents no fundamental challenge to capitalism and its system of class relations. It is, in fact, a specific feature of capitalism that a particular kind of universal equality is possible which does not extend to class relations – that is, precisely, a formal equality, having to do with political and legal principles and procedures rather than with the disposition of social or class power. Formal equality in this sense would have been impossible in pre-capitalist societies where appropriation and exploitation were inextricably bound up with juridical, political and military power.

For these very reasons, the old conception of formal equality satisfies the most fundamental criterion of the new pluralism, namely that it gives no privileged status to class. It may even have radical implications for gender or race, because in respect to these" differences, no capitalist society has yet reached the limits even of the restricted kind of equality that capitalism allows. Nor is it clear that the new pluralism has found a better way of dealing with diverse inequalities in a capitalist society, something that goes consistently beyond the old liberal accommodation with capitalism.

Efforts have been made to construct new 'complex' or 'pluralist' conceptions of equality which acknowledge diverse oppressions without 'privileging' class. These differ from the liberal – democratic idea in that they explicitly challenge the *universality* of traditional liberalism, its application of uniform standards of freedom and equality which are blind to differences of identity and social condition. Acknowledging the complexities of social experience, these new conceptions of equality are meant to apply different criteria to different circumstances and relations. In this respect, pluralist notions claim certain advantages over more universalistic principles, even if they may lose some of the benefits of universal standards.[22] It might be objected here that the dissociation of the new pluralism, from any universal values may permit it to serve as an excuse for suppressing the *old* pluralist principles of civil liberty, free speech and toleration, and that we are in danger now of coming full circle, as respect for diversity turns into its opposite. Yet even if we leave that objection aside, and whatever advantages 'complex' or 'pluralist' conceptions of equality may claim over traditional liberalism, they have left intact the liberal accommodation with capitalism, if only by evading the issue; for at the very heart of the new pluralism is a failure to confront (and often an explicit denial of) the overarching totality of capitalism as a social system, which is constituted by class exploitation but which shapes all 'identities' and social relations.

The capitalist system, its totalizing unity, has effectively been conceptualized away by diffuse conceptions of civil society and by the submersion of class in catch-all categories like 'identity' which disaggregate the social world into particular and separate realities. The social relations of capitalism have been dissolved into an unstructured and fragmented plurality of identities and differences. Questions about historical causality or political efficacy can be evaded, and there is no need to ask how various identities are situated in the prevailing social structure because the very existence of the social structure has been conceptualized away altogether.

In these respects, the new pluralism has much in common with another old pluralism, the one that used to prevail in conventional political science – pluralism not simply as an ethical principle of toleration but as a theory about the distribution of social power. The concept of 'identity' has replaced 'interest groups', and these two pluralisms may differ in that the old acknowledges an inclusive political totality – like the 'political system', the nation, or the body of citizens – while the new insists on the irreducibility of fragmentation and 'difference'. But both deny the importance of class in capitalist democracies, or at least submerge it in a multiplicity of 'interests' or 'identities'. Both have the effect of denying the systemic unity of capitalism, or its very existence as a social system. Both insist on the heterogeneity of capitalist society, while losing sight of its increasingly global power of homogenization. The new pluralism claims a unique sensitivity to the complexities of power and diverse oppressions; but like the old variety, it has the effect of making invisible the power relations that constitute capitalism, the dominant structure of coercion which reaches into every corner of our lives, public and private. In their failure to acknowledge that various identities or interest groups are differently situated in relation to that dominant structure, both pluralisms recognize not so much *difference* as simple *plurality*.

This latest denial of capitalism's systemic and totalizing logic is, paradoxically, a reflection of the very thing it seeks to deny. The current preoccupation with 'post-modern' diversity and fragmentation undoubtedly expresses a reality in contemporary capitalism, but it is a reality seen through the distorting lens of ideology. It represents the ultimate 'commodity fetishism', the triumph of 'consumer society', in which the diversity of 'life styles', measured in the sheer quantity of commodities and varied patterns of consumption, disguises the underlying systemic unity, the imperatives which create that diversity itself while at the same time imposing a deeper and more global homogeneity.

What is alarming about these theoretical developments is not that they violate some doctrinaire Marxist prejudice concerning the privileged status of class. The problem is that theories which do not differentiate – and, yes, 'privilege', if that means ascribing causal or explanatory priorities – among various social institutions and 'identities' cannot deal critically with capitalism at all. Capitalism, as a specific social form, simply disappears from view, buried under a welter of fragments and 'difference'.

And whither capitalism, so goes the socialist idea. Socialism is the specific alternative to capitalism. Without capitalism, we have no need of socialism; we can make do with very diffuse and indeterminate concepts of democracy which are not specifically opposed to any identifiable system of social relations, in fact do not even recognize any such system. Nothing remains but a fragmented plurality of oppressions and emancipatory struggles. What claims to be a more inclusive project than traditional socialism is actually less so. Instead of the universalist aspirations of socialism and the integrative politics of the struggle against class exploitation, we have a plurality of essentially disconnected particular struggles, which ends in a submission to capitalism.

It is possible that the new pluralism is indeed leaning towards the acceptance of capitalism, at least as the best social order we are likely to get. The collapse of communism has undoubtedly done more than anything else to encourage the spread of this view. But in the left's responses to these developments, it is often difficult to distinguish between a panglossian optimism and the deepest despair. On the one hand, it has become increasingly common to argue that, however pervasive capitalism may be, its old rigid structures have more or less disintegrated, or become so permeable, opened up so many large spaces, that people are free to construct their own social realities in unprecedented ways. This is precisely what some people mean when they talk about the vast expansion of civil society in modern ('post-Fordist'?) capitalism. On the other hand, and sometimes in the same breath, we hear a counsel of despair: whatever the evils of a triumphant capitalism, there is little hope for any challenge to it beyond the most local and particular resistances.

This may not be the moment for optimism, but a critical confrontation with capitalism is, at the very least, a useful start. We may then be obliged to differentiate not less but much more radically among various kinds of inequality and oppression than even the new pluralism allows. We can, for example, acknowledge that, while all oppressions may have equal moral claims, class exploitation has a different historical status, a more strategic location at the heart of capitalism; and class struggle may have a more universal reach, a greater potential for advancing not only class emancipation but other emancipatory struggles too.

Capitalism is constituted by class exploitation, but capitalism is more than just a system of class oppression. It is a ruthless totalizing process which shapes our lives in every conceivable aspect, and everywhere, not just in the relative opulence of the capitalist North. Among other things, and even leaving aside the direct power wielded by capitalist wealth both in the economy and in the political sphere, it subjects all social life to the abstract requirements of the market, through the commodification of life in all its aspects, determining the allocation of labour, leisure, resources, patterns of production, consumption and the disposition of time. This makes a mockery of all our aspirations to autonomy, freedom of choice, and democratic self-government.

Socialism is the antithesis of capitalism; and the replacement of socialism by an indeterminate concept of democracy, or the dilution of diverse and different social relations into catch-all categories like 'identity' or 'difference', or loose conceptions of 'civil society', represents a surrender to capitalism and its ideological mystifications. By all means let us have diversity, difference, and pluralism; but not an undifferentiated and unstructured pluralism. What is needed is a pluralism that does indeed acknowledge diversity and difference, not merely plurality or multiplicity. This means a pluralism that recognizes the systemic unity of capitalism and can distinguish the constitutive relations of capitalism from other inequalities and oppressions. The socialist project should be enriched by the resources and insights of the (now not so new) 'new social movements', not impoverished by resorting to them as an excuse for disintegrating the resistance to capitalism. We should not confuse respect for the plurality of human experience and social struggles with a complete dissolution of historical causality, where there is nothing but diversity, difference and contingency, no unifying structures, no logic of process, no capitalism and therefore no negation of it, no universal project of human emancipation.

References

1. For an argument that the Romans, specifically in the person of Cicero, had a concept of 'society', see Neal Wood, *Cicero's Social and Political Thought* (Berkeley and Los Angeles, 1988) esp. pp. 136–42.
2. Much of John Keane's argument in *Democracy and Civil Society* (London, 1988) is, for example, predicated on a criticism of Marxism for its identification of 'civil society' with capitalism, which he opposes by invoking the long tradition of conceptions of' 'society' in the West, reaching much further back than the advent of capitalism.
3. Something like the first conception can, for example, be extracted from Jean L. Cohen, *Class and Civil Society: The Limits of Marxian Critical Theory* (Amherst, 1982). The second view is elaborated by John Keane in *Democracy and Civil Society.* (For his criticism of Cohen's conception, see p. 86n.).
4. John Keane, ed., *Civil Society and the State* (London, 1988) p. 1.
5. *Ibid.,* p. 2.
6. Norman Geras debunks such myths about Marxism in 'Seven Types of Obliquy: Travesties of Marxism', in *Socialist Register* (1990).
7. For the application of 'civil society' to events in Poland, see Andrew Arato, 'Civil Society Against the State: Poland 1980–81', *Telos,* 47 (1981) and 'Empire versus Civil Society: Poland 1981–82', *Telos,* 50 (1982).

8. Keane, *Democracy and Civil Society,* p. 32.
9 Cohen, *Class and Civil Society,* p.192
10. See, for example, *ibid.,* p. 49; Keane, *Democracy and Civil Society,* p. 59; Agnes Heller, 'On Formal Democracy', in Keane, *Civil Society and the State,* p. 132.
11. I have discussed these points at greater length in my *The Retreat from Class: A ,New 'True' Socialism* (London, 1986) chap. 10.
12. Jeno Szucs, 'Three Historical Regions of Europe', in Keane, *Civil Society and the State,* p. 294.
13. *Ibid.,* p. 295,
14. *Ibid.,* p. 296.
15. *Ibid.,* p. 302.
16. *Ibid.,* p. 304.
17. *Ibid.,* p. 306.
18. The defence of formal democracy is sometimes explicitly accompanied by an attack on 'substantive' democracy. Agnes Heller, in 'On Formal Democracy', writes: 'The statement of Aristotle, a highly realistic analyst, that all democracies are immediately transformed into anarchy, the latter into tyranny, was a statement of fact, not an aristocratic slandering by an anti-democrat. The Roman republic was not for a moment democratic. And I should' like to add to all that that even if the degradation of modern democracies into tyrannies is far from being excluded (we were witness to it in the cases of German and Italian Fascism), the endurance of modern democracies is due precisely to their formal character' (p. 130). Let us take each sentence in turn. The denunciation of ancient democracy as the inevitable forerunner of anarchy and tyranny (which is> incidentally, more typical of Plato or Polybius than Aristotle) is, precisely, an anti-democratic slander. For one thing, it bears no relation to real historical sequences, causal or even chronological. Athenian democracy brought an end to the institution of tyranny, and went on to survive nearly two centuries, only to be defeated not by anarchy but by a superior military power. During those centuries, of course, Athens produced an astonishingly fruitful and influential culture which survived its defeat and also laid the foundation for Western conceptions of

citizenship and the rule of law. The Roman republic was indeed 'not for a moment democratic', and the most notable result of its aristocratic regime was the demise of the republic and its replacement by autocratic imperial rule. (That undemocratic republic was, incidentally, a major inspiration for what Heller calls a 'constitutive[1] document of modern democracy, the US Constitution.) To say that the 'degradation of modern democracies into tyrannies is far from being excluded' seems a bit coy in conjunction with a (parenthetical) reference to Fascism – not to mention the history of war and imperialism which has been inextricably associated with the regime of 'formal democracy'. As for endurance, it is surely worth mentioning that there does not yet exist a 'formal democracy' whose life span equals, let alone exceeds, the duration of the Athenian democracy. No European 'democracy', by Heller's criteria, is even a century old (in Britain, for example, plural voting survived until 1948); and the American republic, which she credits with the 'constitutive idea' of formal democracy, took a long time to improve on the Athenian exclusion of women and slaves, while free working men – full citizens in the Athenian democracy – cannot be said to have gained full admission even to 'formal' citizenship until the last state property qualifications were removed in the nineteenth century (not to mention the variety of stratagems to discourage voting by the poor in general and blacks in-particular, which have not been exhausted to this day). Thus, at best (and for white men only), an endurance record of perhaps one century and a half exists for modern 'formal democracies'.

19. This is, for example, the view of Ernesto Laclau and Chantal Mouffe in Hegemony and Socialist Strategy (London, 1955).
20. See, for example, Stuart Hall in Marxism Today, October 1988.
21. The notion of complex equality is primarily the work of Michael Walzer, *Spheres of Justice: — A Defence of Pluralism and Equality* (London, 1983). See also Keane, *Democracy and Civil Society*, p. 12.
22. For a discussion of both the advantages and disadvantages in Walzer's conception of complex equality, see Michael Rustin, *For a Pluralist Socialism* (London, 1985) pp. 70–95.

6

Civil Society and Democracy

Baogang He

The idea and practice of civil societies are important for theories of democracy and for democracy itself. Indeed, civil society is a necessary condition for democratization, for parliamentary democracy to be established and for the boundary question to be peacefully settled. This chapter has three key objectives. First, it aims to review briefly the diverse range of theories of civil society that have been put forward by various thinkers, discuss the recent revival of the notion of civil society and address various disputed interpretations of the concept. Second, the chapter aims to discuss the relationship between different models of democracy and civil society. Finally, it seeks to examine the theoretical question of how civil society can define the political boundary within which national democracy can take place.

The chapter adopts a conventional definition of civil society as de facto autonomous organizations that are independent of direct political control by the state. The notion of the national boundary problem refers to the difficulties associated with the boundaries of nation-states. It is particularly concerned with territorial disputes, such as secession or unification, all of which involve the modification of national boundaries. The boundary problem is also defined as a national identity problem, whereby certain sections of peoples, who do not identify with the existing nation-states in which they reside, seek instead their own political identity through the reconstruction of cultural and ethnic identities.

CONCEPTS OF CIVIL SOCIETY

Classical and Contemporary Meanings

The concept of civil society has diverse and complex meanings. The classical notion, according to Adam Ferguson, for example, refers to state institutions, civic law and commercial economy.[1] For Jean Bodin, the sixteenth-century French philosopher, '[t] he State [*republique* or *res publica*] is the civil society that can exist on its own without associations and other bodies, but it cannot do so without the family'.[2] In the eyes of Hobbes civilized society was seen essentially as the political order and institution which established a sovereign power in order to prevent the war of all against all. As Hobbes said: 'The Multitude so united in one Person, is called a COMMONWEALTH, in latine CIVITAS. This is the Generation of the great Leviathan.'[3] Similarly, Locke stated: 'Those who are united into one Body, and have a common established Law and Judicature to appeal to, with Authority to decide Controversies between them, and punish Offenders, *are in Civil Society* one with another: but those who have no such common Appeal, I mean on Earth, are still in the state of Nature.'[4] However, for Locke, absolute monarchy 'is indeed *inconsistent with Civil Society,* and so can be no Form of Civil Government at all'.[5]

Adam Smith, on the other hand, referred to civil society as commercial economy and the division of labour. He pointed out: 'Nobody ever saw a dog make a fair and deliberate exchange of one bone for another with another dog.' By contrast, 'In civilized society [a person] stands at all times in need of the cooperation and assistance of great multitudes.'[6] Hegel conceptualized civil society as a source of inescapable tensions that embraced the sphere of the market and private interests.[7] He believed these tensions hindered moral development and this led him to synthesize his views on family, civil society and the state into a systematic moral theory.[8] Hegel's views on civil society provided a theoretical basis for Karl Marx, who stressed the means of production behind civil society and the dangers of capitalism,[9] emphasizing class conflict and the built-in crises of capitalism. His alternative was a political society that embodied all economic and political powers in a single institutional framework. But when communist states put Marx's theory into practice, civil society was atomized and ultimately destroyed.[10]

Today, there is a diversity of meanings attributed to the notion of civil society and, as a consequence, there are definitional difficulties associated with the concept. Nevertheless, there are a number of concrete contemporary interpretations of civil society that can be cited. Ernest Gellner, for example, holds a macro-view of civil society, seeing it as 'a society in which polity and economy are distinct, where polity is instrumental but can and does check extremes of individual interest, but where the state in turn is checked by institutions with an economic base; it relies on economic growth which, by requiring cognitive growth, makes ideological monopoly impossible.'[11] At a micro-level, by contrast, civil society is sometimes regarded as the sphere of non-governmental organizations (NGOs). Charles Taylor clarifies three senses of civil society. First, a *minimal sense,* according to which civil society exists where there are free associations, such as the family, church and club, which are not under the tutelage of state power. Second, a *stronger* sense, in which civil society is seen as existing where society as a whole is able to structure itself and coordinate its actions through associations, such as the green movement, which are free of state tutelage. According to the third sense, civil society denotes that ensemble of associations (e.g., interest and pressure groups) that can significantly determine the course of state policy.[12] Similarly, in Schmitter's view, an ideal type of civil society refers to a set of self-organized intermediary groups or organizations which: (1) are relatively independent of both the state and private units of production and reproduction (i.e., firms and families); (2) are capable of taking collective action in defence/promotion of the interests or passions of their members; (3) do not seek to replace either state agents or private (r)eproducers or accept responsibility for governing the polity as a whole; (4) do agree to act in 'a civil fashion' within pre-established rules.[13]

The Revival of the Idea of Civil Society

The failure of the communist system shows that attempts to abandon the liberal separation between state and civil society are dangerous. It is this failure that has done most to revive the notion of civil society, and this is especially so in Eastern Europe.[14] The fundamental theme underpinning the revival of civil society in Eastern Europe was 'the rejection of totalitarianism in favour of the idea that individuals and organizations ought to be free to act autonomously rather than be subject to all-pervasive state direction and control'.[15]

The normative distinction between the state and civil society is also being rediscovered in China. The communist hegemony over mainland China has radically reinforced the age-old tradition of unitary, non-competitive politics, and created a highly centralized, highly dependent society.[16] In a bid to end the invidious and inhuman conflicts, which Marx saw as characteristic of capitalist societies, the Chinese communist system attempted a deliberate connection between the state and civil society. It was on the grounds that the abolition of civil society would remove the divisions and conflicts which bedevil capitalist societies that the Chinese Communist Party (CCP) suppressed and destroyed civil society in the 1950s, a move that has led to the expansion and aggrandizement of the power of the state.

Indeed, it was the failure of communist practices that contributed most to the revived notion of civil society. Most Chinese critics of the CCP consider the distinction between the state and civil society to provide a useful perspective on economic and political reforms. It is this separation – the main feature of any democratic political order – that is seen as the most important step in the revival of civil society, and as a prerequisite to genuine political freedom and economic prosperity in China. The idea of civil society reflects the desire to curb the power of the overweening state through autonomous organizations.[17]

The concept of 'the reconstruction of civil society' has also been revived in the West. In France, for example, there are three justifications for this revival: the statist political culture of the French left; the expansion of the role of the centralized modern state; and the 'totalitarian' expansion of capitalism, which engulfs all spheres of social activity under the single dimension of economic activity. As Rosanvallon writes, the welfare state disorganizes all social networks, associations and solidarity, replacing them by state-administrative relations. He goes on to propose an alternative based on the concept of civil society: 'The reorientation to civil and political society relocates the locus of democratization from the state to society and understands the latter in terms of groups, associations, and public spaces primarily.'[18]

In the former West Germany, the welfare state is seen as a mechanism by which to repoliticize the economy and dissolve the sharp boundaries between state and society. To promote civil society against the welfare state in Germany, the analysis of new social movements emphasizes a model for politicizing civil society ('non-statist socialism' makes no concessions to economic privatization or to statist authoritarianism). Offe argues that civil society must be politicized and emancipate itself from the state. The revitalization of political society or a political version of civil society lies in the form of citizen initiatives and social movements.[19]

A common feature that unites these theories is the separation of the state from civil society. Also, most have an anti-state tendency. Nevertheless, there are substantial differences in their application, as theories of civil society serve different purposes in different environments. For instance, the theory of civil society held by the left in the West tends to relate to a critique of the welfare state. By contrast, the theory held in Eastern Europe and China is directed more towards an attack on totalitarian rather than welfare states. The ideological mobilization power of civil society discourse developed by the Western democratic left, however, is much less influential than its counterpart in Eastern Europe and China. In Eastern Europe and East Asia, the discourse of civil society plays an important role in political mobilization and democratization. By comparison, civil society discourse in the West seems too weak to constitute a political force capable of reforming welfare states. This can largely be understood in an historical and political context: that is, the discourse of civil society has empowered various new social associations that have then challenged the totalitarian or authoritarian societies in Eastern Europe and East Asia. It is no wonder that White, Diamond and Schmitter have theorized the role played by civil society in the process of democratization.[20] They see it providing reservoirs of potential resistance to arbitrary or tyrannical actions by rulers, and contributing to a balanced opposition, thus setting limits on state power. It has also facilitated the development of democratic attributes such as mitigating the principal polarities of political conflicts, enforcing standards of public morality, improving the performance of democratic polities through the articulation, aggregation and representation of interests, and defining the rules of the political game along democratic lines, thereby strengthening the democratic state. Nevertheless, it is suggested that the discourse of civil society will decline in importance when democratization reaches a certain level. This is because social associations will then have become a *normal* part of a new democratic order, and various new problems associated with civil society will have arisen.

Disputes Over the Notion of Civil Society

Should markets be included in the notion of civil society? Classic liberals, such as Adam Smith and David Hume, tend to regard markets as crucial institutions of civil society, and contemporary liberals such as Diamond see productive and commercial associations and networks as part of civil society.[21] By contrast, the left emphasizes equality and democratic control over the market economy. Cohen and Arato, for example, stress the dangers of markets and separate them from civil society in their *tripartite* model, which incorporates civil society, the state and the economy.[22] It is also debatable whether multinational firms can be regarded as part of global civil society.

A further dispute concerns whether or not the notion of civil society contains normative elements or moral judgements about civility. Schmitter, for example, does not consider any rightwing nationalist NGO to be part of civil society.[23] There are others, however, who tend to de-emphasize the moral dimension of civil society and take civil society as a residual concept which includes all autonomous organizations independent of the state, even including organized crime.[24]

In the context of the individualist versus communitarian debate, individualists tend to see civil society as a series of civic associations through which individuals pursue their interests and happiness, agreeing to establish rules and laws to regulate their relations. Communitarians, by contrast, stress the basic ingredients of the concept of civil society: the sense of society's separation from the state, the widespread unity among disparate groups, paternal concern for society's members at risk, trust, mutuality, social connection and cooperation, social fabric and social capital.[25] A similar debate has taken place in China. Thus, while Chinese liberals fight against the legacy of Confucianism in introducing the individualist notion of civil society, Confucian communitarian scholars often dismiss individualist elements of civil society and tend to incorporate civic associations into the scope of state control.[26]

Despite such disputes, liberal and left scholars seem to agree that the normative distinction between civil society and the state is necessary. For the democratic left, the democratic socialist alternative has to confirm the fundamental liberal notion that the 'separation' of the state from civil society must be a central feature of any democratic political order. Nevertheless, they maintain a substantially different attitude towards the relationship between the state and civil society. While some scholars use the notion of civil society in their anti-state projects, others draw on the writings of Kant to stress mutual support and interdependence between the state and civil society.[27] Anthony Giddens, allegedly British Prime Minister Tony Blair's favourite intellectual, stresses the important role that governments can and must play in fostering and renewing civil society.[28] But Foucault sees civil society as the 'correlate of a political technology of government', and the 'distinction between civil society and the state is a form of 'schematism' for the exercise of political power'.[29]

A Sceptical View

A sceptic will offer a critical view of civil society and the organizations that comprise it, suggesting that many so-called civil associations, such as NGOs, lack grassroot support in their own society. For example, some members of NGOs in Cambodia and Eastern European countries speak fluent English and engage in various fund-raising activities. Consequently, they have developed closer links with foreign funding organizations than with their own grassroot supporters. Because they are financially dependent on these foreign organizations, the agendas and activities of NGOs are strongly influenced by their priorities.

A sceptic is likely to venture further, pointing out the illusory nature of civil society discourse.[30] Civil society, it could be suggested, has been interpreted in the West as a type of 'democratic rescue operation', or seen as something that will dictate a new dimension of democratic development in Eastern Europe and East Asia. However, such an idealized view may prove to be illusionary. A lesson from Eastern Europe is that civil society is not an all-purpose political panacea. As Bronislaw Geremek, one of the outstanding proponents of the civil society idea during the heyday of Solidarity and later Speaker of the

Polish Parliament, correctly points out, earlier hopes that the struggle for civil society would yield support for a future democratic order have proved to be mere wishful thinking:

> In light of the dangers that have appeared on the horizon for Poland in particular and for Central and Eastern Europe in general, we must ask whether the idea of a civil society – however effective it was in helping to bring down communism – will turn out to be useless in the building of democracy.[31]

THEORIES OF DEMOCRACY AND CIVIL SOCIETY

Despite these difficulties, it is contended that civil society is a necessary condition for democracy. This can be confirmed with reference to the historical fact that no democracy has existed and developed without the institutions of civil society. Without civil society, communist collectivist 'democracy' is merely one-party dictatorship, as demonstrated by the experience of Eastern Europe and China. Moreover, the development of civil society nurtures a plurality of interest groups, which, when reaching a certain stage in their growth in the economic and other sectors, will in a variety of ways demand to express their interests in the political domain. These aspirations and activities are a powerful impetus towards the creation of democracy. In this sense, then, civil society lays down a solid social foundation for democracy.

Civil society, however, does not constitute a sufficient condition for democracy. This can be demonstrated by the fact that civil society can exist without democracy and that a civil society will not automatically lead to a democratic polity. More importantly, certain types of civil society may distort democratic order, and civil associations may contain many uncivil and undemocratic elements. Even the theory of civil society contains some anti-democratic elements, as, for example, in the Chinese discourse of civil society.[32] Therefore, as Held suggests, civil society needs to be democratized.[33]

Although civil society is an integral part of democratic order, different theorists of democracy prescribe different political roles for civil society. These include maintaining pluralism, assisting democratization, enhancing and providing the basis for associational democracy and furthering global democracy.

Pluralist Democracy and Civil Society

In a model of pluralist democracy, an accountable government is secured by various associations, which are crucial obstacles to the development of excessively powerful factions and an unresponsive state. One of the key features of pluralist democracy is a functioning civil society: 'If men living in democratic countries had no right and no inclination to associate for political purposes, their independence would be in great jeopardy.'[34] Robert Dahl argues that elections and parties alone do not secure the equilibrium of democratic states. Active groups of various types and sizes are fundamental mechanisms that constrain the scope of political leaders. This is an essential difference between democracy by *minorities* and tyranny by *a minority.* For pluralists, the democratic regime is secured by the existence of multiple groups or multiple minorities.[35]

On this view, a highly articulated civil society with cross-cutting cleavages, overlapping memberships of groups and social mobility is a guarantee both for a stable democratic polity, and against permanent domination by any one group. Civil society is, therefore, a necessary condition for a pluralist model of democracy. The dispersion of economic power means that political, economic and legal powers cannot be monopolized, and that checks and safeguards against the abuse of power are able to operate. Thus, liberals see civil society as associations that assist individuals in their pursuit of liberties, interests and happiness and as a key mechanism by which to curb the power of the state. Under this model, civil society has the capacity to check the state, defend the freedom of its institutions from abnormal intervention and infringement by the state and maintain its independence and autonomy. It is in this sense that civil society is seen as the last bastion for protecting freedom and preventing the reversion of political authority to totalitarianism.

Elitist Versus Participatory Democracy and Civil Society

An elitist democratic theory does not trust people and diverse associations. It emphasizes the insulation or autonomy of elites from the influence of peoples and their associations and organizations. It even discourages the direct participation of civil associations and sees an over-politicized civil society as a threat to parliamentary democracy.[36]

Unlike the elitist theory of democracy, a participatory theory stresses the direct participation by citizens in the regulation of the key institutions of society, including the workplace and local community.[37] It is widely contended that without active participation on the part of citizens in civil associations and politically relevant organizations, there would be no way to develop and maintain the democratic character of a political culture or social and political institutions. A classical example is a town meeting and a self-governing urban crisis centre where individuals seek to arrive at a consensus through face-to-face encounters and open debate.[38] Under this model, it is through various associations that individuals participate in democratic life. In this sense then, civil society is seen as an institutional instrument for individuals to advance their interests, develop their political skills and contribute to the improvement of democratic life. Nevertheless, it should be pointed out that when the scope of democracy is local and face-to-face, there is little need for this variety of associations. That is why in village elections in China, associations play a very limited role in developing and promoting village democracy.

Advocates of civil society in Eastern Europe and East Asia reconfirm representative democracy as unsurpassable,[39] a view that is challenged by the civil society discourse of the Western social democratic left, which espouses the principles and practices of participatory democracy. For proponents of this discourse representative democracy is too elitist and fails to deliver accountability to the popular will. They argue that offices should be rotated, and revocable delegates should be preferred to mandated representatives. According to these advocates of civil society, a genuine democracy depends on the existence of a public sphere for the formation of a rational or enlightened public opinion. The free rational formation of a popular will in the public sphere is a condition of genuine democracy.

Sceptics may doubt whether civil associations and social movements do actually challenge parliamentary or representative democracy in the West. Not only have we witnessed the decline of social movements and civil society's lack of success in popular mobilization, but also social movements seem to have given up their pursuit of democracy, participation and equality.[40] Ironically, while the left in the West has celebrated the emergence and development of civil society in Eastern Europe, it does not seem to have understood that the discourse of civil society has served to create a new myth of a non-coercive and non-hierarchical political order, which in a sense reinvents some fundamental ideas of 'communism' at a deeper level.[41] Moreover, civil society in Eastern Europe has undermined communist rule and strengthened international capitalism and representative democracy. As a result, the West, now deprived of rival communist systems, has become dominated by the principle of neoliberal economics, while the principles of social justice appear to be in decline.[42]

Cosmopolitan Democracy and Civil Society

While the civil society project at the level of the nation has become problematic, it has re-emerged with new vigour at the global level. In this context, the cosmopolitan model of democracy aims to democratize the global arenas of decision-making that are now dominated by state and market forces.[43]

When democracy extends to the level of international and global politics, it requires an increasing number of social and political associations to deal with the multiplicity of interests that pertain to a global population. The theory of cosmopolitan democracy, therefore, prescribes a large role for civil society: '[e]nhancement of non-state, non-market solutions in the organization of civil society', and '[c]reation of a diversity of self-regulating associations and groups in civil society'.[44] Held's theorizing of cosmopolitan democracy combines globalization with local civil society. He sees 'the recovery of an intensive and participatory democracy at local levels as a complement to the deliberative assemblies of the wider global order'.[45] Peoples' rule is therefore embodied at different levels, through local participation, global representatives and the restructuring of the UN system. Held writes: 'It is possible to conceive of different types of democracy as forming a continuum from the local to the global, with the local marked by direct and participatory processes while larger areas with significant populations are progressively mediated by representative mechanisms.'[46]

Table 6.1 The role of civil society in different models of democracy

Model of democracy	*The role of civil society*
Pluralist democracy	Curbing the state, constraining the scope of political leaders and securing democratic regime
Participatory democracy	Providing channels for democratic participation, improving people's ability to participate in political life
Elitist democracy	Over-politicized civil society is a threat to a democratic order and therefore should be restricted
Cosmopolitan democracy	Enhancement of non-state, non-market solutions in the organization of civil society, and the increasing role of global civil society

Special attention should be given to transnational of global civic society, which is an integral part of the cosmopolitan model of democracy. Archibugi, for example, asserts that the members of global civil society who represent the peoples rather than their governments ought to constitute the UN People's Assembly or Citizen Assembly. Institutions of global civil society are likely to challenge nation-states through their global activities.[47]

Table 6.1 summarizes the role played by civil society in different theories of democracy.

CIVIL SOCIETY, DEMOCRACY AND THE BOUNDARY QUESTION

Civil societies play diverse roles in developing and maintaining democracy/democratization, as discussed above; they also perform different functions in addressing the boundary question. A growing literature testifies to the emerging importance of the function of civil society in defining the boundaries of political communities,[48] and the participation of ordinary people and the institutions of civil society in defining these boundaries gives rise to the possibility of a democratic approach to this question.

A democratic approach encompasses not only the use of referenda and the right to self-determination, but also the participation of people and the institutions of civil society in the decision-making process dedicated to the peaceful resolution of the boundary question. Under conditions of democratic management, the general public has the opportunity for meaningful participation in defining national boundaries and in the formation of policies. Civil society is an integral part of the democratic project in the sense that it is the main mechanism, apart from referenda, by which the will of the people is expressed. In contrast to management by elites, democratic management encourages the participation of ordinary people and the institutions of civil society.

It has been a longstanding assumption of democratic theory that democracy is incapable of playing a role in addressing the boundary question. However, such a presupposition is no longer able to withstand the challenges put up by the various urgent boundary problems that continue to proliferate around the world. Given the urgency of such problems, it is of critical importance that contemporary democratic theorists develop a theory dedicated to outlining how the boundary question can be democratically managed.

For this purpose, the notion of civil society can be understood not only to include autonomous organizations, but also to embrace normative elements, or moral judgements about civility. As Schmitter stresses, civil society must act in a civil manner within established rules.[49] In this respect, as noted earlier, rightwing nationalist NGOs, for example, will not be regarded as part of civil society.[50] Moreover, with regard to the boundary question, the notion of civil society as an ideal model stresses a way of coexistence between overlapping associations and communities; and challenges the old idea that a unified polity must have a unified ethnic base.

Connecting the Boundary Issue and Civil Society

In the past, national boundaries were largely decided by force, with states claiming their prerogatives and manipulating popular opinions and sentiments. Most nation-states have statutory rights granted by their constitutions to deal with issues concerning national boundaries. Nation-states appear to be the major players in the matter of determining national boundaries. They negotiate with other states, declare wars or sign international agreements to settle certain boundary disputes. The division of the world into states has strengthened claims to state sovereignty and created ongoing pressure for the continuation of the statist approach to the boundary issue. Such an approach tends to deny or exclude civil social groups from the decision-making process, on the grounds that they represent only sectional or private interests, rather than the general interests of bordered nation-states.

The limitations of the statist approach have become increasingly clear in recent decades. The failure to resolve the national identity question in Northern Ireland highlights problems with this approach.[51] The events in Eastern Europe around 1989 demonstrate that civil society has played a crucial role in the struggle against communist states and in the redefinition of national boundaries. Globalization has tended to weaken the power of states and the statist tradition. Global civil society, albeit at a fledgling stage of development, has posed a serious challenge to the arbitrary boundaries of nation-states. States, once seen as the exclusive decision-makers and problem-solvers in boundary disputes, are now seen to contribute to, and even intensify, boundary problems. Faith in the capacity of nation-states to deal with the boundary issue is either completely or at least partially lost, depending on one's view of nation-states. As Freeman points out, the state-centred theories of self-determination neglect the importance of non-state, trans-state and super-state actors. In particular, Freeman argues that there is an inherent contradiction in the theories of self-determination elaborated by Beran, Margalit and Raz, which consider states to be part of the problem and yet offer them as part of the solution.[52] Thus, Freeman calls for a paradigm shift from a state-centred to a society-centred approach.[53]

Given the context outlined above, it is possible to see that the idea of civil society has challenged the state's monopoly of national territory. By competing against nation-states, civil society has become an increasingly important agent in defining national boundaries. The linkage between the boundary issue and civil society is thus established, so much so that civil society is sometimes seen as an alternative or supplement to the statist approach. It is deemed to be one source of legitimacy for the national boundary. Moreover, a state with multiple nationalities requires not only tolerance, but also a public discourse where citizens and civil societies are able and willing to engage in discussion about the social arrangements that hold them together.[54]

A shift in the theoretical paradigm towards civil society can be understood further by an analysis of the strengths of the civil society approach in comparison with the statist approach. First, because their very existence is based on fixed borders, nation-states have a static view of what constitutes the boundary and they are reluctant to make changes. Civil societies, on the other hand, in particular global associations such as human rights organizations, may raise and discuss issues that go beyond the fixed borders of nation-states. Because the organizations or associations of civil societies do not have privileged interests within the nation-state system, they are able to consider issues concerning the justice of national boundaries.

Second, it is argued that the statist approach gives power to a few politicians or representatives, while the civil society approach empowers NGOs and assigns them an important role in the process. In short, the civil society approach enables more people and social organizations to participate in a diversity of spheres, making it much more representative than states in articulating the will of the people.

Third, the statist approach tends to impose a single-state-centred notion of national identity, as demonstrated by the Chinese government's imposition of Chinese national identity on the Chinese diaspora.[55] Nation-states commit themselves to the monopoly of violence: the willingness to use force to manage the boundary problem is a common attribute among nation-states. By contrast, civic associations generally advocate non-violence, new principles of morality and new means for resolving conflicts.

Fourth, nation-states tend to close off the discussion of the national boundary issue. In the eyes of the state, civil society may become a 'troublemaker' and make the boundary issue more complex. When the people are 'sleeping', it is easy for the state to decide the boundary issue, to strike a secret deal and to close off the issue. But if the people are awake, and civil society expresses the diversity of their opinions on the national identity issue, the state is more likely to encounter difficulties in dealing with the boundary issue. From the perspective of civil society, however, civic associations would produce different solutions and proposals, and help create a diversity of political forces. The participation of civil society could knit different ethnic groups together because it promotes the exchange of opinions and mutual understanding between groups, increases overlapping membership and the level of tolerance and provides a public basis for the unity of national identity.

Furthermore, the suppression by the state/party of public discussion on the national identity/boundary problem may lead to trouble and disorder. When a political regime suppresses NGOs, it is likely to face difficulties in solving the boundary problem. Consider, in this context, the breakdown of the former Soviet Union. The state there did not encourage cultural creativity and the free flow of discourse. Only state-sponsored cultural products were used to unify the large and heterogeneous country as a whole. This had enormous negative consequences. As Calhoun points out: 'When the state lost its credibility, so did much of the cultural basis for unity at the largest level.' When discussion and creativity were suppressed in order to maintain ideological conformity, it became difficult to achieve the manifold continuous cultural adjustments that were essential to both legitimization processes and the sense of common membership in a political community. So, ironically, the very attempt to maintain complete conformity undermined identification with the whole, left it superficial and easily forgotten.'[56] Nevertheless, the civil society approach cannot presuppose that the more NGOs there are, the easier it is to solve the boundary problem. Nor can it assume that the members of civil society are unitary rational actors who are able to reach consensus and agreement on the boundary issue.

Fifth, governments and NGOs operate differently. NGOs tend to be more loosely organized, more flexible and less costly than governments. For example, international governmental organizations cannot work at the Thai-Burma Border, nor enter Tigray or Eritrea. They are restricted in their work in Cambodia and do little in Vietnam. In these areas, the private agencies carry the burden; and in some places the NGOs do the bulk of the ork.[57]

A Conceptual Framework Concerning the Role of Civil Society

How does civil society play its actual and potential roles in defining the boundary of a political community? Consideration of the role of civil societies is largely influenced by our view of civil society – as a set of societal conditions, a means of conflict resolution, political actors or transnational phenomena.

Civil society as a set of societal conditions

For the successful operation of civil society, a number of social conditions, including non-segregation, integration and people's contact between divided nations or ethnic groups, are necessary. Such conditions make dialogue and accommodation possible, reduce tension, break down barriers and stereotypes and promote mutual sympathy and mutual understanding. The civil society approach assumes that the more a society is integrated, the more its membership is overlapping or cross-cutting, and therefore the easier the boundary issue is to solve. Conversely, the more a society is segregated, the more difficulty it has managing the boundary issue. Dixon, for example, argues against segregation, which he sees as facilitating fears and suspicions in Northern Ireland. While civil society may not directly solve the boundary problem, it 'appears to at least offer a way out of the current impasses by creating the environment in which accommodation might be possible'.[58] In the context of the two Koreas, Young Whan Kihl also proposes integration and people's contact, including NGOs' involvement in such areas as relief work, environmental protection, religious mission trips and youth exchanges in North Korea.[59]

Civil society as a means of conflict resolution

When civil society is used as a model for conflict management, it celebrates plural, overlapping and cross-cutting associations, while rejecting nationalist principles. The civil society approach appeals to civility, non-violence and dialogue, as opposed to the state's monopoly of violence and its use of force to resolve disputes. If nation-states tend to use whatever methods are necessary, including military force, to solve the national boundary problem, the civil society approach insists that the method of dealing with the national boundary problem does matter. Indeed, it is emphatic that it must be civic and non-violent. As such, it aims to break with the human habit of fighting over territories. It rejects the terrorist view that violence, terror and bloodshed are necessary means of dealing with the boundary issue. It envisages that a civilized way to deal with the boundary issue will bring about a more desirable result. Consider, for instance, the bloody disintegration in Yugoslavia. It could be assumed that with a more developed civil society and civic culture, the disintegration could certainly have been more civilized. The war itself could have been avoided, or it could have resulted in far fewer human casualties and destruction, and less cruelty and war crimes.[60] It was the domination by the strongly rightwing nationalist groups (which should not be regarded as a part of civil society according to the working definition of the concept adopted in this chapter) that made compromise and peaceful settlement impossible. Moreover, the tragedy in Kosovo in 1999 shows that without civil society and a civic culture, ethnic conflict and ethnic cleansing are likely to take place. It also demonstrates that the best solution to the boundary conflict must come from within. NATO's intervention in Kosovo played a limited role in protecting Albanians and it did not prevent ethnic conflict after the withdrawal of Serbian forces in 1999. Intervention alone cannot produce peace.

Those advocating the civil society approach argue further that the articulation of the national identity question by violent groups may undermine civil society, and such groups are unlikely to manage the boundary issue successfully. An example of this can be found in Northern Ireland. When 'uncivil' society prevails over 'civil' society, as demonstrated by the Ulster Workers Council strike in 1974, the power-sharing executive was brought down, and the peace process was blocked.[61] Conversely, if members of civil society are rational and committed to compromise and engage in productive and fruitful debates, the articulation of the national identity issue by civil society helps to manage the boundary issue and will not undermine a community on which civil society depends. A good example is the Corrymeela Community, whose aim is to be a symbol in a divided society that Protestant and Catholic can share together in a common witness to Christ, who transcends division. Its members are both Roman Catholic and Protestant and are encouraged to explore the nature of conflict and to establish mediation networks. It gives us a hope that it will be possible to rebuild a civil society in Northern Ireland, although its role is very limited.

Civil society associations as actors

Associations in civil societies, understood as political actors, can express a collective voice, adopt certain strategies, take certain collective actions, such as demonstrations and petitions, and influence and change state policy concerning the national boundary issue. The idea of civil society implies the 'capacity of ordinary people to join together in associations' and 'to create a public sphere capable of shaping social and political decisions on the basis of rational-critical discourse'.[62] Bleiker, Bond and Lee, for example, discuss an alternative to conventional political approaches for achieving unification and promoting democratization in the Korean peninsula. They focus on the non-violent direct action of non-governmental actors and the general public and continued grassroots support for alternatives to current unification strategies and engagement in inter-Korean affairs.[63]

Various associations in South Korea and Taiwan have mobilized peoples and organized collective action to challenge and break down the monopoly of the boundary issue by the governments. Today, the state alone cannot decide the national identity question. Nation-states cannot simply deny or ignore the roles of civil society in relation to the boundary issue. If the states do not trust people and do not rely on civil society, they will face a legitimacy crisis. They have to think how to co-opt and manipulate civil associations in a skilful way.

Global civil society

Increasing economic and technological globalization has challenged the nation-state system. Global networking and overlapping memberships increasingly make national boundaries unclear and render identities more blurred. Today, minority questions can easily draw international attention and become a global issue and it is becoming increasingly common for minority groups, such as Aboriginal and Torres Strait Islanders in Australia and Tibetans in China, to bring an issue to the international arena.

For some commentators, our awareness of the global village should begin to transform the character of social sciences and influence the structure of our theoretical frameworks.[64] Both state-centred and society-centred approaches are now proving problematic and inadequate. Importantly, the civil society approach is itself problematic if it does not take account of global civil society. It seems that the idea of global civil society combines elements of both anti-state and anti-nation positions. Anti-state because states are seen as part of the boundary problem; anti-nation because nations are deemed to be redundant.

Global civil society includes various international NGOs (INGOs).[65] It is not only subject to international law, but is also an active participant in shaping such law. It is important in shaping opinion and serves as an autonomous actor in competition with states. In other words, global civil society is more concerned with global issues, such as human rights and the global environment, and less concerned with national sovereignty.

Those who are theorists of global civil society see the boundary problem from the aspect of global civil society without adopting the views of states with regard to certain boundary questions. The general consensus is that global civil society plays an increasingly important role in diminishing the sacredness of the national boundary. It challenges the boundaries of nation-states, in that the boundaries and perspectives of global civil society do not coincide with the boundaries of nation-states. It aims to create a global culture, the consciousness of a global village, which overrides the sense of national identity. As Richard Falk puts it:

> [T]he modernist stress on territorial sovereignty as the exclusive basis for political community and identity would be displaced both by more local and distinct groupings and by association with the reality of a global civil society without boundaries.. . . Global civil society treated as the hopeful source of political agency needs to free the minds of persons from an acceptance of state/sovereignty identity, and rethink the contours of community, loyalty, and citizenship.[66]

It should be noted that, although global civil society diminishes the importance of national boundaries, this does not imply that the boundary problem will gradually disappear. Instead the national boundary issue is relocated in local politics with different settings, at least in the case of the European Union. With the increasing importance of local territories and of local associations, the concept of borderlands, in contrast to borderlines, has developed.[67] The idea of the borderline expresses both the dividing line and the sanctuary line, which thus defines nation-states in terms of difference. In other words, the nation-state is defined in terms of what lies on the other side or of what they do not or will not admit. The notion of the borderland, conversely, refers to the border 'that draws all things into it, the place identified with the middle-ground, with the union of opposites, and with mediation'.[68] The idea of the borderland was suggested and championed by a religious studies group which sponsored a series of lectures on regional trade and economic development at Baylor University in Waco, Texas in 1988 and 1989.[69]

Particular attention should be paid to the role of INGOs in managing the boundary issue. Usually, international governmental organizations are averse to, or indifferent towards, boundary issues such as secessionist movements. Before the 1990s, as Heraclides observes: '[T]he UN intervened drastically only once, and in that case decidedly against a secessionist movement (in Katanga in the early 1960s).'[70] The Organization of African Unity is even more firmly committed to the status quo in relation to the existence of national boundaries, and it regards any redrawing of African boundaries as totally unacceptable.[71] By contrast, INGOs have sometimes been involved in secessionist situations, and have even lobbied to support secessionists. Such groups can be outright partisan supporters in a subtle manner, initiators of contacts and then mediators or supportive consultants. They include Amnesty International, the Minority Rights Group, Oxfam and Caritas International (the relief agency of the Roman Catholic Church), the International Commission of Jurists (a quasi-juridical organization), the Roman Catholic Church, the Anglican Church, the World Council of Churches and the World Muslim League.[72]

Laurie Wiseberg summarizes the role of INGOs in secessionist movements in the following way: according legitimacy to the secessionists by dealing with them directly; providing moral support; publicizing the secessionist case through appeals for funds for the starving or displaced or for refugees; providing the secessionist movement, directly or indirectly, with medicine, food, funds, currency or perhaps even fuel or means of transportation or communication; serving as a cover for arms shipments; and providing access to the outside world.[73]

Amnesty International, as a moral agent dedicated to promoting universal human rights, has privileged human rights principles in a way that goes beyond the idea of national sovereignty. It has defended the freedom of speech, which guarantees the right to express dissident views on questions of national identity, such as in South Korea and Taiwan. For many years the annual reports of Amnesty International have challenged the National Security Law (NSL) and its restriction on people's contacts and movements between South and North Korea. On 25 November 1995, the London-based wing of Amnesty International, for example, published a 62-page report urging the South Korean government to amend the NSL.[74] It should be acknowledged that Amnesty does not intend to address the unification question per se. Nevertheless, its primary concern with human rights and its activities against the NSL do have unintended consequences. It has, for instance, facilitated people-to-people contact across borders, reinforced the unification forces from civic groups in South Korea, and provided moral support for NGOs in challenging the government's monopoly of the unification issue.

INGOs are likely to have much more impact on South Korea than on North Korea. This is because, as of the end of 1989, South Korea had 820 INGO memberships, while North Korea had only 141.[75] Moreover, the government of North Korea does not allow Amnesty International to establish branches in its territory, while the government of South Korea does in its. As a democratic regime, the government of South Korea is subjected much more to international pressure than that of North Korea. In North Korea, INGOs only began to operate and exercise influence in the 1990s. The Rockefeller Foundation, for example, funded projects in North Korea, which were initiated by the Asia Society. It is believed that this type of NGO activity will build confidence and facilitate people-to-people exchange before official exchange and cooperation with North Korea.[76]

A Sceptical View

A sceptic is likely to argue, however, that states have been, and will continue to be, key players and decisive forces in dealing with the boundary problem. Civil society does not, and cannot, replace the state. Civil society *alone* cannot resolve or manage the boundary problem and will not eliminate all the deep-rooted problems. It is not a panacea, nor a viable alternative to nation-states. Moreover, states now adopt new strategies, using NGOs for their own purposes. In Taiwan, for example, the government increasingly uses NGOs as an alternative channel to win international space and to promote the national identity and political profile of Taiwan.

Furthermore, the view that civic groups and associations should play their part in defining the boundary question not only brings a new perspective on, and a new approach to, the old problem, but also gives rise to new questions and new problems. First, global civil society goes beyond the nation-state only in the sense that its members are not necessarily restrained by their nation-state. Nevertheless, when they come to support certain groups' effort to establish a new state, such activities presuppose and strengthen the centrality of national boundaries and the nation-state system. In this sense, they are not purely global nor beyond the nation-state system. Second, even the concept of civil society itself begs many questions. As has been discussed before, it is very difficult to define the boundary of civil society, draw the line between civil society and the state and avoid the arbitrary judgement of the 'civility' of civic associations.

CONCLUSION

Civil society is a necessary condition for both established parliamentary democracy and democratization, for it curbs the excessive power of states and enables people to participate in democratic life. It is also a supplement to, and crucial part of, the democratic management of the boundary question. Civil society has played an increasing role in developing and maintaining democracy and in addressing the national boundary issue, not only in Western liberal democratic countries, but also in East Asia. The emergence and rapid growth of civil society might be seen as an 'association revolution', which may prove to be significant in both promoting global democratization and in addressing the national boundary issue well into the twenty-first century.

REFERENCES

The author is grateful for the critical and useful comments and suggestions from Geoff Stokes and April Carter, and assistance from Christine Standish and Yingjie Guo.

1. A. Ferguson, *'An Essay on the History of Civil Society'* Edinburgh, Edinburgh University Press, 1966 [1767].
2. Cited in N. Bobbio, *Democracy and Dictatorship: The Nature and Limits of State Power,* trans. P. Kennealy (Minneapolis, University of Minnesota Press, 1989), p. 35.
3. T. Hobbes, *Leviathan,* ed. C.B. Macpherson (London, Penguin, 1968 [1651]), p. 227.
4. P. Laslett (ed.), *Locke: Two Treatises of Government* (Cambridge, Cambridge University Press, 1960 [1690]), p. 324.
5. Ibid., p. 326.

6. A. Smith, *An Inquiry into the Nature and Causes of the Wealth of Nations,* Vol. 1, ed. R.H. Campbell and A.S. Skinner (Oxford, Clarendon Press, 1976), p. 26.
7. Hegel included in civil society elements we would usually think of as part of the state, e.g., commercial law.
8. See Z.A. Pelczynski (ed.), *The State and Civil Society: Studies in Hegel's Political Philosophy* (Cambridge, Cambridge University Press, 1984); and A.B. Seligman, *The Idea of Civil Society* (New York, The Free Press, 1992), pp. 44–51.
9. Seligman, *The Idea of Civil Society,* pp. 51–8.
10. See E. Gellner, 'Islam and Marxism: Some comparisons', *International Affairs* 67, 1 (1991): 1–6.
11. E. Gellner, *Conditions for Liberty: Civil Society and Its Rivals* (Hamilton, Penguin Books, 1994), p. 211.
12. C. Taylor, 'Models of civil society', *Public Culture* 3, 1 (1990): 95–118.
13. P. C. Schmitter, 'On civil society and the consolidation of democracy: Ten general propositions and nine speculations about their relation in Asian societies', paper presented at an International Conference on Consolidating the Third Wave Democracies: Trends and Challenges, Taipei, 27–30 August 1995.
14. See Z. Rau (ed.), *The Reemergence of Civil Society in Eastern Europe and the Soviet Union* (Boulder, Westview Press, 1991).
15. R. Rose, 'Toward a civil economy', *journal of Democracy* 3, 2 (1992): 13–26, p. 20.
16. See E. Vogel, *Canton Under Communism:.Programs and Politics in a Provincial Capital, 1949–1968* (Cambridge, MA, Harvard University Press, 1969); Tang Tsou, *The Cultural Revolution and Post-Mao Reforms: A Historical Perspective* (Chicago, University of Chicago Press, 1986); and P. Duara, *Culture, Power and the State: Rural North China, 1900–1942* (Stanford, Stanford University Press, 1988).
17. Baogang He, *The Democratic Implications of Civil Society in China* (London, Macmillan, 1997).
18. Rosanvallon, cited in J.L. Cohen and A. Arato, *Civil Society and Political Theory* (Cambridge, MA, MIT Press, 1992), p. 39.

19. See Cohen and Arato, *Civil Society and Political Theory.*
20. G. White, 'Civil society, democratization and development (I): Clearing the analytical ground', *Democratization* 1, 3(199^4): 382-5; L. Diamond, 'Rethinking civil society: Toward democratic consolidation', *journal of Democracy 5,* 3 (1994): 4–17, esp. pp. 7–11; Schmitter, 'On civil society and the consolidation of democracy', pp. 13–14.
21. Diamond, 'Rethinking civil society', p. 6.
22. Cohen and Arato, *Civil Society and Political Theory.*
23. Schmitter, 'On civil society and the consolidation of democracy'.
24. See J.H. Mittelman and R. Johnston, 'The globalization of organized crime, the courtesan state, and the corruption of civil society', *Global Governance* 4 (1999): pp. 103–26.
25. E. Cox, *A Truly Civil Society* (Sydney, ABC Books, 1995).
26. Chen Kuide, 'The misleading conception of clan society and the reconstruction of civil society in China', *Chinese Intellectuals* (Summer 1990): 23–30; Jiang Qing, 'Rujia wenhua: Jiangou zhongguodeshe shimin shehui de shenhou ziyuan' ('Confucian culture: The rich source of constructing Chinese type of civil society'), *Zhongguo shehui kexue jikan* (HK) (15 May 1993): 170–5.
27. R. Madsen, 'The public sphere, civil society, and the moral community', *Modern China* 19, 2 (1993): 183–98.
28. A. Giddens, *The Third Way: The Renewal of Social Democracy* (Cambridge, Polity Press, 1998), p. 79.
29. G. Burchell, 'Peculiar interests: Civil society and governing the system of natural liberty', in G. Burchell, C. Gordon and P. Miller (eds), *The Foucault Effect: Studies in Governmentality* (Hemel Hempstead, Harvester Wheatsheaf, 1991), p. 141.
30. See C. Tempest, 'Myths from Eastern Europe and the legend of the West', *Demoralization* 4, 1 (1997): 132–44.
31. B. Geremek et al., *The Idea of Civil Society* (Research Triangle Park, NC, The National Humanities, 1992), p. 18.
32. See Baogang He, *The Democratic Implications of Civil Society in China.*
33. D. Held, *Models of Democracy* (Cambridge, Polity, 1987), p. 283.

34. A. de Tocqueville, *Democracy in America* (New York, The New American Library, 1956), p. 199.
35. See R. Dahl, *Polyarchy: Participation and Opposition* (New Haven, Yale University Press, 1971) and *Dilemmas of Pluralist Democracy: Autonomy vs. Control* (New Haven, Yale University Press, 1982).
36. For an elitist theory of democracy, see J. Schumpeter, *Capitalism, Socialism and Democracy* (London, Alien and Unwin, 1976).
37. C. Pateman, *Participation and Democratic Theory* (Cambridge, Cambridge University Press, 1970).
38. J.J. Mansbridge, *Beyond Adversary Democracy* (New York, Basic Books, 1980).
39. Rau (ed.), *The Reemergence of Civil Society in Eastern Europe and the Soviet Union;* and Baogang He, The idea of civil society in both China and Taiwan', *Issues and Studies* 31, 6 (1995): 24–64.
40. E. Etzioni-Halevy, 'Have social movements in the West abandoned the quest for equality and democracy?', paper presented at the First Regional Conference on Social Movements, Tel-Aviv, September 1997.
41. As G.M. Tamas argues, 'like communism, the myth of civil society is a tale of a noncoercive political order ... civil society is nonhierarchical'. In this sense, 'Eastern Europe ... has reinvented communism'; see 'A Disquisition on civil society', *Social Research* 61, 2 (1994): 205–22, pp. 216–18.
42. One tragic consequence of this is that the universities' relative autonomy is frequently infringed and the very limited democratic elements and consultative collegiality that have existed in the past have been destroyed by bureaucratic and managerialist control of funding.
43. R. Falk, *On Humane Governance: Toward a New Global Politics* (Cambridge, Polity, 1995).
Post-Cold War Era (Geneva, WCC Publications, 1993), p. 35.
44. D. Held, *Models of Democracy*, 2nd edn (Cambridge, Polity, 1996), p. 158.
45. D. Held, 'Democracy and the new international order', in D. Archibugi and D. Held (eds), (Cambrideg, Polity, 1995), p. 112.

46. Held, *Democracy and the Global Order,* p. 280, p5.
47. D. Archibugi, 'From the United Nations to cosmoplitan democracy', in Archibugi and Held (eds). *Cosmopolitan Democracy*, pp. 135–55.
48. See A. Heraclides, *The Self-Determination of Minorities in International Politics* (London, Frank Cass and Co. 1999); R. Bleiker, D. Bond and Myung-Soo Lee, 'The role and dynamics of non-governmental actors in contemporary Korea', *Korean Studies* 18 (1994): 103–22; M. Freeman, 'Democrar and dynamite: The peoples' right to self-determination', *Political Studies* 44 (1996): 746–61; Baogang He, *The Democratic Implicanons of Civil Society in China;* P. Dixon, 'Paths to peace in Northern Ireland (I): Civil society and consociational approaches', *Democratization* 4, 2(1997): 1–27; and P. Dixon, 'Paths to peace in Northern Ireland (II): The peace processes 1973–74 and 1994–96', *Democratization* 4, 3 (1997): 1–25.
49. Schmitter, 'On civil society and the consolidation of democracy'.
50. It is debalable whether a moderate nationalist NGO can be seen as part of civil society.
51. Dixon, 'Paths to peace in Northern Ireland (III).
52. Freeman, "Democrat and dynamite'; H. Beran, 'A democratic theory of political self-determination for a new world order, in P.B. Lehning (ed.), *Theories of Secession* (London, Routledge, 1998), pp. 32–59. A. Margalit and J. Raz, 'National self-determination', *The Journal of Philosophy* 87, 9 (1990); 439–61.
53. Freeman, 'Democrat and dynamite'.
54. C. Calhoun, *Neirber Gods Nor Emperors: Students and the Struggle for Democracy in China* (Berkeley, University of California Press, 1994), pp. 190-3.
55. Ibid., p. 191.
56. C. Calhoun, 'Nationalism and civil society: Democracy, diversity and self-determination', in C. Calhoun (ed.), *Social Theory and the Politics of Identity* (Cambridge, MA, Blackwell, 1994). 304–35.
57. E.G. Ferris, *Beyond Borders: Refugees, Migrants and Human Rights in the Post-Gold War Fra* (Geneva, WCC Publications, 1993), p. 35.
58. Dixon, 'Paths to peace in Northern Ireland (II)', p. 22.

59. Young Whan Kihl, 'Epilogue: Korean conundrum in the post-cold war era', in Young Whan Kihl (ed.), *Korea and the World: Beyond the Cold War* (Boulder, Westview Press, 1994), pp. 332–3.
60. V. Pavlovic, 'Ethical conflicts and democracy in the suppressed civil society', paper presented at the 17th World Congress of IPSA, Seoul, 17–21 August 1997.
61. Dixon, 'Paths to peace in Northern Ireland (II)', p. 22.
62. Calhoun, 'Nationalism and civil society', p. 306.
63. Bleiker, Bond and Lee, 'The role and dynamics of non-governmental actors'.
64. B. Turner, *Orientalism, Postmodernism and Globalism* (London, Routledge, 1994).
65. P. Ghils, 'International civil society: Internationa: nongovernmental organisations in the international system', *International Social Science Journal* 44, 133 (1992): 417–31.
66. Falk, *On Humane Governance,* pp. 100–1.
67. S.J. Randall, H. Konrad and S. Silverman (eds), *North America Without Borders? Integrating Canada, the United States, and Mexico* (Calgary, University of Calgary Press, 1992), pp. 201–2.
68. Russell Brown, cited in Randall et al., *North America Without Borders,* p. 202.
69. Until independence in 1836, the state was part of Mexico. It has had a strong Mexican heritage and a close relationship with Mexico since the mid-nineteenth century.
70. Heraclides, *The Self-Determination of Minorities in International Politics,* p. 54.
71. Ibid., p. 55.
72. Ibid., pp. 54–7.
73. See ibid., p. 57.
74. D. Cho, 'National security law may be hot issue in general elections', *The Korea Herald* (10 December 1995), p. 2.
75. Samuel S. Kirn, The two Koreas and world order', in Young (ed.), *Korea and the World,* p. 34.
76. Young, 'Epilogue: Korean conundrum in_ the post-cold war era', p. 331.

7

Civil Society

Marina Ottaway

OVERVIEW

The expression 'civil society' has metamorphosed during the 1990s from a relatively obscure concept familiar mostly to scholars of Marxism into a mainstream term freely used by social science analysts in general and by practitioners in the international assistance field specifically. Several factors contributed to these developments. First, there was growing interest by the United States and many European countries in promoting democracy abroad during the 1990s. The demise of the Soviet Union and the Eastern European communist regimes triggered a wave of more or less successful democratic transitions further afield, where regimes formerly influenced by the Soviet model and often by the Soviet government struggled to transform themselves into something both more acceptable to their populations and less anachronistic internationally. This wave of political transformations provided an opportunity for the industrialized democracies to actively promote the spread of political systems similar to their own. As international actors devised democracy promotion strategies, they focused much effort on promoting citizen participation and activism – what quickly came to be known as a vibrant civil society.

Another factor was the changes taking place in the established democracies themselves. Many organizations of what used to be called broadly 'the left', inspired by socialist or social democratic ideals of socio-economic equity and justice, were replaced by newer groups whose concept of justice extended beyond the traditional concerns of socialist parties and labour movements. They embraced a broad array of causes such as environmental protection and sustainability, opposition to globalization, and protection of gay rights. The old left was rooted above all in political parties and labour unions. The new activists were organized in smaller non-governmental organizations, often loosely tied in broad networks, that saw themselves as the embodiment of a mobilized civil society.

Disenchantment with the performance of state institutions was an additional factor, as political leaders made concerted efforts to narrow the functions of government and enlarge the spheres of the private and non-profit sectors. At the same time, the corruption and inefficiency of many developing countries' governments prompted international development agencies to rethink the assumption that development required state intervention. As a result, they sought ways to bypass governments and implement some development projects and programmes through non-governmental organizations.

Needless to say, the popularization of the concept of civil society has led to a blurring of its meaning. It has also led to a blurring of its political connotations: a greater role for civil society is now extolled by conservatives, liberals, and radicals alike as a crucial component of political and even economic reform. Analysts of different persuasions do not agree about which organizations should be considered part of civil society and which should not, but they all agree that civil society is a good thing.

INTRODUCTION: DEFINING CIVIL SOCIETY

Defining the meaning of civil society is difficult because the term is laden with theoretical assumptions, unsolved problems, and value judgements. According to Hegel's oft-cited but ultimately unsatisfactory definition (in his *Philosophy of Right*, 1821), civil society comprises the realm of organizations that lie between the family at one extreme and the state at the other. While superficially clear and logical the definition generates a lot of conceptual confusion and some political booby traps. The result is that very few scholars, and virtually no practitioners of democracy promotion, now accept such a broad definition in practice, even if they cite it.

Intellectual Conundrums

The definition is clear on one point: civil society is not the whole society, the entire web of social institutions and relations, but only one part of it. The problem is how to define that part with any degree of precision. Citing the realm of voluntary associations between the family and the state does not provide sufficient clarification. Three problems deserve special attention: (1) distinguishing organizations that are truly voluntary from those that are not; (2) determining whether all voluntary organizations between the family and the state deserve to be considered civil; and (3) determining whether there is a conceptual difference between civil society and political society, as some argue, or whether this is a distinction with little analytical value, which has gained currency for reasons of political expediency.

The concept of voluntary association contains ambiguities, particularly when applied to the less formal organizations that constituted civil society in the past and are still important in the developing world. According to definitions that stress civil societies' voluntary character, a civil society group is a formally constituted association of which individuals become members as part of a completely free choice – a club, for example, is undoubtedly a voluntary association. The family is not, because membership in it is not chosen. But there is a grey area of groups in which membership is not formally compulsory, but is not completely a matter of free choice, either. Religious associations offer one example. Very often people are born into a church or another type of religious association by virtue of having been born in a family, and inertia explains continued membership; in other cases, membership in a religious group is a truly voluntary choice. Similarly, people are born members of a clan, tribe, or ethnic group, but membership in an organization that claims to represent that group is a political choice made voluntarily and deliberately by some but by no means all members of that particular group. South Africa provides a telling example of how membership in an ethnic group can be an accident of birth or a voluntary decision to join a group. In the early 1990s, at a time of intense fighting between the supporters of Inkatha, a political party with a Zulu nationalist agenda, and other black South Africans, ethnic Zulus who did not support the party and its agenda referred to Inkatha supporters, but not to themselves, as Zulus.

The ambiguities even extend to organizations that appear at first sight to be clearly voluntary, such as political parties. In the early twentieth century many Europeans were born as members of social democratic parties, figuratively, because of their families' allegiances, or even literally, being delivered by 'mid wives' paid by the party as a service to their members. Membership was voluntary in that anybody could stop paying dues and quit the party, but, for many, membership became part of an identity acquired at birth. A contemporary example of this phenomenon is offered by the Sudan, where major religious brotherhoods, into which people are born when families belong, have formed political parties to which adherence is equally automatic.

Another common problem in determining whether an association is voluntary or not arises in relation to ruling political parties and the mass organizations they control. Membership in the party or mass organization is rarely compulsory, but the absence of membership has negative consequences and many are forced to join. One of the difficult tasks faced by the United States as the occupying power in Iraq in 2003 was to distinguish between committed members of the Baath Party, who were part of the defunct regime of Saddam Hussein, and those who had joined in order to keep their jobs so as not to attract undue attention to themselves.

A second thorny problem in determining the boundaries of civil society is ideological in nature, hinging on the interpretation of the word 'civil', which can mean both 'relating to citizens or the general public' and civilized'. The expansive definition of civil society as comprising all voluntary associations between family and state is based on the first meaning. For many, this is an unacceptable approach because it combines in one category, for example, human rights groups and terrorist organizations. In practice, the word civil society is almost invariably used to denote organizations that share certain positive, 'civil' values. But there is no consensus on that point. During the 1980s, Scandinavian countries considered the organizations fighting apartheid in South Africa as 'civil' and provided support. The United States defined them as terrorist organizations and refused to help; Nelson Mandela, the much acclaimed first president of post-apartheid South Africa, was once considered a terrorist by the United States. Many liberals or radicals have no problem accepting labour unions as organizations of civil society, but are often reluctant to see a federation of employers in the same light.

Another controversial issue influenced by political and policy consideration is whether it is valid to draw a distinction between civil and political society. Those who defend the distinction, first made by Gramsci (in 1929–35 in *Prison Notebooks)*, admit that both civil society and political society play a political role and seek to influence policy decisions. But the political role of civil society is indirect: civil society groups do not aspire to control the government and exercise power, but see their role as that of influencing policies in the public interest. Political society organizations – essentially, political parties—want to control the government. A corollary of this view is that the civil society is virtuously dedicated to giving citizens a voice, while political society is power-hungry, self-interested, and considerably less virtuous. A second corollary is that international agencies seeking to promote democracy can and should provide assistance to civil society organizations; supporting political society, which aspires to power and thus is partisan by definition, would be morally questionable and would also represent unjustifiable interference in the domestic politics of another country.

The distinction between civil and political society has theoretical justification. Its usefulness, however, is scant, because most civil society organizations are, overtly or covertly, more partisan and political than they claim to be. True, there are organizations of civil society that act purely as pressure or advocacy groups and have no intention of contesting public office. But civil society activists are often close to specific political parties, and many move freely between civil society organizations and parties. Furthermore, many political parties, including some in power, set up organizations of civil society in an attempt to capture some of the assistance that is available only to civil society organizations.

Examples of the blurring of the lines between political and civil organizations exist in most countries, though more pronounced in some than in others. Civil society organizations may be pushed into close alliance with political parties by government repression. Many non-governmental organizations (NGOs) in Zimbabwe, for example, developed during the 1990s as bona fide, non-partisan civil society organizations lobbying for improved human rights, constitutional reform, better legal services for the poor, and a variety of similar causes. As the government, when challenged by the opposition party, the Movement for Democratic Change, turned increasingly repressive, violating laws and human rights principles in order to stay in power, civil society organizations increasingly became part of the political opposition. Formally organized NGOs operating at the national level are particularly likely to become politicized when confronted by a repressive regime. But less formal, local groups, sometimes referred to as Community-Based Organizations (CBOs), rarely become openly political. CBOs are usually concerned about local level development and welfare issues, focusing on service delivery or simply self-help.

Politics and Expediency

The abstract problems of how to define civil society remain a source of debate among academics, but in the meantime, civil society is being defined in practice by the policies of bilateral and multilateral aid agencies, by the governments of countries receiving democracy assistance, and by civil society organizations themselves.

Bilateral and multilateral international aid organizations define the boundaries of civil society when they decide which organizations are eligible for assistance under democracy promotion programmes or should be consulted in the preparation of an assistance strategy. This definition is based on a mixture of political considerations and administrative requirements. The major political requirement is that such organizations focus their activities either on civic education or advocacy for democratic reform. Civic education programmes, particularly common in countries in the early stages of political transition, seek to convey the basic meaning of democracy as well as teach about the political and institutional mechanisms of democratic systems. In its more sophisticated, advanced form, civil education is *also* training for political activism: citizens are encouraged to scrutinize the action of politicians, to lobby them to enact reforms, and to hold them accountable by voting them out of office. Advocacy organizations that attract international support focus on human rights, women's rights, legal reform, judicial reform, and, occasionally, environmental sustainability. To be part of civil society thus means to belong to one of these types of organizations.

The aid agencies' definition of civil society is further narrowed by their administrative requirements. The groups must be organized in a formal way because donors cannot provide support for an organization that is not registered in some way, that does not have a name and address, or that cannot be audited. Informal networks or vaguely organized civic movements may play an important part in a society or a democratic transition, but they do not meet donors' needs and only some foreign funders will provide support for them on an exceptional basis. For practical reasons, donors also prefer to deal with organizations that speak, literally and figuratively, the same language.

As a result, the donors' civil society is an entity very different either from the society at large or from civil society as the realm of voluntary organizations between the family and the state. The term civil society as used, and financed, by the international aid agencies refers to 'a very narrow set of organizations: professionalized NGOs dedicated to advocacy or civic education work on public interest issues directly relating to democratization, such as election monitoring, voter education, governmental transparency and political and civil rights in general' (Ottaway and Carothers 2000 : ll).

Direct funding of civil society is not the only way in which international assistance agencies define that society. Their influence is strengthened by the requirement under which many now operate that they consult with local civil society in implementing a wide variety of development and democracy aid programmes. The World Bank has such civil society requirements and many bilateral agencies also hold wide consultations. In practice, many of the groups so contacted are the same organizations the assistance agencies helped set up or fund in the first place – the ones they know and are capable of sending representatives to meetings.

The governments of countries that are recipients of democracy assistance also try to shape the definition of civil society by imposing registration requirements, which are sometimes very strict and used to prevent the formation of antagonistic organizations. Many also try to limit the access to donor funding to only some categories of organizations or to prevent it outright. Some international agencies are willing to circumvent such regulations and provide funding covertly, others are more anxious not to antagonize the government.

Civil society activists have also played a very important part in determining which organizations are recognized as part of civil society. Transnational networks of NGOs, usually led by the better-funded groups of the industrialized countries, have been particularly influential here. For example, they successfully pressed the United Nations to accept their presence at international meetings; and the World Bank agreed to undertake re-evaluations of some of its practices, particularly lending for the construction of dams, and to consult with the NGO sector before reaching decisions on certain issues. For example oil companies in Chad are now required to pay royalties into specially controlled funds where they are administered under strict controls with the participation of civil society organizations. These examples of success are counterbalanced by more numerous examples where the militancy of transnational civil society networks has failed to earn them recognition as rightful participants.

Key Points

- The widespread agreement about the importance of civil society is accompanied by a great deal of controversy about what civil society is, not only among theorists but also among practitioners.
- The term has been given a concrete meaning by the policies of international assistance agencies and to a lesser extent by the efforts of civil society organizations.

TRADITIONAL AND MODERN CIVIL SOCIETY

It is common for donors to bemoan the weakness, or even the absence, of civil society in countries where they try to promote democracy. This concern has spurred governments of industrialized countries, as well as international NGOs and private foundations, to launch an array of civil society assistance programmes to strengthen what is invariably referred to as a 'fledgling' civil society. In many instances, even after years of effort, donors express concern about the slow progress of civil society development and its continuing need for support. Paradoxically, in the countries where civil society is deemed at its weakest, for example in war-torn African countries, the population relies for survival on civil society networks that go well beyond the family and reveal a high degree of sophistication and organization. One of the problems faced by countries undergoing political upheaval is that some civil society networks quickly establish themselves in major fields of economic activity and even within parts of the government. The criminalization of the state that has been witnessed in failing states in West and Central Africa is the result of the disparity between the power of civil society organizations and that of a duly constituted government and administrative structure.

These considerations point to the need to put the discussion of civil society in a broader perspective. Following the current use of the term, the discussion so far has dwelt on 'modern' civil society, that is, the part of civil society organized into formal, professionalized NGOs typical of the late twentieth century. But in all countries, including the industrialized ones, there is another civil society – 'traditional society'. This society is organized more informally, often through networks rather than formally structured organizations, and often following patterns that existed in earlier times.

Traditional forms of civil society exist in most countries today, but particularly so in countries where the state is weak. Organizations that are traditional in form do not necessarily perform only traditional roles. On the contrary, they grow in new directions in response to contemporary needs and requirements. West African Sufi organizations such as the Mourides are ancient, but they establish control over the wholesale rice trade in Senegal, or set up mechanisms to help members of the brotherhood emigrate to the United States and find jobs there: they are performing definitely non-traditional functions in response to new challenges.

Modern and traditional civil society stand in inverse relation to each other. In countries where the state is strong, traditional civil society is weak and modern civil society is strong. If the state is weak, so is modern civil society but traditional civil society strengthens (Migdal *1988b).* This explains the paradox outlined above: in countries in the throes of a difficult, state-weakening transition, citizens rely on civil society networks in many aspects of their lives even as donors bemoan the weakness of civil society.

Traditional Civil Society

Organizations of civil society have taken a great variety of forms traditionally, from the very informal to the highly structured. Loosely structured but culturally sanctioned mechanisms for swapping labour and joining efforts in the performance of large collective tasks exist in all societies, as do more structured mechanisms – for example, the rotating credit associations that exist, under different names, almost everywhere. Compared to modern ones, traditional civil society organizations were less specialized and formal. They were extremely unlikely to have full-time organizers and certainly not offices. Even in industrial countries, the professionalization of civil society, hence its separation from the society at large, is a recent phenomenon. When Alexis de Tocqueville visited the United States in the first half of the nineteenth century and wrote *Democracy in America* (published in two volumes, in 1835 and 1840) he was struck by the American propensity to form intermediate associations in the pursuit of a wide range of interests and projects; he was looking at loosely structured, ad hoc groups, not at formal organizations with professional staffs.

Modern civil society defined as a set of NGOs has clear boundaries that separate it from the family and indeed from the rest of society as well as from the state. The expression 'members of civil society' refers to a rather small number of people who belong, and very often work for, such NGOs, not to all citizens. Traditional civil society has no such clear boundaries, but fades into the larger society at one extreme and non-state forms of political authority on the other. In non-state societies, governance was an extension of the overall social organization, not the activity of specialized institutions.

The blurring of the lines between the society at large, more organized associations within it, and political authority is not completely a thing of the past, but can reappear in extreme situations of state collapse, as in Somalia.

Traditional civil society performed important economic activities that today are considered to be the responsibility of state authority. For example, long distance trade was once organized and carried out through private, civil society networks that extended over long distances. States took over much of the responsibility for protecting trade routes and otherwise making large-scale economic activity more feasible. In places where the state has collapsed or is severely weakened, civil society is taking on again some of those functions. This has been the case in the Democratic Republic of the Congo (formerly Zaire) since at least the 1980s, for example.

Traditional Civil Society and the State in the Contemporary World

Some traditional forms of civil society exist even in the industrialized countries and they pose no problem. On the contrary, they contribute to the reservoir of what Putnam (1993) calls social capital. When traditional forms of civil society grow very strong as a result of the weakness or total collapse of the state, however, they can become highly problematic. Traditional civil society in the contemporary world is both indispensable and dangerous. Where the state is incapable, it can help people survive and maintain a semblance of normal life under very difficult conditions. But in the absence of a strong state, civil society networks can also turn into a source of power and domination for an oligarchy, become estranged from the broader society, and thus prevent the rebuilding of the state and the introduction of democratic forms of governance (Migdal *1988b:* 24–41).

The benign side of the reappearance of traditional civil society is apparent every day in countries where government is unable to perform functions expected of a modern state. The government cannot fund schools for all children, and civil society responds by setting up alternative schools. State collapse forces banks to close, and civil society responds by setting up informal systems that may not be officially recognized or formally registered. Noteworthy particularly in the Arab world (the *hawala* system), they move money rapidly and efficiently across continents and into remote villages. The formal economy cannot provide jobs for everybody, and civil society develops an informal sector that provides the livelihood of the majority of the population.

But there is unfortunately also a malignant side to the reappearance of traditional civil society, because it can further undermine the failed state institutions for which it is trying to compensate. During the transition from apartheid in South Africa, a weakened government lost its capacity to enforce the laws that kept peddlers away from the business district of Johannesburg. Informal sector businesses took over the sidewalks, to the benefit of the people who were trying to make a living by selling vegetables and braiding hair on the street. But the informal marketplace also became the territory of criminal gangs, legitimate businesses were driven out, and the once thriving business district became a 'no-go' area.

And parts of the civil society that flourish because of the absence of the state may be hostile to efforts to revive it. The trading networks that form in war-ravaged countries respond to a need, but they can also become profitable organizations that resist the efforts of the new, stronger government to revive institutions. Vigilante groups, such as those that operate in many parts of Nigeria, are a civil society response to insecurity. But they tend to turn into criminal organizations that end up by preying on those they were supposed to defend. In extreme cases, the re-emergence of traditional civil society is a threat to the continued existence of the state or can challenge its reconstruction, as in Somalia today where the clans, who constitute the traditional organizations of civil society, resist any transfer of power to the state.

The tension between traditional civil society and the state is also evident in the cultural domain. Traditionally, civil society has always been a major vehicle through which culture has been transmitted. In many countries public education has deliberately sought to create a new culture, different from that transmitted by civil society and in many ways alien to it. A central part of the new public education was the effort to create a new national identity, different and often hostile to the local identities transmitted by traditional civil society. Public education historically was part of a struggle between state and traditional civil society. Thus in Turkey under Kamal Ataturk the state tried to impose secular values on a traditional society that upheld Islamic ones. This cultural conflict between states and traditional civil society continues today even in the most industrialized, democratic societies—it is evident for instance in the disputes in France over the right of Muslim girls to wear a headscarf in school. In societies where the state is weaker, or less determined to influence the culture, the battle is often won by civil society – the re-Islamization of culture in Egypt after decades of secular public education is a striking example (Wickham 2002).

Key Points

- Traditional forms of civil society exist in all countries, but they do not necessarily perform traditional functions.
- When the state is weak, traditional civil society tends to be strong.
- Traditional forms of civil society help alleviate certain problems created by the weakness of the state, but they can also prevent the strengthening of the state.

THE MODERN STATE AND CIVIL SOCIETY AS A SPECIALIZED ENTITY

The rise of civil society as an entity separate from the broader society and from the state is part of an overall process of specialization that has affected all social and political institutions, particularly in the later part of the twentieth century. This specialization of functions has been accompanied by a formalization of the organizations that discharge those functions.

The phenomenon of specialization and formalization is visible everywhere. Governments are spawning increasing number of agencies and bureaux in order to perform a growing number of intricate functions. Although more evident in industrialized than in developing countries a trend towards specialization exists in the developing countries too, driven in part by similar factors: economic change and urbanization. The multiplication of government functions is made necessary by the increasing complexity of the economy and the requirements of more urban societies. The change in lifestyles resulting from industrialization creates the need for new social institutions while reducing the importance of others. In developing countries these trends are also driven by the example of the industrialized countries and by the direct pressure exercised by international development agencies that seek to reproduce familiar forms of organization.

Such pressure is entirely understandable and probably useful in some cases, but it can also create distortions. For example, the insistence by international financial institutions such as the International Monetary Fund and the World Bank that aid recipient countries set up special anti-corruption agencies could prove beneficial, at least if the agencies were to work efficiently. However, the creation of specialized organizations in this way can lead to development of a civil society sector that is poorly suited to the prevailing conditions and financially unsustainable. It may undermine forms of civil society organizations that are more in line with the resources and needs of the developing countries (Ottaway and Chung 1999).

Contemporary Civil Society: Myths and Realities

In order to address the problem of whether the emergence of a specialized civil society in developing countries is a positive phenomenon or a distortion created by international development agencies, it is necessary to consider the main functions that civil society organizations perform in the contemporary world. This section focuses on three major functions of civil society and asks whether the new, specialized, and professionalized civil society can perform them in developing countries. The first and vaguest of these functions is the generation of social capital; the second, somewhat more specific, function is the representation of the interests and demands of the population; and the third, quite concrete, function is the provision of goods and, above all, services for the population. The specialization of civil society alters the way in which civil society performs these functions in all countries, but raises particularly serious problems in developing countries.

Take first the widely held view that civil society organizations generate social capital, a concept first set forth by Putnam (1993) in a study of regional government in Italy, as an explanation of why the same institutions functioned differently in the north and south of the country. He observed that the inhabitants of the northern region shared a civic culture rooted in earlier experiences with self-government and sustained over the centuries by a rich associational life. These attitudes constituted the social capital that determined the way people viewed government and related to its institutions. This social capital was scarce in the southern regions, which had both a different historical experience and a dearth of associational life.

It is open to question to what extent the more specialized civil society organizations of today, with their professional staffs and narrow focuses, generate social capital. Professional, specialized organizations tend to have small or even non-existent membership and thus they do not reach many people. Even if they do, they engage them only on very specific issues. They probably do not inculcate in their members the attitudes of trust and cooperation that constitute social capital. Putnam argues that professional NGOs, even if devoted to democratic causes, contribute less to the social capital that supports democracy than seemingly irrelevant associations such as bowling leagues or the charitable and social clubs once widespread in American towns. He even sees in the decreasing popularity of these organizations a harbinger of the decline of American democracy.

Putnam's concern about the capacity of specialized and professionalized NGOs to generate social capital may be exaggerated in the case of the United States. There, many types of voluntary associations thrive and NGOs are numerous, extremely varied in their ideological and policy positions, and draw support widely, thereby contributing to pluralism. But in developing countries, many NGOs have small memberships, focus on a narrow range of issues and are highly dependent on foreign governments or international NGOs. Their contribution to social capital is highly questionable, particularly when compared to the social capital generated by more traditional social institutions. Such traditional institutions also teach values and attitudes, but not necessarily those extolled by Putnam as necessary for democracy. They may include, for example, extremely negative views of other ethnic or religious groups, deep distrust of all strangers, or demeaning attitudes towards women. The fact that the content of this social capital is different and may be contrary to democratic values does not alter the fact that it is deeply embedded in social relations and not easily erased, particularly by professional NGOs with weak social roots.

The second of the three functions attributed to civil society – the representational function – raises the question whether or how far such groups can actually represent the society vis-a-vis the government. The simple answer is that specialized civil society organizations do not represent society as a whole in any country. But in developing countries and within non-democratic international institutions, however, civil society organizations do broaden the range of interests that are expressed. Yet they do so in a lopsided way that favours groups with the capacity to organize and to access resources, even if their ideas are not widely held.

In well-established democracies, the problem of representation is solved by the existence of elected officials, freely chosen by the voters to represent their interests. Organizations of civil society are simply one among many types of organized interest group that put pressure on the elected officials to adopt the policies they favour. Professional NGOs are numerous and hold a variety of conflicting positions, as already stated, and compete for influence with a lot of other groups including paid lobbies; thus, they cannot advance a credible claim to represent the interests and the will of the entire population.

But in many developing countries representative institutions are often weak and elections fall short of being free and fair; as a result, civil society organizations may more credibly claim to represent voiceless citizens. Civil society organizations also have a degree of credibility when they claim to speak for unrepresented constituencies in international institutions, which are designed to represent states, but provide no formal channels through which popular demands can be expressed. Because lack of popular representation is a real problem in many developing countries and in international organizations, NGOs' claims that they voice the voiceless have won a degree of acceptance in recent years, and even gained them a place at the table in many policy discussions.

The issue whether NGOs should be consulted despite their lack of representativity remains highly controversial, and unlikely to be resolved soon. As long as countries do not have truly democratic institutions, the voice of NGOs adds an element of pluralism to the political system, and the distortions created by this imperfect form of representation may be an acceptable price for such a broadening of the political process. On the other hand, there is an element of risk in mandatory consultations with organizations that are not representative and above all not accountable to the people in whose name they claim to speak.

The third function performed by modern, professional civil society organizations is the provision of goods and services to the population. Many voluntary organizations provide a wide range of assistance—from the very basic, survival-oriented food distribution or provision of emergency shelter to the funding of research on rare diseases or the formation of support groups for people facing an almost infinite variety of problems. In this field too, there are considerable differences between the importance of this civil society in industrial and less developed countries, as well as in the issues raised by the existence of these organizations. On the one hand, these civil society organizations are much more numerous, better organized, and more capable in the industrialized countries. In developing countries they are usually highly dependent on external funding and very often find themselves in a subordinate position to the more affluent international NGOs that can access with greater ease money from rich countries and international organizations.

On the other hand, professional NGOs delivering goods and services often have a more important role in developing countries compared to richer counterparts in the industrialized West. In the poorest countries, for example, the assistance provided by NGOs is the main form of assistance available to the population, while in the richer countries NGOs supplement rather than replace the safety net provided by the government. This gives the foreign organizations that provide the funding for activities in developing countries a role that is often more important than that of the government. In extreme cases, the imbalance between the capacity of a developing country's government and that of the foreign and domestic NGOs operating there becomes dramatic and can hollow out the role of the government. To illustrate, in Afghanistan between January 2002 and March 2003, foreign donors channelled $296 million in assistance through the Afghan government and $446 million through international NGOs.

Key Points

- Professionalized and specialized civil society organizations generate little social capital.
- Specialized civil society organizations are not truly representative, but they broaden the range of interests expressed in the political process.
- Professional organizations can play a crucial role in the provision of services.

CIVIL SOCIETY AND THE STATE IN THE DEVELOPING WORLD

Relations between state and civil society, both in its traditional and modern forms, are quite complex in the developing world, more so than in industrial countries. Political systems are undergoing change in many countries, some states are still consolidating or conversely are on the verge of failure, modern civil society is a recent construct, and traditional forms of civil society are still making adaptations to a changed social and political environment. As a result, relations between state and civil society are in flux. In consolidated democracies, the relationship is more stable and thus more predictable.

Civil society organizations relate to state institutions and officials in one of three different ways: they ignore them and try to avoid their control; they oppose them and work for their replacement; or they seek to influence their policies. The pattern of avoidance is most often found in countries where the state is incapable of delivering services or other public goods. Civil society organizations give up on the state and seek to provide essential public goods on their own. Some of these activities are benign, for example the organization of alternative self-help schools for children neglected by the public system. Others are quite problematic; for example, in countries where the police force is incapable of ensuring a minimum of security for citizens, vigilante groups sometimes degenerate into protection rackets or become predatory. The organizations of civil society that flourish in the space left by a failing state are unregistered and unlicensed, often illegal. In terms of structures, they thus fall into the category of traditional civil society, although the functions they perform are a response to contemporary problems created by state collapse and/or political repression.

When the state is capable of performing its functions, but the government is repressive and unresponsive, civil society organizations are more likely to take an antagonistic position. Some civil society organizations that take on an opposition role are simply fronts for political parties, deliberately set up to circumvent donors' rules against funding political organizations. As mentioned earlier, in some countries civil society organizations have strong party links. In others, civil society organizations turn into opposition groups after trying to influence the government and discovering they cannot do so. Many NGOs in Zimbabwe developed in the early 1990s as bona fide civil society organizations lobbying for improved human rights, constitutional reform, better legal services for the poor, and a variety of non-partisan causes. By the end of the decade, many had turned into anti-government forces as President Mugabe's government became increasingly repressive. Organizations that see themselves as guardians of universal principles – human rights organizations for example – are particularly likely to turn antagonistic when the government continues to violate those principles. Civil society groups that oppose the government can be organized as professional NGOs or along less formal lines as broad social movements or loosely structured networks. Such a broad, loosely structured alliance of hundreds of small local organizations or 'civics' formed in South Africa during the 1980s. The existence of this many-headed and elusive hydra was crucial in convincing the apartheid regime that peace could not be restored by repressive measures and that a political solution was necessary.

Finally, the relationship of civil society to state and government can be a cooperative one. This is the ideal promoted by democratization programmes. There are various forms of cooperation. Civil society organizations, which possess a degree of expertise in their specialized area, lobby the government to promote specific policy reforms and even provide the government with the expertise to implement the reforms, like helping to write legislation. Women's organizations, which are not usually seen as particularly threatening by governments although they may antagonize conservative social forces, are adept at this advocacy role. For example, they helped craft legislation in Uganda that expanded landownership rights for women, as well as a new divorce law more favourable to women in Egypt.

Another form of cooperation between government and civil society is found when the government contracts out the delivery of services to non-profit non-governmental organizations. This is rarer in developing countries than in Europe because it requires strong governments, capable of establishing a regulatory framework and providing supervision, and strong civil society organizations capable of delivering complex services. The existence of a weak government on one side and strong international NGOs, often backed by large amounts of foreign money, gives rise to the common complaint that in such conditions international NGOs de facto make policy, further weakening the government and undermining its capacity.

The relationship between state and civil society in developing countries is rarely an easy one. This explains why many governments see civil society organizations as dangerous enemies to be tightly controlled. In democratic countries, setting up and registering an NGO is an easy process and regulations aim above all at preventing abuse of tax-exempt status or the misuse of donations. By contrast, in many developing countries NGOs are subject to complicated regulations aimed at suppressing groups that aspire to an advocacy role, instead of merely dispensing charity. An important issue that emerged in the 1990s in some countries is whether organizations of civil society should be allowed to receive foreign funding. Most governments welcome foreign funding of charitable organizations – for example, groups that provide assistance to AIDS orphans in Africa. Foreign funding of advocacy organizations, on the other hand, is very controversial.

Key Points

- When the state is repressive, civil society organizations are usually antagonistic to it.
- When the state is weak and incapable of delivering services, civil society organizations seek to ignore the state and avoid its control, rather than press for reforms.
- When the state is strong and civil society organizations are well developed, relations tend to be cooperative and constructive.

CIVIL SOCIETY AND DEMOCRATIZATION

The rapid transformation of the term civil society from an obscure concept known to a few scholars to one that finds its place in all discussions of political transformation is due to the rapid spread of democracy assistance initiatives that followed the end of the cold war. However, by the end of the 1990s it was clear that many so-called democratic transitions had led at best to the formation of semi-authoritarian regimes rather than democratic ones (Ottaway 2003). Furthermore, the reform process was losing momentum almost everywhere (Diamond 1996). Nevertheless, democracy promotion abroad remains on the political agenda of most industrial democracies. And leaders in the developing world, including many with no democratic credentials and no visible intention of acquiring them, embraced the rhetoric of democracy.

The concept of civil society became an important part of all discussions of democratization for reasons grounded to some extent in theory – as discussed earlier – and to a larger extent in pragmatism. In order to provide democracy assistance, aid agencies had to break down the abstract idea of democracy into concrete component parts that could be supported with limited amounts of aid. Civil society was such a component, and a particularly attractive one. Developing civil society meant promoting government by the people and for the people. And when civil society was defined as a narrow set of professional NGOs, it was also an entity to which assistance could be easily provided.

NGOs are easy to organize and cheap to fund; small grants go a long way. Professional NGOs were also a new type of association in many countries. Without roots in the traditional civil society and the culture of their countries and highly dependent on outside funding, professional NGOs were easy to train and influence to conform to the funders' concept of what civil society should do. With donor support, NGOs multiplied rapidly in all regions of the world, displaying remarkably similar characteristics. This made the aid agencies' job of supporting civil society-easier. It also raised the question whether these organizations were truly addressing the specific challenges of democratization in their countries.

Many studies of the donor-assisted civil society have reached the conclusion that pro-democracy NGOs tend to be quite isolated from the society at large. For instance this was a nearly unanimous conclusion of the contributors to *Funding Virtue* (Ottaway and Carothers 2000), with the only exception being two experts on the Philippines, where the growth of civil society was an indigenous process that owed much less to foreign assistance. This suggests that donor support is an important contributor to the isolation of civil society organizations. Many professional NGOs have small or no membership. They are often exclusively urban organizations with little reach in the countryside – only the best organized are able to extend their reach through networks of less formal Community-Based Organizations (CBOs). Exchanges (often called 'networking') among the NGOs from different countries provide an opportunity for organizations to discuss their problems and learn from each other, but they also contribute to creating a special international NGO world whose inhabitants talk to each other more easily than they do to their

Box 7.1 Civil Society in the Philippines

In the Philippines, the NCO community has long played a significant political role – helping bring down the Marcos regime, challenging and helping define the national political agendas under presidents Aquino, Ramos and Estrada, and taking sides in the 1998 presidential elections to support Estrada over Ramos ... a reason for the unusual strength of civil society is that the focus of most NCOs in the Philippines is not the promotion of a formal democratic system but the participation of citizens in promoting economic development and tackling the social problems that affect them directly. Democratic participation is thus not an abstraction but a means to an end that is directly important to the lives of people. Democratic participation becomes an extension of such efforts to improve one's life chances.

(Ottaway and Carothers 2000: 297; 302)

compatriots. These observations do not call into question the genuine commitment of many NGO leaders to democracy, human rights, or other causes. They do call into question, however, the capacity of these so-called organizations of civil society to influence their societies.

Democracy NGOs have other problems worth mentioning briefly. One is the opportunism that exists in the NGO world alongside genuine commitment – when assistance is available, setting up an NGO can simply be a way of making a living. Corruption also exists in the NGO world, which is unsurprising in view of its very rapid growth. And many, as mentioned earlier, become partisan organizations affiliated with political parties. These problems are tangible, but also inevitable to some extent and not particularly worrisome unless they are extremely widespread. They are simply part of the inevitable imperfection of the real world.

What is more worrisome is whether the growth of a small professional civil society actually contributes to democratization and whether the attention lavished on these organizations has led to the neglect of organizational forms that might have greater popular appeal and greater outreach within the population. Democracy promoters recognize the weakness of the NGOs they support and they equate it with the weakness of civil society. And yet, in many of the countries where the organizations officially designated as civil society are weakest, for example in many war-torn African countries, informal civil society organizations have proven very resilient in trying to address the most severe difficulties created by state collapse. In their search for a society that is civil by their definition and assistable in terms of its formal characteristics, aid providers may have marginalized groups with a proven record of effectiveness.

Arab countries, with their contrast between a vast Islamic civil society and their struggling official civil society, illustrate the problem particularly well. In Egypt the world of Islamic civil society is large and multifaceted. It includes charitable groups, organizations that provide free of charge medical services the state has stopped delivering, organizations that offer some educational opportunities for students under-served by failing public schools, groups that provide textbooks for university students who cannot afford them. It also includes organizations with political goals that do not satisfy the principles of liberal democracy, and terrorist groups that can only be defined as uncivil.

This Islamic civil society is well rooted in the society at large. Even organizations that are by no means traditional, but represent a contemporary and, from a religious point of view, aberrant response to contemporary problems, can cast themselves as part of a well-established tradition. They are certainly better rooted in the society than the modern, professional, pro-democracy NGOs favoured by donors. But the new, donors' civil society espouses the values of liberal democracy, while the more traditional Islamic civil society is at best ambiguous on this point. In the end, neither an isolated modern civil society nor a well-rooted Islamic one are good vehicles for democratic transformation.

Box 7.2 Policy and advocacy NGOs only a part of civil society

The case studies make clear the assumption of NGOs' centrality is questionable. Other kinds of civil society groups frequently drive political change, eclipsing what is often the circumscribed role of policy or advocacy NGOs. In South Africa a social movement brought down apartheid. In Egypt, traditional professional associations are major players in the struggles over political liberalization. In Latin America, the profound struggles of the 1980s against dictatorship and repression were conducted by many social and political forces very different from the technocratic advocacy NGO donors would favour, in the 1990s. And in the Philippines, Bangladesh, and elsewhere in Asia, citizens' groups focused on socio-economic issues are having major effects on long-term processes of societal change.

(Adapted from Ottaway and Carothers 2000: 295)

Key Points

- The difference between traditional organizations well rooted in the society, relatively close to the population, but not necessarily democratic or official and the civil society recognized by international democracy promoters may be starker in the Muslim world than elsewhere at this time, but is found in all parts of the developing world.
- Democracy requires a large, active, democratically oriented civil society, but what is found in most countries is a bifurcated situation: an official civil society – small, democratic, but essentially elitist; and a less formal, traditional civil society – large, popular, well rooted but of dubious democratic credentials.
- How to combine the democratic commitment of the former to the popular roots and outreach of the other is a major conundrum for democratization.

CONCLUSIONS

The chapter started with an acknowledgement of the ambiguity of the concept of civil society and of its lack of definitional clarity. It ends on the same note, but with a normative addendum. Not only the concept of civil society is an imprecise, ambiguous one, but it must be accepted as such. The more strictly the concept is defined, the less it helps understand how people come together voluntarily to address problems that they cannot solve as individuals and that the state cannot or does not want to help solve for them.

It is of course possible to narrow down the definition closely. This is what the international development agencies do all the time when they pick the organizations to support on the basis of the civility of their goals and the adequacy of their organizational structures. But what is gained in terms of clarity is lost in terms of the understanding of the society. First, the narrow definition loses sight of the many ways in which people in any society organize themselves to pursue their interests and satisfy their needs. It may reduce the effectiveness of any outside intervention, by focusing attention on groups that may be quite marginal to the society but happen to appear all-important to aid agencies. Second, a definition that separates a democratic, virtuous civil society acting in the public interest from a non-democratic, uncivil one, selfishly promoting narrow interests is more normative than analytical. The idea of the common good and the public interest obfuscate the reality that all societies are made up of groups with different and often conflicting interests, and that all groups are equally part of the society, whether their goals conform to a specific idea of civility or not.

In conclusion, despite the caveat expressed at the outset, from an analytical point of view we need to accept that we cannot do better than accept that civil society comprises the entire realm of voluntary associations between the family and the state. It is a vast and complex realm. Voluntary associations take many different forms, ranging from small, informal self-help groups and ad hoc committees with narrow goals to large, professional and bureaucratic organizations with large budgets. In developing countries, civil society organizations perform a wide range of functions. At one extreme, there are narrowly focused groups that seek, for example, to provide support for AIDS orphans in a community or raise money to improve the track that connects a village to the nearest highway. At the other, there are organizations tied into transnational networks with goals such as changing the World Bank's outlook on the construction of dams or delivering humanitarian assistance to populations in need. Many voluntary associations in developing countries try to provide services the state is unable to deliver. Others form to help citizens resist pressure from predatory governments. Organizations citizens develop voluntarily are not always 'civil' in the normative sense of the word. The realm of civil society comprises organizations that promote human rights and vigilante groups that prey on the people they are supposed to protect. While it is tempting to narrow the definition of civil society to organizations with commendable goals, this is not helpful. If we want to understand how people come together to defend their interests or pursue their goals, we need to accept the diversity, the complexity, and in many cases the flaws of the associational realm that has become known as civil society.

References

Florini, Ann M. (ed.), *The Third Force: The Rise of Transnational Civil Society* (Washington: Carnegie Endowment for International Peace, 2000). Case studies of the role of transnational networks of civil society including the global anti-corruption movement, human rights movement, organizations for democracy, and against dam-building and for environmental sustainability.

Hann, Chris, and Dunn, Elisabeth (eds.), *Civil Society: Challenging Western Models* (New York: Routledge, 1996). A critical account.

Kasfir, Nelson (ed.), *Civil Society and Democracy in Africa* (London: Frank Cass 1998). A critical view of conventional Western attitudes towards civil society in Africa.

Ottaway, Marina, and Carothers, Thomas (eds.), *Funding Virtue: Civil Society Aid and Democracy Promotion* (Washington: Carnegie Endowment for International Peace, 2000). A critical examination of civil society aid drawing on cases in Africa, Asia, the Middle East, and Latin America.

_______ and Chung, 'Debating Democracy Assistance: Toward a New Paradigm', *Journal of Democracy*, 10/4 (1999): 99–113. A cautious view of international 'democracy assistance' to civil society and to elections and parties too.

Putnam, Robert, *Making Democracy Work: Civic Traditions in Modern Italy* (Princeton: Princeton University Press, 1993). A seminal work on social capital.

Wickham, Carrie Rosef sky, *Mobilizing Islam: Religion, Activism, and Political Change in Egypt* (New York: Columbia University Press, 2002). A highly acclaimed analysis of the role of cultural identity, political economy, mobilization and organization in political Islam in Egypt.

8

Interpreting the Notion of Civil Society

Jean Cohen

I will address three questions disturbing to those who make use of the concept of civil society,

1. Is the term 'civil society' really a code word for the market, private property, capitalism?
2. If not, is the discourse of civil society necessarily traditionalistic – does it ignore hierarchies and forms of domination on the terrain of the social?
3. Is the politics of civil society necessarily a- or anti-political?

What is the relation between a politics of civil society and the state or the economy?

The concept of civil society has recently become fashionable thanks to struggles against communist and military dictatorships, first in Eastern Europe and the Soviet Union, and second in Latin America. Accordingly, to some, it seems to indicate what the West\has already achieved, and thus the concept appears to be without any critical potential vis-a-vis the dysfunctions and injustices in our type of society. I believe this mistaken view relies on a two-part model that opposes civil society to the state. And I want to argue that no version of the two-part model, whether liberal and/or Marxian, whereby civil society includes everything outside of the state sector, is helpful today. The stark polemical opposition between civil society and the state can only be a slogan, a starting point for analysis or for mobilization against statist regimes, but it is certainly not adequate for serious analysis or politics within civil societies.

Nevertheless, I do believe that the discourse of civil society involves a politics, a democratic politics potentially more engaging and mobilizing than the slogan 'Join the association of your choice' (Michael Walzer).

I begin from a three-part model which differentiates between civil society, the state, and the economy. Its roots lie in Hegel, but theorists as different as Gramsci, Parsons and Habermas also make use of it. The three-part model has two advantages. First, it avoids an unpleasant ambiguity in the programme of the defense of civil society against the state, for it allows one to distinguish between the 'civil' and the 'bourgeois.' On a three-part model, the autonomy of civil society is not the same as the autonomy of the market. To put it another way, a bourgeois society that places the market and property rights at its centre is only one version of this, and a problematic one at that. The advantage of a three-part model is that it allows us to differentiate between the task of establishing or maintaining viable market economies (whatever the forms of property) and the project of strengthening civil society vis-a-vis the state and the liberated market forces. As we know from the West, economic power can represent as great a danger to social solidarity, social justice, and autonomy as the power of the modern state. So only a concept of civil society differentiated from the economy could become the centre of a critical theory in societies where the market economy has already developed its own autonomous logic or is in the process of doing so.

Second, the three-part model also helps us to counter conservative conceptions of the social life. It allows us to see that the defense of civil society does not have to entail a traditionalistic hierarchy as opposed to a modern (egalitarian) life world. If civil society can take many forms, then it can also be a target of democratization. The politics of civil society can try to change the institutions of civil society in a direction away from hierarchical, inegalitarian, patriarchal, nationalist, racist versions toward egalitarian, horizontal, non-sexist, open versions based on the principles of individual rights and democratic participation in associations, and public. No one can argue convincingly that such a movement is realized anywhere in the West. However, with the demise of Marxism and the revolutionary rhetoric of communism, the question confronting political theorists everywhere is whether Utopian thought and meaningful political projects are conceivable at all. Or are the great mobilizing ideals embedded in the earlier Utopias consigned to the dustbin of the history of ideas?

The ideals generated in the age of democratic revolutions – liberty, political equality, solidarity, justice – were each embedded in totalistic Utopias: anarchism, libertarianism, radical democracy, Marxism. Sober reflection on the history of the past century and a half should dissuade responsible persons from trying to revive any of these utopias in their original form. Yet a society without action – orienting ideals, without political projects, is equally undesirable, for the civil privatism or 'realism' that would result, would involve a political culture unable to generate enough motivation to even maintain, much less expand, existing rights, democratic institutions, social solidarity, or justice.

I believe that the discourse of civil society helps here. This discourse reveals that collective actors and sympathetic theorists are still oriented by the Utopian ideals of modernity, even if die fundamentalist revolutionary rhetoric within which they once were articulated is on the wane. Indeed, the movement of civil society is itself a new kind of Utopia: the normative principles underlying it, plurality, publicity, legality, equality, justice, voluntary association, and individual autonomy, constitute a self-limiting utopia that calls for a plurality of democratic form, a complex set of social, civil, and political rights compatible with a highly differentiated society. It also calls for what I label a self-limiting, radical politics.

Let me briefly redefine more clearly my conception of civil society and point to the possible politics this entails. I understand civil society as a sphere of social interaction distinct from economy and state, composed above all of associations (including the family) and publics. Modern civil society is created and reproduced through forms of collective action, and it is institutionalized through laws, especially subjective rights that stabilize social differentiation. While the active and institutionalized dimensions can exist separately, in the long run both independent action and institutionalization are necessary for the reproduction of civil society.

I do not, however, identify civil society with all of social life outside the state and economic spheres. First, one must distinguish civil society both from what I call a 'political society' of parties, political organizations, and political public spheres (parliaments) and from an 'economic society' composed of the organizations of production, distribution, and associated publics, usually firms, cooperatives, institutions of collective bargaining, unions, councils, etc. The actors and institutions of political and economic society are directly involved with state power and economic production. They cannot afford to subordinate strategic and instrumental criteria to the patterns of normative integration and open-ended communication characteristic of civil society. While the associations of civil society are communicatively coordinated, modern political and economic institutions must be coordinated through the media of power and money, however much communicative interaction can be found there. Even the public spheres of political society involve important formal and temporal constraints in processes of communication. In turn, the political role of civil society is not directly related to the conquest of power, but to the generation of influence, through the life of democratic associations and unconstrained discussion in a variety of cultural and informal public spheres. Thus, the mediating role of political society between civil society and the state (political society sets up receptors for the influence of civil society) is indispensable, but so is the rootedness of political society in civil society. In principle, similar considerations pertain to the relationship of civil and economic society, even if historically, under capitalism, economic society has been more successfully insulated from the influence of civil society than political society, despite the claims of elite theories of democracy. Of course, I have now apparently replaced a three-part with a five-part model, but it should be obvious that the concepts of political and economic society are mediating categories between the three core terms of my framework.

Indeed, I want to stress that under liberal democracies it would be a mistake to see civil society in opposition to economy and state by definition. My notion of economic and political society refers to mediating institutions through which civil society can gain influence over political/administrative and economic processes. An antagonistic relation of civil society or its actors to economy and state arises when these mediations fail, or when economic or political institutions insulate decision making and decision makers from the communication with and influence of social organizations, initiatives and discussions.

This conceptual framework obviously translates categories of general social theory into political sociology. The point of this translation is to get beyond a strictly dichotomous framework and the one-sided models of politics that flow from it. On the dichotomous model we are left with a rather varied set of theoretical choices: the defense of civil society against the state, participation in the political system on strictly strategic terms, or attempts to dispense with the opposition altogether in the name of a republican model of participatory democracy. The first position is typical of the anti-politics of some components of the new social movements, the second of elite theorists of democracy. What both have in common is a view that severs the link between civil and political society. The third model is based on a republican conception of political society, which tends to denigrate civil society as individualistic, apolitical, and privatistic. The politics of civil society looks far more promising on the three-part model. As I said at the beginning, civil society is a project, a terrain and target of democratic politics. The institutions of civil society can and ought to be the target of democratization, of egalitarian projects aimed at expanding rights and solidarities and the institutions of political and economic society can and ought to be the targets of actors in civil society seeking to render them more receptive to their influence, in short, I can identify, on my conception, four types of politics which I call the politics of identity, influence, inclusion, and reform, which address civil, political and/or economic society, the economy, and state, respectively. All of these comprise the policies of civil society.

Contemporary collective actors consciously struggle over the power to construct new identities, and to reshape institutions, cultural and normative expectations accordingly. Civil society proper is the terrain and target of this politics of identity. It is here that collective actors defend spaces for the creation of the new identities and seek to render more egalitarian and democratic the institutions and social relations in which identities are generated. It is through such action that traditions are reassessed, renewed, or revised, and inegalitarian social relations or forms of domination within civil society properly challenged.

The target of the politics of influence is public opinion in civil and political society. Or rather, the politics of influence aims at making the actors in political society (or in economic society) responsive and receptive to those in civil society. In short, the politics of influence seeks to alter the universe of political discourse such that it keeps up with the basic principles and cultural changes articulated in civil society. The politics of influence indicates how actors of civil society can accomplish something on the level of the political or economic system without losing their identity as civil actors or social movements.

In political society, actors get to participate through political inclusion in the form of parties, lobbies, and recognized partners in bargaining forums. A similar point can be made for economic society. Collective action aimed at the expansion of political or economic society to include new actors, in order to gain access to power or benefits, is what I call the politics of inclusion. Finally, recognized actors seek to accomplish some of their goals through strategic action in order to make policy: this is the politics of reform, at least in the case of actors arising from social movements.

I believe that all of the important contemporary movements can be analyzed in these terms. I also believe that construed in this way, the concept and politics of civil society take us beyond the unattractive alternatives of soulless reformism and revolutionary fundamentalism. Utopian ideals are not on the wane, political projects are still possible, we need not indulge in resignation, for a democratic and egalitarian civil society is still a project worth fighting for.

9

Reconceptualizing Civil Society for Now: Some Somewhat Gramscian Turnings[1]

Kai Nielsen

I

'Civil Society' much more than 'state,' 'government,' 'power' or even 'democracy', is a term of art in political theory. There is no discovering what the concept means, let alone what it 'really means,' what instead is to be done is to see if we can forge some conceptualization or reconceptualization of civil society which would be useful, given, on the one hand, some important political or ethical purposes or, on the other, some theoretical purposes.

In ancient usage, *civilis societas* (in Cicero, for example) referred to the condition of living in a civilized political community: a community with a legal code cities, commercial arts, and the refinements of living, For there to be a civil society, according to the ancient conception, is for there to be this kind of political community. Skipping a few centuries, by the time we get to contractarian thought, there is a considerable change. In John Locke, for example, political and civil society were taken to be the same thing (whether it was a society of refinement or not) and this contrasted with paternal authority and the state of nature. But still there remained the identification of political society and civil society. With Hegel and Marx, the conception of civil society (*burgerliche Gesellschaft*) underwent a much greater change. For them, civil society was contrasted with political society. Civil society referred to a social order, and most fundamentally, an economic order operating according to its own principles, independent of the ethical requirements of law and political association. It was, for both Hegel and the early Marx, part of social life where avariciousness and egoism, sometimes accompanied by economic rationality, were the order of the day.[2] This part of social life lacked all the qualities of warmth, solidarity and moral cohesion at least supposedly characteristic of the *Gemeinschaften* of simpler societies.

Today many political theorists of rather different theoretical orientations and political commitments rather uncontroversially think of civil society as the non-political and non-private aspects of society. It is located in a conceptual space distinct from, and between, the state and the at least supposedly private sphere of the family and spousal arrangements and the like. As opposed to ancient usage, where 'civil society' was synonymous with a certain sort of 'political society,' the contemporary use of 'civil society' generally refers to economic and other social arrangements whether they be practices, codes, institutions, or organizations, as long as they are apart from the state and also apart from the private sphere of the family. Still, economic institutions remain the central element in civil society so conceived. Thus I do not think much, if any, exception would be taken to Michael Walzer's remarks that 'the line between political community and civil society was meant to mark off coercive decision-making from free exchange,'[3] and that 'the separation of civil society and political community creates the sphere of economic competition and free enterprise, the market in commodities, labour, and capital.'[4] This, of course, as Walzer is perfectly aware, is only the civil society of our bourgeois societies. Civil society here is quite literally just a *burgerliche Gesellschaft*. But the point is, that it is in such societies that these forms of life have gained prominence. Moreover, there are analogies in earlier pre-capitalist societies and in what once were State Socialist societies.

However, this by now rather orthodox conception of civil society is not the only way civil society has been conceptualized. Antonio Gramsci, from an historicist but still thoroughly Marxian perspective, reconceptualized civil society into a tripartite conception in which civil society is juxtaposed not only against the state, taken as a coercive governmental apparatus, but, strikingly, against the economy and the private sphere of the family as well.[5] Although he was thoroughly Marxist, he is not to be understood here (Noberto Bobbio, to the contrary, notwithstanding), as having abandoned historical materialism for a kind of Crocean historical idealism.[6] He did take the state, civil society, and the economy to be distinct elements in the social fabric, but he also stressed that they were methodological (analytical) distinctions used for purposes of perspicuous representation, analysis and critical praxis. In the real world their boundaries are blurred, indeed they even flow into each other, and are not separable. He might have even taken a page from that great 'atomist,' David Hume, and have reminded us that everything that is distinguishable is not separable: being physical and being extended or being an equiangular triangle and being an equilateral triangle, for example. They are not like a chair with its various parts or a human body with its various parts. In societies complex enough to have a state there can be no state without civil society and no economic relations without both and no private sphere without all of these elements. They are analytically separable (distinguishable) but not separable in reality. They are not like the parts that make up an automobile. Still, there are important systematic connections between these elements of society. In reality they form a continuous whole. But it is often useful to make these analytical distinctions.

It is not only Gramsci that has in general terms such a conception but also ex-Marxists such as Leszek Kolakowski, neo-Marxists such as Jurgen Habermas, and social theorists influenced by Habermas such as Andrew Arato, Jean Cohen, and Claus Offe.[7] It is my hunch – a hunch I will pursue to see if it is anything more than a hunch – that a clarified form of this conception of civil society is both politically and theoretically more useful than the more standard conceptions. It helps us to understand what makes societies tick. I shall turn to that after I have characterized rather more fully what this Gramscian conception of civil society comes to.

II

Walter Adamson aptly defines this Gramscian conception of civil society as follows: 'By civil society... I mean the public space between large-scale bureaucratic structures of state and economy' on the one hand, and the private sphere of family, friendships, personality, and intimacy on the other.'[8]

We need an adequate conception of civil society. In addition, we need to understand the politics of civil society in order to provide a corrective for a characteristic failure of liberalism, namely, that of operating with a simplistic conception of the distinction between public/private, state/society, and social/individual, liberalism lacks, or at least seems to lack, the conceptual resources to make clear how there is a non-governmental public sphere, a civil society, which, though closely related to the state, is still not a part of the state apparatus. But this non-governmental public sphere is nonetheless a vital force in forming public opinion, constructing consent and generating a de facto legitimation.[9] Here we need to think of organizations such as schools, churches, labour unions, businessmen's clubs, ethnic associations, the media, various professions like medicine with its institutional setting, the legal profession with its institutional setting, and the like. Just what role to take the most obvious example – do the media and the schools play in the forming of individuals (that is, in the forming of them as persons) or in the stabilizing or destabilizing of the state or the economy, and how does the economy interact with these institutions? Would a newspaper of any extensive circulation or a television network last long, indeed any time at all, if it took a persistently oppositional stance to the economic order of the time? Indeed it is very unlikely it would even come into being. Do we tend, when there is little conflict between the forces of production and relations of production, to have a nice functional meshing between the economic structure of society and the way its schools or media operate, or do we not? And if there is a meshing, just how does it work? Our political thinking tends to be so individualistic, with (as Ronald Dworkin puts it) individual rights taking centre stage, that these problems tend not even to surface, to say nothing of being carefully and clearly examined in a way that might be helpful in the creation of a good or at least a just society.[10]

In locating civil society we must look for those organizations or practices that are not directly governmental or economic but which generate opinions and goals, in accordance with which people who partake in these practices and are a part of these organizations seek not only to influence wider opinion and policies within existing structures and rules, but sometimes also to alter the structures and rules themselves.[11] Such a conception of civil society is valuable in coming to understand how the dominant classes often, indeed typically, rule by something other than force, how they achieve and sustain hegemony – that is, cultural leadership – across the society in which they are dominant, and how subaltern classes constitute themselves politically and mount challenges to the dominant political and economic order.

For Hegel, and for Marx as well, civil society was most centrally the sphere where the economic struggles of public life were played out. For Gramsci, by contrast, 'the conflicts of civil society are centrally political... their point is not merely the making of economic contracts and dividing of the existing labour product' – something which Gramsci took to be both economic and political – but in civil society, what is both more characteristic and more central is the formation of and the giving expression to political points of view by parties, religious groups, organs of information, and so forth deployed to 'influence the political identification of the masses and the institutional nature and boundaries of civil society itself.'[12]

III

At this juncture, a brief digression is in order on historical materialism, on how Gramsci's historical materialism is to be understood, and on its relation to how he conceptualized and on how we should conceptualize civil society. Gramsci was not an historical idealist, but what G.A. Cohen and Andrew Levine have aptly characterized as someone reasoning in accordance with a weak and restricted form of historical materialism.[13] Historical materialism, let us remind ourselves, is a theory of epochal social change. From epoch-to epoch, human history has a determinate structure and a direction resulting from an endogenous dynamic process in which social relations of production rise and fall in order to maintain functional compatibility with developing material forces of production. During a given epoch the relations of production exist as they are because they facilitate and do not fetter the development of the forces of production. Similarly, the political, legal, moral, and religious institutions exist as they are because they sustain the relations of production (the economic structures) that occur during that period. Restricted historical materialism restricts the explanatory scope of historical materialism. On the standard unrestricted account, economic structures (relations of production) explain all superstructural phenomena; on the restricted account, historical materialism only seeks to explain the superstructural facts which, via their effect on the relations of production, are required to explain how the distinctive dynamic forces of production remain in place, which in turn cause the rise and fall of economic structures. Restricted historical materialism seeks to be a general theory of history by explaining general trends, namely, epochal social change, but it is not a theory of general history; it does not try to explain all historical phenomena. However, it is still a strongly foundational theory for it explains how it is, from epoch to epoch, that there are major structural changes in our social life. Though Gramsci did not put things in this way, he was (and I think to his credit) a restricted historical materialist.

Gramsci also operated with what I shall characterize (following Levine) as a weak historical materialism. Traditional historical materialism (strong historical materialism, if you will) purports to give an account of the necessary and sufficient conditions for epochal social transformation. Traditional historical materialism purports to explain how we go from one set of relations of production, from one economic structure to another. It holds that certain levels of development of productive forces are both necessary and sufficient for the inception and reproduction of particular and distinctive economic structures or sets of production relations and that 'continuous development ... generates structural instabilities between forces and already existing relations of production.'[14] Traditional historical materialism holds that the development of the productive forces is sufficient, as well as necessary, to explain the movement from one set of production relations to another; weak historical materialism, by contrast, only claims that the development is necessary for such a movement,. 'Weak historical materialism,' as Levine well puts it, 'does not advance sufficient conditions for epochal historical change but only necessary material conditions. It does not purport to explain what actually happens, other things being equal (or nonexistent), but only what is (materially) possible.'[15] But it still yields a determinate historical agenda, something that is essential for Marxian praxis, by giving us a characterization of (a) historically possible epochal economic structures (a typology if you will) and (b) a characterization of the possibilities of moving from one epochal structure to another. The rest, on a Marxian account, is a matter of political action in class struggle. And it is here, of course, that a good account of civil society, and most particularly of civil society in industrialized societies, is of crucial importance.

If historical materialism is to stand much chance of being a true account of epochal or social change, it should be a restricted weak historical materialism. It is that form that fits very well with Gramsci's historicism, his activism, and his account of civil society.

Marxist fundamentalists (if there still are any) believe in the inevitability of socialism and that, in some sense of 'inevitability,' fits well with traditional historical materialism, Where these beliefs – historical materialism and historical inevitability – are well-entrenched, there is a tendency for Marxists to move toward economism or pessimistically, to self-consciously abandon class struggle and to content themselves with social democracy, while patiently waiting for the forces of production to develop. There are, however, as has been evident for a long time, good reasons, both political and theoretical, for not endorsing socialism's inevitability. But a Marxian revolutionary, which was what Gramsci was, need not and indeed should not believe in socialism's inevitability, but only that it is a feasible historical possibility, and thus on the historical agenda – and so, given that it is also desirable, something to strategically plan for and to struggle for.

IV

With this construing or perhaps in effect rational reconstructing, of Gramsci as an historical materialist in the weak and restricted sense, let us return to his account of civil society. Walter Adamson, one of Gramsci's most astute interpreters, remarks:

> Gramsci wanted to preserve both the Marxian insight that the forces of production (not the state) are the primary determinant of modern social evolution, and the Crocean insight that civil society is primarily a sphere of ethical-political contestation among rival social groups. The first point implies that the widening contradiction between the forces and relations of production remains the most basic precondition for the historical realization of a new socialist mode of production. But the second point implies that the fundamental political contest is unlikely to be a direct confrontation between capital and labour for control of the state and, thus, the means of production, at least not in the near term. Rather, the contest is likely to be a 'positional' one for civil society conceived essentially as a cultural-political domain, indeed the sole public domain where mass consent is at issue.[16]

This whole passage fits very well with restricted weak historical materialism. The first point in the passage, with its talk of basic preconditions, brings out the necessary conditions side; the second point provides a plausible and politically fruitful way to proceed for someone who was such an historical materialist. In the situation we are now in, the political context would be that of the class politics of civil society. What specific struggles and what kind of politics – that is concrete political strategies – would obtain will be strongly conditioned by what is possible at a given time and place. And intelligent moral agents should keep that firmly in mind. But that leaves plenty of Lebensraum for particular political strategies, for contestations of how civil society is to be forged. It provides conceptual space for what a Marxian politics or any other politics should be. So it is sensible enough to call Gramsci (as he has been called) a Marxist of the superstructures without at all suggesting (as has also been suggested) that he has set aside the bedrock of historical materialism for a Crocean historical idealist framework.[17] Keeping this in mind will help us to understand better the importance of his account of civil society.

Much of Gramsci's discussion of civil society, understandably enough, was focused on the Italian society of his time. A critical question we need to consider is how much of his analysis can more generally be extended to our present burgerliche Geselllschaften. In Italy, since its unification, no group, not even the Catholic Church, had gained cultural leadership – what Gramsci called hegemony. The principal players here were Fascism, traditional Catholicism, laical liberalism led by Croce as a kind of 'lay Pope,' and Marxism. In the struggle to gain hegemony in civil society and to extend this to the state and to the economy, Croce understood (and Gramsci took keen note of this) that 'the great problem of the modern age was to learn to live without religion, that is, without traditional confessional religion,'[18] Croce thought that traditional religion was, as such a social force, dead, but he also believed that the liberal tradition could be revived and refurbished and made to serve as a secular 'religion of liberty': an ersatz religion, if you will. He thought his History of Europe in Nineteenth Century (1932) provided the kind of narrative that would advance that.

Gramsci thought that Croce had posed the problem in the right way. Some form of secular religion was a key element in achieving a hegemonic culture in Italy – though, of course, he differed with Croce about what the content of this new secular equivalent of a religion should be. But he believed as firmly as Croce that Italy needed one, and that more generally modern societies need one. Gramsci wrote that Italy needed, a 'coherent unitary, nationally diffused 'conception of life and man,' a 'lay religion,' a philosophy that has become precisely a 'culture,' that has generated an ethic, a way of life, a civil and individual form of conduct,'[19] He agreed with Croce that there was then in Italy a crisis in authority, what we would now call a crisis in legitimation. The Church and the ruling classes had lost their firm hold on the populace. These authorities could no longer rely on a consensus in society in which the allegiances and behaviour of the masses were predictably stable. He further agreed with Croce that as a consequence the Italian state was forced into operating more and more by something approximating pure force. The masses had become 'detached from their traditional ideologies' such that they 'no longer believe what they used to believe etc.'[20]

In formal terms, then, Gramsci agreed with Croce about the need for a secularized religion as the functional replacement of traditional religion, which in Italy was Catholicism, and, if he had known of his work, he would have agreed with Emile Durkheim as well about the role of religion in our social life. About such matters Durkheim more than anyone else in the twentieth century probed very deeply. He saw how very much modern society was in need of a secularized religion, in a world, as Durkheim put it, in which 'the old gods are growing old or already dead, and the others are not yet born'[21] But in content, as I have noted Gramsci differed from both of them. What was needed, he believed, was not liberalism's religion of liberty, which Gramsci thought was little more than an 'atheism for aristocrats,' It neither could nor should succeed as a secular religion; what was needed instead was Marxism, what Gramsci, under the eye of the censors, called 'the philosophy of praxis.' It, he said, was an 'absolute secularization and earthiness of thought, an absolute humanism of history'[22] .What Marxism needed to do was to form its own intellectual body to 'combat modern ideologies In their most refined forms.' This he thought would take time and strategic and organizational skill. Moreover, the central struggle in civil society was not with liberalism, which he saw as having no mass backing, but with the Catholic Church with its long tradition and complex entrenched organization. But, historical materialist that he was, he thought a nontranscendental conception of religion, an utterly secularized religion, was on the historical agenda and that, as the struggle in civil society played itself out for our time, it would become gradually apparent that Marxism was the 'only religious faith that is adequate to the contemporary world and can produce a real hegemony.'[23]

This is surely a remark that would startle analytical Marxists and scientific socialists, but I think Adamson rightly remarks that for Gramsci 'Marxism is less a philosophy, political strategy, or understanding of history than a new religion which integrates its world view and practical ethic into a distinctive culture.'[24] So viewed, it could facilitate the acquisition of class consciousness in ways similar to the way any religion socializes its members. And what we get, when a population achieves class consciousness, is not just a knowledge of what a class is and what our particular class position is (though we do gel that) but also, by what Gramsci regarded as a catharsis, a vivid feeling of group solidarity with a keen sense of 'them' and 'us,' a feeling for and a sense of 'the collective power of a mutually shared vision of what the future can be and a mutually shared faith in the group's ability to arrive at that destination'[25] Marxism's power, Gramsci believed, derives not from science or from its having a set of firmly warranted beliefs, but from culture, from a collectively shared faith.

Gramsci saw Marxism, in the political struggle for hegemony, as 'containing in itself all the fundamental elements needed to construct a total and integral conception of the world,' but, even more importantly, he saw Marxism as having the cultural arid intellectual resources needed 'to give life to an integral practical organization of society, that is to become a total integral civilization.'[26] In short, he saw Marxism, far in advance of Fascism, Catholicism, and liberalism, as offering a new and higher principle of civilization.[27]

V

How much (if any) of this Gramscian conception of the politics of civil society makes sense for us standing where we stand? How much of this, if much of anything, answers to our needs both purely intellectual and political? Adamson, a knowledgeable and sympathetic – interpreter of Gramsci, writing in 1987, remarks, 'In today's world, of course, the possibility that Marxism represents history's anointed successor to Calvinist Christianity appears extremely unlikely. That such a world-historical vision was still plausible in the 1930s dramatizes the very great political and cultural distance we have travelled in the last half century.'[28] As a cultural force communism, and probably socialism too, is, for the present at least, a spent force.[29] Great masses of people may well never again march under red banners or sing *The Internationale.* Gramsci's 'new religion' seems not to have stuck – I say this with 'what for me is a deep sadness, I have very little hope that the world we can reasonably expect to obtain during our lives will resemble even a minimally decent world. It will not be just and it certainty will not be humane and probably not even be very intelligently ordered. But, aside from fears – I think not unfounded – about the uncontrolled and now hardly effectively opposable, American domination of the world – or (alternatively) trilateralism (the joint American-cum-European-cum-Japanese domination of the world) – I have no sorrow at all for the passing of the Russian Thermidor, along with its client communist (pseudo-communist is more accurate) regimes. But I had hoped – a hope that proved illusory – that something would be salvaged of a genuine socialist tradition from the ashes and that there would not be in those countries a capitalist restoration. But the capitalist countries won the Cold War and a capitalist restoration is well in progress, though not without opposition, along with an American or at least a trilateral world domination. Communism and socialism appear at least to be conceptualizations, culturally speaking, of times past. (Still, this may be too hasty a judgement. In many ways, things look uncertain.)

There is an irony in this for Marxian theoreticians. Marxism as a social force is dead, for the present at least, just as we are gaining from the work of such analytical Marxists as G.A. Cohen, Andrew Levine, Erik Olin Wright, and John Roemer a sophisticated and appropriately rigorous Marxian social theory that is arguably the best holistic social theory in or out of town.[30] Marxism has always been something more (indeed very much more) than a theory, even a good theory, and now it will have no basis for its praxis. It will, whatever its intentions, not be a theory in the service of a revolutionary movement. But this is to take away its very underlying rationale.

So the wheel of the world having turned, our analysis of the politics of civil society will have to be somewhat different from Gramsci's, Still, deploying the notion of civil society may continue to be useful, perhaps even more useful than before, for analyzing and critiquing the contemporary world.

For the institutions of civil society to be in place and properly functioning, two essential preconditions must be met: (a) the society must be a complex society with many different social functions and roles into which people are slotted and (b) the state and economic organizations cannot incorporate or even completely control the various practices, organizations, and institutions of the society that are non-economic and non-governmental. Vulgar Marxism with its economic determinism and reductionism sees the state and other non-economic institutions as utterly in control of the ruling class that goes with the economic structure. But Gramsci plainly was not such a Marxist and, even if he were, such a Marxism is plainly false.[31] In our societies these two essential preconditions for the possible viability of civil society are met, albeit perhaps insecurely. The key critical question for us should be: how should the politics of civil society appear, given present-day social realities? Put differently: what practices, organizations, and institutions should the particular civil society that is ours have and what kind of life together for ourselves should we seek to achieve? We, of course, cannot sensibly answer the latter question without a good understanding of what is feasibly possible: of what is on the historical agenda.

The preconditions for civil society are met in our world, but it is also true that the strength, and so far the growing strength, of economic-corporate and political-bureaucratic organizations threatens to undermine the institutions of civil society. There is, as Habermas puts it, a colonization of the life-world. Adamson is only being slightly hyperbolic when he remarks that 'we face a social world in which the power of corporate-bureaucratic structures is so great as to threaten the very existence of civil society and even the private sphere as we know them.'[32]

A viable civil society as a kind of third force between the state and economy, on the one hand, and the private sphere, on the other, seems to require some effective sense of community and of there actually being a community to which people are committed. That was plainly Gramsci's hope and indeed he thought that it would come about with the establishment of communism. In the long war of position for the challenging class – the working class – it can, in that struggle, forge partial structures of community within civil society, though this will not be achieved without class struggle. But an overarching sense of community is what he thought, with the entrenchment of socialism, the new religion of Marxism would articulate and enhance for us. Remember that this community would be a total integral civilization rooted in a total and integral conception of the world, with a-unitary conception of the common good supported by an integral practical organization of society, yielding when fully developed, a regulated society but a society that is regulated for the common good – a common good that would be so comprehensive that it would articulate justified norms for what Gramsci called a total integral civilization. It is understandable that this, given our past history, would give some people the jitters. For others it will just seem thoroughly unrealistic given the diversity of present day complex societies.

Hitler made the word *'Gemeinschaft'* a dirty word and Stalinist and neo-Stalinist realities in what once were the actually existing socialisms have stamped that feeling in. We have a well-warranted aversion for total ideologies, grand meta-narratives, or comprehensive totalizing theories. Yet what are the goals of our civil society, if indeed there is any consensus about this at all, in the really existing capitalist world? What conception of a truly human community can we plausibly come up with that we could aim to have instantiated and that could gain our reflective allegiance? Such a conception, if we can forge one, must not only be normatively warranted, it must as well be something that is feasible: that there could actually be such institutions, organizations, and practices in our world as distinct from their simply being something of which we dream – create in our philosophers' closets – for an ideal but unachievable world. When we are talking about such an unachievable world, the fact that we do this with elegance, rigor and adroit conceptualization matters very little. We are – if this is how we proceed – just playing little games. (Doing that is an old philosophical pastime.) The norms of a viable civil society must be justified and the conceptualized civil society must really be a civil society that could come to be in our world or at least in a near possible world that could actually come to be our own. But there is the rub, for I do not believe that a humanly viable civil society is on the historical agenda *for* at least the foreseeable future. Our societies are pretty rotten, to put it crudely and bluntly, but I think correctly, and I do not see much prospect for them being changed for the better.[33] I think Michel Foucault and Noam Chomsky, in their different ways, are nearer to the mark about the prospects for a just and humane world order than social democratic communitarians such as Charles Taylor and Michael Walzer or Habermasian neo-Marxists-1 would, of course, very much like to be mistaken and perhaps I am too pessimistic, too derailed by the death of anything like a Marxian Utopian vision for a future society, I will close by giving some reasons for my pessimism while quite sincerely wishing to be shown that things are not as bleak as I am about to portray them.

VI

There are a number of not so pessimistic, roughly social democratic moves that could be made here, including Habermasian ones and Rawlsian ones. I shall not consider the Habermasian and Rawlsian ones here. I shall, rather, consider only one such attempt to defend a conception of civil society for our time and a social democratic political culture: namely, the communitarian attempt. Sometimes, such an orientation, taking as it does some clues from Machiavelli, Montesquieu, and Tocqueville, has been called (more ambiguously I believe) the civic humanist tradition, defending in its contemporary forms republicanism, industrial democracy, and with the latter a kind of democratic socialism.

Such communitarian accounts, and Habermas's as well, seek to reinvigorate the public sphere, to make us conscious again of how 'politicized civil society is, to make it self-consciously and overtly politicized, and to render it a viable mediator between the private sphere and the corporate-bureaucratic state apparatus with its linked capitalist economic order (by now a world order). I choose to examine communitarian defenses of social democracy because they are more directly normative and political than the more procedurally based accounts we have in Habermas and Rawls. But any detailed examination of the rationale for social democracy and the role civil society plays in that would have to include them too. I leave that for another day.

What centrally sets communitarian social democrats apart from social democratic liberals such as Ronald Dworkin and John Rawls is that the latter pair believes that the state should be neutral between different conceptions of the good life espoused by individuals, while the former group believes that a good society, including a genuinely constitutional democracy, needs some commonly recognized, socially sanctioned, conception of the good life.[34] The communitarians believe that without that there will be no viable community, including a political culture. Without such an authoritative conception of the good life there will not be the social cement to make us an *us* (a distinct people) and without such an *us* there will be no viable civil society.

What is needed in a good society (including, of course, a just society), communitarians argue, is an identification with others, in particular others in a determinate society or a cluster of closely related societies. The attachment needs to be to some particular community or cluster of communities (say, for a Dane the Scandinavian communities) and only secondarily, if at all, to some universal moral principle or set of moral principles, e.g., Stoic, Kantian or utilitarian principles. 'Functioning republics are like families,' Taylor remarks, In this crucial respect, that part of what binds people together is their common history.'[35] 'Only when this obtains can there be a viable community, including a viable civil society. To have this is to have a common identification with an historical community founded on certain values.'[36]

In the individualistic tradition – what Taylor misleadingly calls the atomistic tradition – of Hobbes, Locke, and Bentham, common institutional structures are conceived of as collective instruments: as things that have instrumental value only. The only good reason for having them is that we, as collections of individuals thrown together as we are, can attain benefits and avoid distresses that we could not secure or escape individually. 'The action,' as Taylor puts it, 'is collective but the point of it remains individual. The common good is constituted out of individual goods, without remainder.'[37] This is the only kind of common good that such individualists acknowledge or in some instances can even make sense of. Indeed it is the only kind that their methodologies allow them to recognize. Taylor thinks these methodologies are fetters and that they are arbitrary and confused. He also believes, though he thinks the methodological fetters keep many from being self-conscious about this, that in reality (though sometimes unwittingly) people in such societies as ours (as in all societies) do have, at least in practice, a richer conception of the common good than that purely instrumental one, though admittedly some kinds of common good are just instrumental goods. But there are other kinds that are not. This richer conception of the good shows itself in the very way we talk and act and in some quite mundane and unproblematic practices. What should be obvious is obscured from us by the atomistic individualistic theories that are pervasive in our societies; theories that in reality are little better than distorting ideologies.

That we have a conception of the common good that is not just constituted out of our individual goods can be shown in the following way. We need to distinguish between I-identities and we-identities and 'between matters which are for me and for you, on the one hand, and those which are for us, on the other.'[38] Suppose one member of an academic department, namely myself, notes that it is raining and observes as well that a colleague is looking out the window and sees that it is raining. I see him, as he is about to go to the Faculty Club, go to his office and get his umbrella. I then say to him, 'Lousy weather we are having. It's raining again,' and he acknowledges that it is and we go on for a bit about how this year has been very unusual. Prior to that remark, I was attending to the weather and so was he, and I was also aware that he was attending to the weather. It was a matter for him and a matter for me but they were distinct matters. What, as Taylor puts it, 'the conversation opener does is make it now a matter of us: we are now attending to it together'. It is important to see that this attending-together is not reducible to an aggregation of attending separately.'[39] Plainly, it involves something more than each of *us* noting the bad weather alone and just silently noting that the other notes it.

Now consider matters of genuine importance. When I talk about things that matter to me, those to whom I talk are my intimates. But it is important to note that intimacy Is essentially a dialogic phenomena: it is a matter of what we share, of what's for us,'[40] The 'move from the for-me-for-you to the for-us, the move into public space, is one of the important things we bring about in language and any theory of language has to take account of this.'[41]

The same thing holds for goods. Some things, like health, have value to me and to you as well and to everyone individually. We can have health and value it individually but it is not essentially linked to us. But there are some things that essentially have value for us. We cannot have diem individually, Their being for us, and not just *for* you and just for me, enters into and constitutes their value for us. Friendship is a good example, as is intimacy. What 'centrally matters for us is just that there are common actions and meanings.'[42] The good in such contexts is what we share. We cannot have it alone. There is nothing there, as there is for goods like health or pleasure, which we could just have and of which our individual having would, just for us, quite alone as individuals, constitute a good. With friendship and intimacy we have a kind of good that is a common good, that is not just an instrumental good to individual havings. It is something we essentially have to have together if we are going to have it at all.

Taylor transfers this talk of such a common good to what he takes to be a similar political common good. In a good republic, a good polity, its citizens are animated by such a shared common good. Where there is a friendship between Jane and Janet, there is a shared common good. Similarly 'the identification of a citizen with the republic, as a shared common enterprise, is essentially the recognition of a common good.'[43] Compatriots in a functioning republic have a bond of solidarity that 'is based on a sense of shared fate, where the sharing itself is of value.'[44] What the civic humanist tradition or communitarian social democracy seeks is a government and civil society that would instantiate that tradition: that would nurture and sustain or, if necessary, bring into being a political culture where the citizens of that community had that kind of solidarity, and where such common goods were acknowledged and prized. The political culture of such a republic would be one in which there would be a socially sanctioned conception of the common good and, as well, political liberty, namely, its being the case that all citizens will have a say in the decisions made in the political domain and in the sphere of civil society. And, with these democratic collective decisions, things they do as a people, they will shape their lives together. Everyone, where political liberty obtains, would have an equal say in how their common life together is to be ordered. There would, with such political liberty, be a sense that the political institutions and the institutions of civil society were expressions of themselves as citizens, as a people, and there would, as well, be an identification with the political community.[45] In sustaining political liberty, there would have to be a well-functioning public sphere where there would be debate and discussion, where the interchange would not principally, or perhaps even at all, be a matter of bargaining and compromise, but would be a genuine matter of citizens deliberating together, as we might as individuals deliberate with ourselves over what to do or seek or, with the same ends in view, deliberate in the private sphere with people with whom we are intimate. There would crucially in this public sphere be genuine citizen deliberation over the refinement, reconceptualization, the applications and implications of then shared conception of the common good. They would not bargain but instead morally deliberate together about it. There would, linked with that, be a participating in self-government and in such a situation the common actions of a free citizenry would be animated by common identifications.

Every political society, despotic or democratic, requires some sacrifices and restraints and demands some discipline from its citizens. Citizens have to pay taxes serve in the armed forces, do jury duty, pick up after their dogs, and the like. In a despotic society these sacrifices, restraints, and disciplines are obtained by coercion or the threat of coercion. In a free society, where there is citizen dignity, these disciplines are willingly accepted as the doing of one's share in maintaining the commonwealth. It isn't that we like doing them—most of us do not—but that we realize we have a duty to shoulder our fair share of the burdens, where what is to count as a fair share has in turn been subject to democratic discussion and decision in a genuine public sphere. Where, that is, there is dispute about what these sacrifices and restraints should be, and how we should respond to them, this will be deliberated over and decided on by a free citizenry reasoning and deciding together. What is done, what is mandated, is what is freely consented to after free and fair deliberation, approximating, as much as possible, conditions of undistorted discourse and carried out in a public sphere.

Such a democratic regime calls on its members to do things that mere subjects would avoid and, in that way, by requiring service in public life, it is more onerous and demanding than in despotic or managed regimes whose citizens are treated as mere subjects; but, though it is more onerous, citizens in a genuine republic will have control over their own lives, have reasons for being loyal and not merely obedient to the regime and will have reasons, as well, for identifying with their state. In being such (if indeed it could be that) the state would be an ethical state. Hegel's conception is not conceptually incoherent.

This civic humanism is indeed an attractive picture, but it seems to me to be in fact only that. It is as unrealistic and unworldly as the classical normative theories of democracy. Just think how far we are from having anything like this public sphere and of what it would be like to achieve it in mass societies such as our own. The very idea of getting from here to there is staggering. We haven't any good sense of what would be an effective means here. Whether this civic humanism takes the communitarian form described above or a more Habermasian form, it is unrealistic, given contemporary, large-scale, bureaucratically organized and inegalitarian societies – inegalitarian in almost all spheres – but particularly deeply inegalitarian and hurtful about the distribution of power; power being in the hands of a few.[46] But this is the reality of our societies.

Such civic humanism is in a bad sense Utopian, taking us away from the grim realities of political life, realities it is urgent to attend to if-we are ever to have decent societies. What might have worked in a small scale, face-to-face society is utterly unworkable in large-scale societies such as our own. Perhaps it would work in Iceland but never in Germany, the United States, or Canada. It is unworkable not because we are ideologically blinded by ontological theses about atomistic individualism but because of (a) the inescapability of powerful and dominating bureaucracies (both state and capitalist) and (b) the plain and inescapable fact – a feet stressed by John Rawls – of the extensive and entrenched de facto pluralism of our societies.[47] Our societies have a rich variety, and not always a harmonious variety, of people with different ethnic backgrounds, religious identifications, moral outlooks, political orientations, class positions, and the like. There is not much reality to the melting pot or die vertical mosaic metaphors of the United States and Canada respectively. There is no chance at all that in such societies – that is, in our societies – that there will be anything like a consensus about a conception of a common good. One could perhaps, just perhaps, be imposed by a despotic or authoritarian state (though even that is rather doubtful), but one would not be accepted as part of what constitutes the citizens' moral point of view, even by an active citizenry – even if, counterfactually, we could galvanize citizens of such societies into participation, (Gunther Grass was appropriately and effectively ironical about such participation.) Furthermore, when we consider citizens' feelings about their society, what we need to note is that very widely there is no such sense of loyalty, there is no such identification with contemporary governments even in the constitutional democracies there is no such actual public sphere in which to exercise such republican virtues and there is little likelihood that such institutions are coming into being. Philosophers can deliberate about what die common good of their society is or over whether there is such a good or should be. With some groups of philosophers, it just might be possible to secure, after much deliberation, a conception that was recognized for a short period of time by these philosophers to be nearer to the mark than others, but even if, as is very unlikely, there could be a kind of local philosophical consensus here there still would be no chance at all of there being a general consensus across the society of the various people that inhabit those societies. Pluralism, for the foreseeable future, is just an inescapable social fact in societies such as ours. Whether it is or isn't a desirable thing is quite another matter; desirable or undesirable, we will have to live with it.

That, in the United States, some citizens responded with outrage to the Vietnam War, to Watergate, to the Iran-Contra affair, perhaps shows there are some residues among some citizens of a concern about republican virtues, some rather attenuated sense of citizen dignity, of what it is for a country to behave honourably, but the evidence that there is a commitment to anything like civic humanism is rather slim, given the quiescence over the Persian Gulf affair and over the not infrequent American military interventions in the world, over the racism of American society coupled with the indifference to widespread poverty and in other ways extensive inequalities in the society. That the sight of the homeless evokes anger directed at the homeless and not at the society that allows this is symptomatic of the sickness of our societies. There is very little civic humanism in our societies and there is nothing to be patriotic about.

If to such considerations we add facts about voter turnouts and additional facts about the number of corrupt or incompetent politicians that get elected and re-elected, we seem at least to have rather strong disconfirming evidence concerning the existence of anything like the polity that Taylor and other social democratic communitarians regard as existent. The ship of state isn't what the communitarians take it to be. It is a nice ideal but ideals need to be tied to the real world. We need something more than pretty dreams. Moreover, to put the point directly normatively, why should one have any loyalty, patriotic commitment, or identification with such regimes? Obedience can be, and is, achieved out of fear, prudence, a recognition that there are no better alternatives around, and from a bitter recognition that the Marxian Utopian visions of society are just that: at least supposedly unfeasible Utopian visions that show no prospect of being realized or even approximated in a form that would yield human emancipation.[48] But the tradition of civic humanism is every bit: as much an unfeasible Utopian vision. It is a conception of a political culture that could have no instantiation in our complex societies, and it does not bring with it a civil society that is much of a bulwark against the economic order or a state that is anything but the realization of an ethical ideal.

References

1. Portions of this article have previously appeared in print in Arena Journal No. 2 (1993/94), 159–174.
2. In Marx's mature thought the term disappears. It is a moot point how much of the concept remains.
3. Michael Walzer, 'liberalism and the Art of Separation.' *Political Theory* 12, No. 3 (August 1984), 321.
4. Ibid 316.
5. Jean Cohen and Andrew Arato, 'Politics and Reconstruction of the Concepts of Civil Society.' in Axel Honneth, et al., eds.. *Zwischenbetrachtungen: Im Prozess der Aufklarung* Frankfurt am Main: SuhrkampVerlag. 1989).
6. Noberto Bobbio, 'Gramsci and the Conception of Civil Society,' in Chantal Mouffe, cd., Gramsci and Marxist Theory (London; Routledge & Kegan Paul. 1979), 21–47. For a well-reasoned rescuing of Gramsci from the charge of being an historical idealist, see Jacques Texier. 'Gramsci, Theoretician of the Superstructures: On the Concept of Civil Society.' 48–79, in the same volume. For a clear articulation of the difference between historical materialism and historical idealism, see Allen W. Wood. Karl Marx (London: Routledge & Kegan Paul, 1982).
7. Jurgen Habermas, *The Structural Transformation of the Public Sphere: An Inquiry into a Category of Bourgeois Society,* trans.

Thomas Berger (Cambridge. MA: MIT PRESS, 1989) (This book was originally published in German in 1962.); Arato and Cohen, 'Politics and Reconstruction of the Concepts of Civil Society'; Jean Cohen$_t$ *Class and Civil society* (Amherst. MA: The University of Massachusetts Press, 1982); and Claus Offe, *Disorganized Capitalim.* (Cambridge. MA: MIT Press, 1985). I should add that Arato and Cohen do not. 1 think rightly, follow Gramsci in taking the family to be part of the private sphere.

8. Walter Adamson, 'Gramsci and the Politics of Civil Society,' *Praxis International* 7$_t$nos. 3/4 (October 1987 and January 1988). 320. See also his *Hegemony and Revolution: Antonio Gramsci's Political and Cultural Theory.* (Berkeley: University of California Press, 1980).
9. For the distinction between de facto and de jure authority and legitimation see Robert Paul Wolff, 'Violence and the Law.' in Robert Paul Wolff, ed., The Rule of Law (New York: Simon and Schuster, 1971). 54–72, and Kai Nielsen, 'Legitimation in Complex Societies: Some Habermasian Themes.' Annals of Scholarship 7, No. 1 (1990). 51–89.
10. Ronald Dworkin, Taking Rights Seriously (Cambridge, MA: Harvard University Press. 1977). 171–77.
11. Adamson, "Gramsci and the Politics of Civil Society." 321.
12. Ibid.. 322.
13. GA. Cohen: Karl Marx's Theory of History: A Defense (Princeton: Princeton University Press, 1979); History, Labour, and Freedom: Themes from Marx (Oxford: Oxford University Press, 1988). 'Reply to Four critics.' Analyse & Kritik 5 (1983). 195–222. Andrew Levine: Arguing for Socialism: Theoretical Considerations (London: Roudedge & Kegan Paul, 1984); The End of the State (London: Wso. 1987), 'Review of Jon Elster's Making Sense of Marx,' Journal of Philosophy LXXXIIII No. 12 (Dec 1986), 721–25; and 'Review of G.A. Cohen's History, Labaur, Freedom.'1 Journal of Philosophy (1990), 267–75. Joshua Cohen: -Minimalist Historical Materialism' in Rodger Beehler. et al. eds.. On the Track of Reason: Essays in Honor of Kai Nielsen (Boulder:Westview Press. 1992). 155–174.
14. Levine. 'Review of History, Labour and Frtmdom,' 273.
15. Ibid., 277.

16. Adamson, 'Gramsci and the Politics of Civil Society.' 325.
17. This is done very well by Jacques Texier. 'Gramsci, Theoretician of Superstructures: On the Concept of Civil Society;' in Chantal Mouffe. Ed., Gramsci and Marxist Theory (London: Routledge 8c Kegan Paul, 1979). 48–74. See also Anne Sasson. "Civil Society." In Tom Bottomore, ed., A Dictionary of Marxist Thought (Cambridge. MA: Harvard University Press. 1983). 72–74.
18. Benedetto Grace's views, taken up by Gramsci, were most succinctly stated in his 'Religione e serenita,' *La Citicas* 23(March 20,1915),153–55. Gramsci republished in his own journal, La Citta Futura (Feb.11,1917).Croce's article is available in English translation in Croce's Ethics and Politics. See Adamson, 'Gramsci and the Politics of Civil Society', 326.
19. Antonio Gramsci. Quaderni del Carcere, 4 Volumes, V. Gerrantana, ed. (Turin: Einaudi. 1975). 2185–86. See Adamson, Gramsci and the Politics of Civil Society.' 327.
20. Gramsci, Quaderni del Carcere, 311, Sec Adamson* 'Gramsci and the Politics of Civil Society,' 327.
21. Emile Durkheim, Elementary Forms of the Religious Life, trans, J.W. Swain (New York: Free Press, 1965). 475–76.
22. Gramsci, Quaderni del Carcere , 1854–64. See Adamson, 'Gramsci and the Politics of Civil Society.' 328.
23. Gramsci, Quaderni del Carcere 1295. 1319–20, and 1380–81, Adamson. 'Gramsci and the Politics of Civil Society, 328.
24. Ibid 328–29.
25. Gramsci. Quaderni del Carcere 1505. 1682–83 and 1860. Adamson, 'Gramsci and the Politics of Civil Society,' 329.
26. Gramsci, Quanderni del Carcere, 1434–35 and Adamson. 'Gramsci and the Politics of Civil Society', 329.
27. Gramsci, Quaderni del Carcere, 1434 and Adamson, 'Gramsci and the Politics of Civil Society,' 329.
28. Adamson. 'Gramsci and the Politics of Civil Society,' 331.
29. About communism as a viable intellectual conception what needs to be said is much more complex. See Andrew Levine, 'Communism after Communism' (unpublished manuscript). The conception of communism in Marx. Luxemburg, and even Lenin may very well

have been more confirmed than refuted by recent events. Russian and similar communisms are so different from the communism envisioned by Marx that the collapse of the terrible authoritarian statism of Russian communism may have, theoretically speaking, made no difference at all to Marx's communism, to genuine communism. Russian communism, to say nothing of what went on in Romania, was at best a grotesque caricature of communism. But as Levine well realizes, things are not that simple. As a political-cultural phenomena, these regimes represented themselves, and were in some sense accepted as, the embodiment of Marxism. But it is these 'embodiments' that have been so thoroughly rejected by their own populations, including their own working class. Given such considerations, where will the political clout come from to move societies along to a genuine socialism? What, practically speaking, will take the place of a class-conscious proletariat? What will fuel the drive for proletarian emancipation through revolution? Given that there is a proletariat (even though it does not see itself as such) how is that proletariat given the turning of the 'world, going to come to see itself as a proletariat and take matters into its own hands and thereby emancipate itself, or more accurately begin the process of emancipation? Have we the slightest reason to think that anything like that will happen in the foreseeable future? Things look very bleak, but there are some hopeful signs as well. Things are working badly in capitalist societies and alienation is extensive. And so far at least, the turn to capitalism in the formerly state socialist societies has in most respects made matters even worse in those societies. Circumstances could arise in which that alienation would be transformed into opposition to the capitalist order. See here Russell Hardin. 'Efficiency vs Equality and the Demise of Socialism,' *Canadian Journal of Philosophy*, Vol. 22, No. 2 (June 1992), 149–161. See also the reference in footnotes 30 and 48.

30. See references in note 12 and Erik Olin Wright. 'What is Analytical Marxism?' Socialist Review 19. No. 4 (Oct-Dec. 1989); Erik Olin Wright, Class (London: New Left Books, 1985); and John Roemer, *Free to Lose* (Cambridge, MA: Harvard University Press. 1988), and Kai Nielsen. 'Analytical Marxism; A Form of Critical Theory.' *Erkennis.* Vol. 39 (1993), 1.21.

31. It should be added that Marx was not such a Marxist., See Cohcn. *Karl Marx's Theory of History: A Defense.*
32. Adamson. 'Gramsci and the Politics of Civil Society,' 335–36.
33. Indeed in many respects things seem to be getting worse. In the United States between 1977 and 1987 the real income of the poorest 20 percent of the population fell by 9 percent, while for the richest 5 percent the real income went up nearly 53 percent. Homelessness and child poverty increased. Among homeless children, once declining diseases like whooping cough and tuberculosis are becoming common again. The United States is strikingly bad in these respects but similar phenomena occur in the other rich capitalist countries. When we turn to the Third World, things get dramatically worse. Given *the* productive wealth of the world, these things are not necessary, but these things go right along without much in the way of an outcry. People seem, for the most part, to accept them like they accept the onset of winter. William Plowden, 'Welfare in America,' London Review of Books 13. No.13 (July 11.1991). 8. See Howard Karger and David Stoesz, *American Social Welfare Policy: A Structural Approach* (London: Longman, 1990) and Theodore Marmor, et al., *America's Misunderstood Welfare State* (New York: Basic Books, 1990), The best that we can hope for, is that because things are so rotten, so irrationally structured, that the capitalist societies will begin, with their citizens becoming increasingly disenchanted and disgusted, to collapse from within.
34. Ronald Dworkin: *A Matter of Principle* (Cambridge. MA: Harvard University Press. 1985), 181–233. and 'Liberal Community,' *California Law Review 77,* No. 3 (1989). 479–507. John Rawls: 'Justice as Fairness: Political not Metaphysical,' *Philosophy and Public Affairs* 14, No. 3 (1983), 223–51: 'The Idea of an Overlapping Consensus,' *Oxford Journal of Legal Studies* 7. No. 1 (1987), 1–25; and The Domain of the Political and Overlapping Consensus,' New York *University Law Review 64* . No. 2 (1989), 233–55, For communitarians sec Charles Taylor, 'Cross-Purposes: The Liberal-Communitarian Debate.' in N. Rosenblum, ed. *Liberalism and the Moral Life* (Cambridge, MA: Harvard University Press, 1989), 159–82; Charles Taylor, The Nature and Scope of

Distributive Justice,' in Frank Lucash, *cd.. Justice and Equality Here and Now* (Ithaca; Cornell University Press. 1986), 34–67; Michael Walzer, The Communitarian Critique of Liberalism,' *Political Theory* 18, No. 1 (1990), 6–23; Michael Walter, 'Justice Here and Now/ in Frank Lucash, ed.,/*Justice and Equality Here and Now* (Ithaca: Cornell University Press, 1986), 135–50; and Michael Walzcr, *Spheres of Justice* (Oxford: Basil Blackwell. 1983).

35. Taylor, 'Cross-Purpose: The Liberal Communttarian Debate,' 166, Taylor has a very naive and unrealistic picture of families as havens of trust and love.
36. Ibid., 178.
37. Ibid., 166.
38. Ibid., 167.
39. Ibid.
40. Ibid., 168.
41. Ibid.
42. Ibid.
43. Ibid., 170.
44. Ibid.
45. Ibid., 165, 170.
46. See Kai Nielsen, *Equality and liberty: A Defense of Radical Egaltarianism* (Totowa, NJ: Rowman and Allanheld, 1985). and Richard Norman. Free and Equal, (Oxford: Oxford University Press. 1986). Michael Walzer perhaps does not stress this as much as he might. Commonly liberals ignore it or downplay it. However, Walzer does rightly remark:.... it is a false view of civil society, a bad sociology, to claim that all that goes on in the marketplace is free exchange and that coercion is never an issue here. Market success overrides the limits of the (free) market in three closely related ways. First of all, radical inequalities of Wealth generate their own coerciveness, so that many exchanges are only formally free. Second, certain sorts of market power, organized, say, in corporate structures, generate patterns of command and obedience in which the formalities of exchange give way to something that looks very much like government. And third, vast wealth and ownership or

control of productive forces convert readily into government in the strict sense: capital regularly and successfully calls upon the coercive power of the state. Walzer. 'Liberalism and the Art of Separation.' 321–22. But Milton Friedman's dreams to the contrary notwithstanding, this is the name of the game *for* really existing capitalisms, even capitalisms with a human face such as Sweden's. What the liberal needs *to* tell us is how capitalist societies of any complexity can be reformed so that that will no longer be the case. It seems to me that a necessary condition for that ceasing to be the case is the public ownership and control of the means of production. But that is socialism. It baffles me why committed socialists such as Jurgen Habermas no longer see things in these terms.

47. John Rawls. 'Justice as Fairness; Political not Metaphysical.' 223–52. See also Kai Nielsen – Rawls and the Socratic Ideal.' *Analyse & Krittk* (Fall 1991) and Kai Nielsen, 'Philosophy within the Limits of Wide Reflective Equilibrium Alone,' *lyyun. The Jerusalem Philosophical Quarterly.* Vol. 43 (Juli/Vol. 13, 67–93, 1994) 3–41. For some cautionary notes, not as distant from Rawls as he seems to believe about the power of philosophy, see Michael Walzer. 'Flight from Philosophy,' *The New York Review of Books* (Feb 2. 1989), 42–43.

48. I do not mean to give to understand that I think there is anything drastically wrong or in a bad sense Utopian about sophisticated forms of Marxian theory either in their weak historical materialism, class analysis, more generally in their political sociology, or (in some cases) in their understanding of the role of moral notions in social life. On the contrary, these accounts seem to me realistic and reasonable. Indeed, seeing Marxian theory, principally through the work of analytical Marxians, as a developing theory being repeatedly refined, it seems to me that that account, though of course flawed (what account isn't?), is the best account we have to date of large-scale social phenomena.

49. For the case for socialism, no matter how well it is articulated and defended – That is unfortunate, but that is the way it is. The world has turned, but it can turn again in ways that are not so uncongenial to the possibility of worker self-emancipation. Tough-minded

idealists can hardly fail to be pessimistic, the way things stand. But that need not be crippling either for thought or struggle. See here GA. Cohen, 'The Future of a Disillusion', in Jim Hopkins and Anthony Savile: Psychoanalysis, Mind and Art: Perspectives on Richard Wallham (Oxford: Blackwell's, 1992) .147–160.

10

Civil Society: Theory and Practice

Michael Edwards

Civil society is much talked about, but rarely understood. Michael Edwards explores the practical and theoretical significance of civil society – and suggests some ways through the issues surrounding its use.

It is impossible to have a conversation about politics or public policy these days without someone mentioning the magic words 'civil society', so one might think that people are clear what they mean when they use this term and why it is so important. Unfortunately, clarity and rigour are conspicuous by their absence in the civil society debate, a lack of precision that threatens to submerge this concept completely under a rising tide of criticism and confusion.

THE CIVIL SOCIETY PUZZLE

According to whose version one prefers, 'civil society' means 'fundamentally reducing the role of politics in society by expanding free markets and individual liberty' (Cato), or it means the opposite – 'the single most viable alternative to the authoritarian state and the tyrannical market' (WSF), or for those more comfortable in the middle ground of politics, it constitutes the missing link in the success of social democracy (central to Third Way thinking and supposedly-compassionate conservatism), the 'chicken soup of the social sciences' – you know those books that provide much-needed comfort without that much substance, so if you can't explain something, put it down to civil society! Adam Seligman, tongue firmly in cheek, calls civil society the 'new analytic key that will unlock the mysteries of the social order', Jeremy Rifkin calls it 'our last, best hope', the UN and the World Bank see it as the key to 'good governance' and poverty-reducing growth, and even the real reason for war against Iraq – to kick-start civil society in the Middle East, according to Administration officials in Washington DC. As a new report from the Washington-based Institute for Foreign Policy Analysis puts it, 'the US should emphasize civil society development in order to ensure regional stability in central Asia' – forgetting, of course, that citizens groups have been a prime cause of destabilization in every society since the Pharaohs.

Some claim that civil society is a specific product of the nation state and capitalism; others see it as a universal expression of the collective life of individuals, at work in all countries and stages of development but expressed in different ways according to history and context. Some see it as one of three separate sectors, others as intimately interconnected or even inter-penetrated by states and markets. Is civil society the preserve of groups predefined as democratic, modern, and 'civil', or is it home to all sorts of associations, including 'uncivil' society – like militant Islam and American militias – and traditional associations based on inherited characteristics like religion and ethnicity that are so common in Africa and Asia?

Are families in or out, and what about the business sector? Is civil society a bulwark against the state, an indispensable support, or dependent on government intervention for its very existence? Is it the key to individual freedom through the guaranteed experience of pluralism or a threat to democracy through special interest politics? Is it a noun – a part of society, an adjective – a kind of society, an arena for societal deliberation, or a mixture of all three? Can you build a civil society through foreign aid and intervention, or is this just another imperial fantasy? What is to be done with a concept that seems so unsure of itself that definitions are akin to nailing jelly to the wall? And in any case, do these questions really matter, except to a small band of academics who study this stuff for a living?

CIVIL SOCIETY – GAINING SOME CLARITY

When an idea can mean so many things it probably means nothing, so I think the time has come to be rid of the term completely or, now that it has acquired a life of its own, to at least be clearer with each other about the different interpretations in play. Consensus is impossible given the range of views on offer, but clarity is not, and greater clarity can be the springboard for a better conversation about the promise and potential of civil society as a basis of hope and action for the future, *and* about the pitfalls of using this term as a political slogan or a shelter for dogma and ideology. Recognizing that civil society does indeed mean different things to different people is one of the keys to moving forward, because it moves us beyond false universals and entrenched thinking. And for those who want to discard the term completely my plea would be, not yet – 'don't throw the baby out with the bathwater.' As I show in *Civil Society* (Edwards 2004), ideas about civil society can survive and prosper in a rigorous critique.

In part, the fog that has enveloped this term is the result of an obsession with one particular interpretation of civil society as a *part* of society – the world of voluntary associations – forgetting that there are earlier and later traditions that have just as much to offer. It was Alexis de Tocqueville [the man you probably all remember from your schooldays] that started this craze on his visits across the Atlantic in the 1830s, who saw America's rich tapestry of associational life as the key to its emerging democracy. 'Americans of all dispositions have an incurable tendency to form voluntary associations.' Originally however, civil society, from Aristotle to Thomas Hobbes, represented a *kind* of society that was identified with certain ideals. And in modern societies, realizing these ideals – like political equality or peaceful coexistence – requires action across many different institutions, not just voluntary associations. Most recently, philosophers have developed a new set of theories about civil society as the *'public sphere'* – the places where citizens argue with one-another about the great questions of the day and negotiate a constantly-evolving sense of the 'common' or 'public' interest.

Civil Society as Associational Life

My starting point in *Civil Society* (Edwards 2004) is to deconstruct the existing, confused conversation about civil society and then reconstruct the relationships between these different schools of thought in a new, and I hope more convincing synthesis. The first school believes that voluntary associations act as gene carriers of the good society

– microclimates, if you will, for developing values like tolerance and cooperation, and the skills required for living a democratic life. The trouble is that real associational life is home to all sorts of different and competing values and beliefs (think pro and anti-choice groups, for example, or peaceniks and the NRA). There's another problem with this thesis too, because the values and beliefs we want to see developed are fostered in all the places where we learn and grow, and where dispositions are shaped, which means families, schools, workplaces, colleges and universities, and political institutions large and small. We actually spend a lot more time in these places than we do in voluntary associations, so these experiences are especially important. For the same reason, by themselves, NGOs and other voluntary associations can rarely secure the level of political consensus that is required to secure and enforce broad-based social reforms – there's too much difference and diversity of opinion. That's why civil society, to quote the British writer John Keane 'is riddled with danger, since it gives freedom to despots and democrats alike.'

Civil Society as the Good Society

So my second school of thought – civil society as the good society – is very important, because it sets the contributions of voluntary associations in the proper context and guards against the tendency to privilege one part of society over the others on ideological grounds – voluntary associations over states for example, or business over both. Good neighbours can't replace good government, and nonprofits shouldn't be asked to substitute for well-functioning markets. Historically (think of the US in the twentieth century and East Asia after World War II), success in achieving good society goals has always been based on social contracts negotiated between government, business and citizens.

However, if the good society requires coordinated action between different institutions all pulling in the same direction, how do societies decide which direction in which to go, and whether it is the right one as conditions and circumstances continue to change over time? How are collective choices made, tradeoffs negotiated, and ends reconciled with means in ways that are just and effective? For answers to these questions, we have to turn to my third school of thought and consider civil society in its role as the public sphere.

Civil Society as the Public Sphere

The concept of a 'public' – a whole polity that cares about the common good and has the capacity to deliberate about it democratically – is central to civil society thinking. The development of shared interests, a willingness to cede some territory to others, the ability to see something of oneself in those who are different and work together more effectively as a result – all these are crucial attributes for effective governance, practical problem-solving, and the peaceful resolution of our differences. In its role as the 'public sphere', civil society becomes the arena for argument and deliberation as well as for association and institutional collaboration, and the extent to which such spaces thrive is crucial to democracy, since if only certain truths are represented, if alternative viewpoints are silenced by exclusion or suppression, or if one set of voices are heard more loudly than those of others, the 'public' interest inevitably suffers. When all politics are polarized, public policy problems become embedded, even frozen, in polities that cannot solve them – think health care and welfare reform in the US, for example. Breaking the resulting gridlock requires the creation of new publics in support of broad-based reform – exactly what is missing in the US right now.

FINDING A WAY THROUGH THE 'CIVIL SOCIETY PUZZLE'

All three of these schools of thought have something to offer, but by themselves are incomplete and unconvincing. So the logical thing to do is to connect them so that the weaknesses of one set of theories are balanced by the strengths and contributions of the others. What does that mean in practice?

Civil society as the good society keeps our 'eyes on the prize' – the prize being the goals of poverty-reduction and deep democracy that require coordinated action across different sets of institutions. However, the vision of the good society says little about how such goals are going to be achieved, and associational life does seem to be an important – if incomplete – explanatory factor in most contemporary settings. Structural definitions of civil society – the first approach I described – are useful in emphasizing the gaps and weaknesses of associational life that need to be fixed if they are to be effective vehicles for change. However, the differences and particularities of associational life generate competing views about the ends and means of the good society, anchored in religion, politics, ideology, race, gender and culture. Without our third set of theories – civil society as the public sphere – there would be no just and democratic way to reconcile these views and secure a political consensus about the best way forward. In turn, a healthy associational ecosystem is vital to the public sphere, since it is usually through voluntary organizations and the media that citizens carry on their conversations. Finally, the achievements of the good society are what make possible the independence and level playing field that underpin a democratic associational life – by reducing inequality, for example, and guaranteeing freedom of association, anchored in the law.

So it's not difficult to see how each approach builds on the others in order to offer a more compelling explanation of civil society's significance. One can construct a similar tripartite relationship at the global level too – 'global civil society' as an additional layer of transnational associational activity, a new kind of global society or form of International Relations marked out respect for human rights and the peaceful resolution of differences, and as an emerging global public sphere exemplified by events like the World Social Forum, Internet sites like open Democracy and open source technology.

CIVIL SOCIETY – THE WAY FORWARD

Thinking about the issues in this way helps us to pose an actionable set of questions instead of arguing in the abstract over which theory is correct. Most importantly, how do shifting patterns of associational life help or hinder the realization of good society goals, and what can we do to revive the public sphere if we believe it is an important transmission mechanism between the two?

This question generates a rich agenda for public policy discussions, though a complicated one since there is no obvious consensus on the answers and the evidence is very muddy – three schools of thought. The social capital school – like Robert Putnam [whose work I'm sure you all know well] – sees associational life in general as the driving force behind the positive social norms on which the good society is founded – things like cooperation, trust and reciprocity. So the logical policy is to encourage as much volunteering and voluntary action as possible even if some of it is used for nefarious purposes. Somewhat magically in my view, these differences will, Putnam argues, work themselves out in the general scheme of things.

The comparative associational school – like Theda Skocpol – see particular configurations of associational life as the key to securing the public policy reforms the good society requires - the nationally-federated mass-membership, cross-class groups like PTAs, labour unions, elks and other forest creatures, that have declined so much over the last 50 years and which used to provide strong bridges between citizens and government that led to reforms like the GI Bill of 1944; and the school of skeptics – like Nancy Rosenblum – don't see any reliable link between the structure of civil society and its achievements. All these positions are analyzed in my book, but none is completely convincing, especially in contexts other than the US. And obviously the appropriate policy depends on which position one subscribes to.

There are some interventions, though, that would be useful across the board. The first thing we need to do is to strengthen the pre-conditions for a healthy civil society in all three senses by attacking all forms of inequality and discrimination, giving people the means to be active citizens, reforming politics to encourage more participation, guaranteeing the independence of associations and the structures of public communication, and building a strong foundation for institutional partnerships, alliances and coalitions. Inequality is the poison of civil society because it endows citizens with different levels of resources and opportunities to participate, so things like support for childcare and a living wage – which are not usually seen as civil-society building interventions, may be the most important areas of all.

Second, we need to support innovations in associational life that encourage citizen action to operate in service to the good society, rather than as a substitute for politics, market reform and the demands of democratic state building. That doesn't mean turning the clock back to the 1950s and forcing teenagers to join the Moose or the Elks (the Norman Rockwell school of civil society thinking), but reinventing associational life to suit the realities of a very different era in which time and energy are more limited, worn down by the demands of work and unsupported family obligations.

For example, we need to build stronger links between policy groups, organizing groups, service deliverers and the media; we need to link associations across different interests and agendas and get progressive organizing out of its silos (issues and identities); we need to encourage a more democratic relationship between grassroots constituencies and those in the non-profit sector who claim to speak on their behalf. We need to reduce the costs and risks of citizen participation(for example, making it easier to organize at the workplace), and we need to honour and connect different forms of participation so that service doesn't become a substitute for political engagement, as is happening among many younger people in America today.

It's also important to make room for surprises – like the potential political effects of self help groups like Alcoholics Anonymous and Weightwatchers (the largest category of voluntary associations in America with over 25 million members), or the boy scouts and mosque associations in Lebanon (which turn out to be among the most progressive), or burial societies in South Africa (which played a major role in the fight against apartheid), or labour unions in France and Brazil which have given an important stimulus to new and less hierarchical forms of transnational organizing.

TO CONCLUDE

To conclude, civil society is simultaneously a goal to aim for, a means to achieve it, and a framework for engaging with each-other about ends and means. When these three 'faces' turn towards each-other and integrate their different perspectives into a mutually-supportive framework, the idea of civil society can explain a great deal about the course of politics and social change, and serve as a practical framework for organizing both resistance and alternative solutions to social, economic and political problems. Many of the difficulties of the civil society debate disappear when we lower our expectations of what each school of thought has to offer in isolation from the others, and abandon all attempts to enforce a single model, consensus or explanation. This may not deter the ideologues from using civil society as a cover for their own agendas, but it should make it easier to expose their claims and challenge the assumptions they often make.

This is one reason why, to answer the question I raised at the outset, getting clearer about civil society *does* matter in more than the academic sense. When, as recently reported in the press for example, the

National Endowment for Democracy claims to be building civil society in Venezuela but is only supporting groups mobilized against President Hugo Chavez, or politicians on both sides of the Atlantic continue to be engaged in a forced march to civil society in the Middle East, it is clear that the ways in which these ideas are interpreted *does* have a real impact on the lives of real people in the here and the now. As Keynes's famous dictum reminds us, 'practical men in authority who think themselves immune from theoretical influences are usually the slaves of some defunct economist', just as present-day civil society builders are motivated by ideas deeply rooted in different schools of thought, but often unacknowledged, untested and insufficiently interrogated.

The second reason why this debate matters is that lasting solutions to problems of poverty, discrimination and exclusion are impossible to conceive of, at least for me, without a full appreciation of the roles of civil society in this new, threefold sense, especially when we compare these ideas to the failings of their competitors such as neo-liberalism, nationalism resurgent, legalism, centralized planning or continued authoritarian rule.

In all three schools of thought, civil society is essentially *collective* action – in associations, across society and through the public sphere – and as such it provides an essential counterweight to individualism; as *creative* action, civil society provides a much-needed antidote to the cynicism that infects so much of contemporary politics; and as *values-based action*, civil society provides a balance to the otherwise-overbearing influence of state authority and the temptations and incentives of the market, even if those values are contested, as they often are. Warts and all, the idea of civil society remains compelling, I think, but not because it provides the tidiest of explanations or the most coherent of political theories – it doesn't and probably never will. It remains compelling because it speaks to the best in us – the collective, creative and values-driven core of the active citizen – calling on the best in us to respond in kind to create societies that are just, true and free.

REFERENCES

This discussion and argument around civil society is developed in: Edwards, Michael (2004) *Civil Society*, Cambridge: Polity. (Go to Polity for a full description of the book).

See also: Putnam, Robert D. (2000) Bowling Alone. *The collapse and revival of American community*, New York: Simon and Schuster.

Skocpol, Theda. (2003), *Diminished Democracy. From membership to management in American civic life*, Norman, Oklahoma: University of Oklahoma Press.

11

Civil Society Debates in India

Civil Society Against Political Society?

Bruno Jobert

Civil society has been a key issue in Indian public debate ever since the state of emergency period in the 1970s. The state of emergency was declared by Indira Gandhi in June 1975 in order to cope with internal disturbances, and it ended in March 1977 with the election victory of the opposition. During that 19 month authoritarian interlude, when Prime Minister Indira Gandhi ruled by decree and civil liberties were suspended, civil society provided a symbolic framework of opposition to the authoritarian practices of the government. In order to fully understand the significance of this upsurge of a civil discourse, we need to go back further in history, however, to the phase of tutelary modernization and even to the struggle for independence.

We share the hypothesis exposed in the writings of Partha Chatterjee (2001) that the Indian case can only be understood by making a distinction between civil society and political society and by analysing its inter-relationship. The civil society appeared in the small circle of the elite leading the national struggle: 'these elites were thoroughly wedded to the normative principles of modern associational public life and criticized the colonial state precisely for not living up to the standards of a liberal constitutional state' (Chatterjee 2001: 175). The political society corresponded to a mode of political mediation that had first developed in the anti-colonial struggle and then in Indian democracy when mobilization spread to broader circles of the population, well beyond the elite. The modes of action in political society were profoundly different from those of associational life. Demands stemmed not from citizens but from a population struggling to 'survive by side stepping the law' (Chatterjee 2001: 177). These demands were expressed in terms of collective rights attached to a 'community'. As Chatterjee puts it, state agents dealt with these people 'not as bodies of citizens belonging to a lawfully constituted civil society but as a population deserving welfare' (Chatterjee 2001: 177). We would add here the following nuance to Chatterjee's analysis: all the examples he gives refer to clear violations of the law by those in need – squatters, encroachers of public properties, unauthorized users of public utilities. But we should be more precise in that the most important source of uncertainty toward the law lies in the elites' frequently used strategy of denial of citizens' rights to subaltern groups.

'Subaltern Studies' (Guha 1983), the well-known school of historiography from below, have shown that these competing modes of political mediation were present within the Congress Party from the time of the anti-colonial struggle onwards. This chapter will analyse this uncomfortable coexistence which persisted through the various stages of India's political evolution, although the configurations varied. We will start with the emergence of a tutelary model after independence, when civil society organizations were clearly subordinated to the political institutions. The following sections will delineate the various answers given to the ongoing expansion of political participation and their impact on civil-society frames. The political consecration of civil society after emergency was followed by alternative patterns of political mediation, when Hindu nationalism and the castes appeared on the political scene. Finally, the economic reforms of the 1990s modified the stakes and fields of action for the civil society organizations, bringing the question of the civilization of the state to the fore.

THE TUTELARY MODEL

Under the impetus of Mohandas K. Gandhi, the national movement set out to link the struggle against colonial domination to a social reform of Indian society. At the time of independence, this combination of political action and social work was the main subject of a debate between Gandhi and the party leaders J. Nehru and V. Patel on the future of the Congress Party. Gandhi wanted the Congress to devote itself to social work and to decentralize its efforts to bring about social reform. He envisaged the building of institutions bottom-up from the village level to the national level. The independence leaders, on the other hand, preferred a top-down approach driven and directed by the state. Contrary to many other cases, the groups spawned by the colonial state - in particular Indian civil service senior officials – did not play a significant part in the struggle for emancipation. Nevertheless, they were instrumental in the process of nation-building after independence.

This change of attitude toward the state bureaucracy can be partly explained by the challenges the Congress leaders were confronted with in the wake of independence: the crisis of the partition of the country, communist insurrection, the partitioning of federated states, and so on. The emerging state-centrism was not just a response to political events, however, but was firmly rooted in the conceptions of the founding fathers of the nation. For instance, the constitution adopted in 1950 put great emphasis on fundamental rights and on guarantees by the judiciary for upholding them, and it also assigned the state to play a key part in social reform. Besides the fundamental rights that were guaranteed by law, the constitution cited a long list of 'directive principles of state policy' asserting the economic and social rights of the citizens. Job reservation for 'scheduled castes and tribes' in public educational institutions and in the civil service was enshrined in it and it instituted the protection of minority rights. By combining universalism with the granting of collective rights connected to ascriptive identities, the constitution outlined the rifts and contradictions inherent in Indian politics.

The weak role conceded to the institutions of India's decentralized democracy was reflected in a top-down modernization project, it was not until the 1990s and 2000s that decentralization was significantly boosted. Until then, the reign of the district magistrate, inherited from the colonial period, was not only extended but even affirmed in a model of planned development that was based on the existing administrative apparatus. The Nehruvian model of development was devised at central-government level by an elite administrative body, i.e. the Planning Commission chaired by the prime minister, and its implementation in the states was carried out via the regular channels.

The tutelary nature of this development model was further accentuated by the modernization ideology that it conveyed. In an early book, Rajni Khotari (1970: 133, 134) defined the community development programme, which was launched in 1952, in the following terms:

> this combination of simple administrative expansion and verbal rhetoric, exhibiting high-minded conviction at the top, unrelated to the realities on the scene, was the biggest weakness of the community development movement. The rhetoric itself was ambivalent. It spoke of the innate capacities of the rural masses but decried their apathy; it wanted the people to come forward but also believed that only government action could produce results.

Throughout this period, most of the associational movements remained under party leadership. The neo-Gandhian social institutions received support from the Congress Party, while the Hinduists relied on Rashtriya Swayamsevak Sangh (RSS) volunteers (Weiner 1962: 65). Trade unions were divided along party lines and civil society was under state control and supervision, restricted by the particularisms and cronyism of political society. The significance of universal suffrage was limited by 'vote banks', i.e. the clientelistic control of a certain section of the electorate. In practice, the execution of the state's modernization programme was largely influenced by the negotiations that eventually took place between the political factions dominating the states and districts, and the administration that was supposed to implement it.

The authoritarian populist period of the first Indira Gandhi government (1966–1977) restricted the space open to civil society even more. Indira Gandhi owed her victory over the Congress barons to a campaign designed to capture the masses' votes by bypassing existing networks of factionalism, in the name of the war against poverty. But the policies adopted retained the top-down modernization model. Authoritarian family-planning and urban renovation policies increased the population's mistrust of state agents. In a context of economic crisis, social movements consequently started to challenge the legitimacy of a state known to be corrupt.

THE RETURN OF CIVIL SOCIETY?

Against a background of unrest over prices and speculation, the neo-Gandhian leader J.P. Narayan became the head of a movement advocating 'total revolution'. He wanted to apply the lessons learned from the two-fold failure of the state-centred development model and of the Gandhian movements through which Vinobha Bhave, another major Gandhian leader, had tried to achieve social reform by appealing to the dominant classes' sense of morality. The aim here was to bring about radical change through the people's own mobilization and to limit the discretionary power of the state and its representatives. The demands of Narayan's movement in Bihar and Gujarat were oriented towards the dissolution of the state assembly. Narayan:

> believed democracy was in danger. He felt that the weakening of democracy had reached a point where the mechanism of self-correction had completely broken down. It was necessary to develop Jan Shakti, people power. The right to recall the elected representative was demanded, repressive measures to curb the agitations were opposed. And the right to speak, assemble and hold demonstration was asserted.
>
> (Ghanshyam Shah 2002: 349)

Threatened by these movements and by a court ruling that challenged her election as a Member of Parliament, Indira Gandhi proclaimed the state of emergency, which suspended the freedoms guaranteed by the constitution. The state of emergency period (1975 to 1977) played a fundamental role in the return of a civil-society discourse within the Indian political scene. The state could no longer be presented as the guarantor of civil rights; instead, it was perceived as a threat to be countered by collective action. Human-rights movements grew rapidly during that period, especially the People's Union for Civil Liberties (PUCL) and later the Peoples' Union for Democratic Rights (PUDR). However, civil society did not find a suitable mediator on the political scene.

The political opposition united in the Janata Party won the 1977 elections. However, the government soon disappointed those who had hoped to see the beginning of a new political era with civil society playing a leading role. Participatory policies were boosted, nevertheless. The new discourse on these policies was grounded on the assumption that the success of redistributive policies was contingent on a collective organization of users: 'Critical for the success of all redistributive law, policies and programmes is that the poor be organized and made conscious of the benefits intended to them' (GOI 1978: 15). Planners, therefore, conceived of placing the implementation of all programmes under the surveillance of beneficiary organizations, including the sensitive area of land reform. This strategy is founded on Indian socialist traditions, but was also influenced by critical international currents, such as Paolo Freire's consciousness raising for instance.

The forms of participation that were effectively implemented under the Janata (the People's Party) government were far removed from this perspective of radical transformation. Projects for collective organization of the poor were opposed by conservative currents within the ruling party itself. Only those participatory devices endured that were no threat to the powers-that-be (Jobert 1984, 1985). They were, nevertheless, the first in a long series of programmes to promote participation in public policy-making. We will see below how these programmes used Non-Governmental Organizations (NGOs) in a far more systematic way, in order to try to counterbalance the pressures of influential citizens and bureaucrats.

On the political scene, the civil liberties and popular organization rhetoric barely concealed the cracks in a governing coalition bound together by little more than their opposition to Indira Gandhi.

> The Congress-I abuse of power under the emergency regime gave the Janata government a historic opportunity to 'restore democracy' and non-partisanship in the use of public authority and resources. It restored the first, but its standards with respect to the second were hard to distinguish from those of the Congress-I.
>
> (Rudolph and Hoeber Rudolph 1987: 160)

Although it had been brought to power by rejecting the abuses suffered under the state of emergency, the Janata government, nevertheless, failed to alter the rules of the political game marked by particularisms and factionalism. Hindu militants did not want to be hampered by the civil-rights movements that they had supported as long as they were in the opposition. They tried to obtain the self-dissolution of the PUCL and were unable to accept the criticisms of the state governments that they controlled. They also refused to sever the umbilical cord binding their party, the Jan Sang, ,to their volunteer movement, the RSS. The divisions between other components of the Janata – senior Congress members, peasant leaders and socialists – ended up tarnishing the image of a completely fractioned party, thus allowing for Indira Gandhi's return to power in 1980 under the minimalist slogan 'government that works'.

Hence, the crisis triggered by the erosion of the tutelary model did not lead to the institutionalization of an alternative model for civil-society involvement. However, it initiated a new period in which different civil frames confronted each other in the political arena. From then on, the question of the social underpinnings of democracy was at the centre of controversies and revealed new rifts.

The Hindu nationalists called for a reconstruction of the Indian nation around its cultural majority. By contrast, the subordinate castes exerted strong pressure towards a stricter application and extension of the positive discrimination model established for the untouchables and tribes. The new social movements mobilized the victims and outcasts of the market-oriented development model of the mid-1980s. Thus, the difficulties and shortcomings of the administration opened a vast field in which protest movements rubbed shoulders with voluntary associations around a common reference framework: the civilization of the state.

CIVIL SOCIETY AND DICTATORSHIP OF THE MAJORITY

The crisis of the tutelary state had favoured the upsurge of Hindu nationalism. This ideology was embodied in organizations inspired by a particular version of democracy and civil society, based on the cultural majority's demand for hegemony. Arun Shourie, one of the thinkers of Hindu nationalism, synthesized the theses of this current in a widely-read book (Shourie 1997). He contended that the state's action had been perverted by 'minoritism', i.e. the granting of exorbitant advantages and exemptions to minorities, especially the Muslim minority. Shourie claimed that it was necessary to reconstruct the Indian nation around its cultural majority which, in his mind, had been marginalized for too long, through centuries of foreign domination. He postulated that its unity should not be based on the action of partisan or administrative elite, but on a cultural tradition binding peoples from the Ganges to the Southern end of the Deccan. He saw the Brahmins as the bearers and guarantors of this tradition who had to reverse a secular current: 'for seven hundred years, talking of the essence of tradition was blasphemy, for one hundred years a stupidity, and for forty years revanchism, jingoism and, finally, communalism' (Shourie 1997: 22). Shourie concluded, therefore, that the minorities should have their privileges withdrawn and should only be tolerated in the country on the condition that they comply with the rules of the majority.

The Hindu nationalist movement's power originated from its electoral base and its grassroots organizations, especially the RSS. If civil society was defined only in terms of associational life and the creation of social capital, these organizations could have been considered as powerful components of Indian civil society. But such a definition would conceal the absolutely uncivil nature of Hindu militantism, consisting of an authoritarian internal organization and paramilitary formation that subjected its members to the ideals of the organization,' violently confronting and intimidating anyone standing in their way (Basu et al. 1993). The reconversion of tribal peoples or untouchables who had turned to Christianity or Islam was achieved through intimidation and violence. The repressions also did not spare cultural communities, in which artists who were deemed to lack respect for tradition were harassed. Hindu nationalist troops played a decisive role in the dramatic events in Gujarat in 2002, when the violence between Hindus and Muslims turned into a full-blown massacre. In all these areas, the collusion between militant Hindus and the government, that was controlled by the Bharatiya Janata Party, attested to the significance of this 'majoritarianism'. The political community that the 'Hindutva' militants wanted to build was not a 'civil' community, but rather a nation cleansed of what were considered to be 'foreign elements' spoiling it. The means used to that end met no criterion of civility whatsoever, even if the rhetoric of majority democracy was omnipresent.

DEMOCRACY THROUGH CASTES?

The parties based in the lower castes used the rhetoric of majoritarianism for different purposes. The victory of parties that advertised their caste membership in the large states of Northern India raised the question of whether the revenge of the oppressed was inevitably to be identified with an advancement of civil society. The Congress' inability to make the alliance between the upper castes, the untouchables, the tribes and the Muslim minority actually work, opened the field for new caste-based parties. Caste politics were fuelled by the debate on 'reservations' that aggravated the country in the early 1990s. The main issue was the extension of job quotas in the public service and education system, reserved until then for the untouchables (or 'scheduled castes') and tribal natives (or 'scheduled tribes'), to 'Other Backward Classes' (OBC). The V.P. Singh government's decision in 1990 to increase the quota to the benefit of the OBC from 23 per cent to 50 per cent, lead to what Indian observers have called the 'Mandalization' of political life (after the Mandal Report which inspired it) – a reference to a fragmentation of political life along the lines of caste. Competition was rife between the lowest castes, however, certain excluded groups, such as Christian and Muslim untouchables, and even members of upper castes in economic difficulties, also demanded reservations for themselves. The scramble for public positions and benefits intensified, as the liberal policies of state withdrawal got under way. But the starting economic growth of the country also facilitated the exit of the upper castes towards more lucrative positions in the private sector, which explains why the coalition led by the Bharatiya Janata Party (BJP) did not step down on the issue of reservations.

The intense competition was further enhanced by the parties trying to instrumentalize it in their election campaigns. According to Zohia Hasan, the main challenge to state governments elected by the lower castes was to obtain proportional representation of all groups in government, in the administration and in educational institutions (Hasan 2000). The formation of an elite derived from these subordinate castes took precedence over substantial policies to improve the fate of the lower castes in general. Sudipta Kaviraj noted that 'an enormous amount of the energy of the new politics of the disadvantaged is spent in symbolic acts of retaliation which have tended to replace substantive measures directed against inequalities' (Kaviraj 2001: 113).

This explains why the 'Mandalization' of political society put movements that were rooted in civil society in an uncomfortable position. Their discretion in this debate probably reflected the ongoing disagreements regarding the criteria for positive discrimination. While the Marxist currents argued in favour of affirmative action on the basis of economic criteria, those close to Gandhian socialism supported the 1990 reform. The growth of caste-based democracy had certainly called into question classical discourses on the virtues of empowerment for excluded groups. As Sarah Joseph explains, 'there seems to be an implicit assumption that social movements and political initiatives which genuinely involve the deprived would necessarily be radical, progressive and democratic in character. This assumption may not always be justified' (Joseph 2002: 302).

This mobilization seems to have impeded the constitution of collective actors capable of changing the social situation. Based on a study of two Indian cities, Frederic Landy et al. conclude that:

> considering governance in general, it appears quite illusory that more openness in society brings more equity and efficiency. The segmentation of local society along religious and caste lines as well as the less visible faults made by economic disparities prevent users from behaving collectively and equally. The unity of civil society is a myth even at this local level.
>
> (Landy 2007: 27)

The structuring of political society along caste lines clearly represented an obstacle to the constitution of a public sphere open to civil-society organizations.

THE TRANSFORMATION OF CIVIL SOCIETY BY THE GRASSROOTS

It is not only Hindu nationalists that have invoked the notion of tradition, certain thinkers of the new social movements that have developed since 1980 refer to it as well. In fact, since then, militants disillusioned by the parties have initiated new forms of political actions, based on the decentralized mobilization of the oppressed. Theorized by R. Kothari (1988) and D.L. Sheth (2004), the concepts of 'non-partisan political formation' or 'grassroots polities' entered the political discourse. Their main claim is that the new movements should always be rooted locally. The positivist knowledge of experts, bureaucrats, capitalists or elected representatives is, thus, opposed to the knowledge derived from the practical experience and values underlying in traditional cultures, along with the ethnic assertion of oppressed groups.

From the emancipatory struggles of the marginalized segments of the population a new conception of democracy can emerge. The aim is not to replace representative democracy and political parties, but to tip the balance of power in favour of the most disadvantaged sections of the population. In order to do so, it is, nevertheless, necessary to overcome the risks of sectarianism and localism in the grassroots movements. Therefore, different networks aiming at coordinating the popular movements were set up. In the view of Rajni Kothari, the characteristics of the Indian tradition seem conducive to the integration of very diverse elements because it is 'based on social pluralism, on a conception of unity built on the dispersion of shared identities and values, as well as on the absence of a clergy and orthodoxy, and, consequently, on tolerance (Kothari 1988: 35). We can, thus, see the difference between the Hindu nationalists' perception of Indian tradition, and the one promoted by the theoreticians of grassroots politics. Nevertheless, they share the same basic assumption on the intrinsic virtue of the traditional society that they defend.

The new movements put their hopes in these communities' capacities to live on their own resources, and by the rules and values of their own cultures. They invoked a civil society as distant as possible from the state and the market. This juxtaposition of civil society and the state has been strongly criticized by Neera Chandhoke (Chandhoke 2003). Above all, however, it was challenged by the actual experience of the new social movements. The opposition to new economic policies of deregulation and liberalization triggered general protests from organizations claiming to represent civil society. Their efforts dealing with the destabilizing effects of new economic policies caused them to switch from global protest to more focused actions aimed at obtaining precise measures to protect the victims of globalization. For instance, the large federation of Indian voluntary organizations, VANI, initiated a vast debate on the structural-adjustment programme decided by the government in 1992. The climax of this campaign was the presentation of an alternative budget for the Union for 1993.

Mobilization has mostly been organized around the territorial dimensions of these liberalization policies, the aim being to defend the interests of those groups of the population that are victims of evictions and upheavals in their environment, due to development programmes concerning dams, mining, industries in the Special Economic Zones (SEZ), forestry or commercial fish culture. The social movements in question claim that such programmes destroy the resources and lifestyles of the concerned people. They defend the victims in two stages, first, by directly challenging programmes, although this has rarely prevented their continuation; and, second, by drawing attention to the needs of the affected group. The latter constitutes the core of the struggle and includes, among other measures, compensation and rehabilitation.

Another emblematic example is the renowned movement against the Narmada Valley dams (NBA). The movement's opposition to these cathedrals of modernization was acknowledged even by the World Bank, and the leader of the movement, Medha Paktar, was chosen to be one of the representatives of civil society on the 'world dam commission'. Faced with the fact that despite their protest, the project still was carried out in the end, the NBA organized local and national support for compensation and relocation of the inhabitants evicted from flooded areas. Summarizing, we can see that constrained by events, these movements have shifted from global protest to the struggle for the incorporation of the interests of disadvantaged people.

THE CIVILIZATION OF STATE INSTITUTIONS

Against this background, a new reference framework of civil action emerged: the Utopia of a stateless civil society was replaced by a vision of civil society as a transformation agent of the state. This new framework of reference was conveyed not only by the heirs of Gandhian socialism, but also by the militants of other ideological movements. The particular idea of this project of civilizing state institutions was not to compensate for the shortcomings of the state, but rather to pressurize it into becoming more civil-oriented. This framework applied to two different areas, the involvement of civil society in participatory policies and civil-society organizations' contribution to key political debates.

BUREAUCRATIC SHORTCOMINGS AND VOLUNTARY ORGANIZATIONS

Civil-society organizations' involvement in public policy-making has been justified by the fact that the states are unable to provide basic services to those parts of the population that need them most. Hence, the blueprint for the llth Five-Year Plan for 2007–2012 points out a fact that has been constantly repeated: in the sectors of primary education and health the diagnosis is severe, many positions are vacant while at the same time absenteeism is a major problem among teachers and doctors (GOI 2006: 59, 68). One may assume that the poor quality of these services is the result of cronyism which strongly limits the emergence of professionalism. Notwithstanding that the quality of the service of both sectors is rated as very weak by the Planning Commission, there is no indication, however, of the Commission's intention to address these well-known shortcomings by implementing internal reforms in these sectors.

Recognizing the incapacity of centralized regulation to obtain more efficiency among staff, planners are calling, moreover, for a mobilization of decentralized authorities and committees of beneficiaries to monitor their performance. In this particular regard, civil-society organizations have been granted an important role:

> The CSO works in the remotest of remote areas where even the Government has no reach ... In addition to capacity-building, many CSO have a proven track record of creating awareness, mobilising social capital and implementing programmes at the grass roots level ... Recognising this experience, the llth Plan should aim at encouraging partnership between CSOs and PRI [decentralized authorities] which also extend to joint implementation.
>
> (GOI 2006: 94)

In this respect, the 11th Plan is a continuation of its predecessors which introduced participatory measures in many fields, such as primary and secondary education, water management, or health services. But the problem of these programmes harnessing local elites – political and social leaders, bureaucrats – still remains unsolved.

Therefore, an alliance is advocated between local councillors and associations in order to spur the bureaucrats into action. For it to be effective, the councillors would have to oppose the cronyism that is hindering the work of civil servants in the field. In this respect, Kerala's experience, in which strong decentralization was combined with intense training and leadership by a militant organization, has attracted a great deal of attention. The 'Power to People Campaign' has been saluted by theoreticians as a model of radical democracy (Fung and Wright 2003). The particularity of this campaign was the combination of massive decentralization with mobilization and training of those concerned by militant networks – a paradoxical situation in which a party devoted to democratic centralism used planning services to achieve the decentralized participation of certain parts of the population. The interpretation of this operation is rendered even more controversial by the electoral defeat of the government that carried the reform (Chatukulam and John 2002).

In order to avoid to be caught in these games of connivance, certain movements have voluntarily situated themselves outside the bureaucracies that they want to monitor. In this respect, innovative practices have proliferated, from citizen juries to citizens' 'report cards on public services', initiated by Paul Samuel (2006) in Bangalore. Another example is the 'movement for the right to information', led by Aruna Roy, which prompted government to substantially amend the conditions of access to public documents. This movement resulted eventually in legislation allowing citizens to call state agents to account more easily.

Under pressure from donors who were eager to short-circuit the Indian bureaucracy and with the support of participatory programmes launched by the government, the associational sector has grown considerably since the 1980s. Currently, it comprises close to one million organizations, providing the equivalent of 2.7 million full-time jobs in 2002 (Planning Commission, Government of India 2005). Over the years this sector has structured itself around coordinating bodies such as the Voluntary Action Network India (VANI), which have the dual role of organizing the sector and negotiating the conditions of their collaboration with the government. The name adopted by this network is no coincidence, it is intended to distinguish it from the spurned world of NGOs. Denunciation of NGOs has become common in Indian political discourse, where arguments against 'NGO-ization' are always more or less the same (see, for instance, Kothari 1988; Chandhoke 2003). Certain NGOs are said to be nothing more than the hidden instruments of politicians, the so-called GONGOs (governmental non-governmental organizations). Others are alleged to be the new vehicles of neo-liberal hegemony, they are said to undermine the sovereignty of the state by short-circuiting the direct relations established with their financiers, and to legitimate the state's withdrawal by promoting private services in order to replace public services. It is, thus, claimed that by this depoliticizing development, NGOs impede the necessary opposition to the neo-liberal model, and they are seen to form an opaque sector which secures its leaders a good standard of living. These widespread allegations explain why many civil-society organizations take great care to refer to themselves as 'movement' or 'voluntary association'.

GRASSROOTS AT THE SUMMITS OF THE STATE

While the Indian state has been willing to grant considerable space to the voluntary sector in the implementation of its policies, it has been far less tolerant of that sector's intrusion in the political debate. For at least a decade, national political mobilization has proliferated around the main topics of social protest. It has taken the form of campaigns bringing together multiple organizations in loose networks, for instance the national campaigns for people's right to information, or the right to food and to education, or campaigns driven by the National Alliance of People's Movements, coordinated by Medha Paktar, the leader of the movement against the Narmada dams. At the international level, these movements have actively participated in attempts to build a global civil society, primarily through world social forums but also via the committees created by international institutions.

This politicization of social movements is often not tolerated by the Indian state. Governments brandish the terrorist threat in order to justify tight regulation of foreign donations and even banning them for political organizations. But from the point of view of voluntary organization, leaving the task of defining what a political organization is to the government, can lead to serious abuses. In some cases, these movements' support is, nevertheless, sought by certain public actors who wish to assert their autonomy. The experience of a 'judiciarization' of collective action and of the National Advisory Council chaired by Sonia Gandhi, is a telling illustration.

Judicial Activism and Civil Society Organizations

With the support of a particular faction of the judiciary, human-rights movements were able to achieve an official recognition of the uncivil excesses of the Indian state. These judges wished to erase the memory of the judiciary's leniency towards the government during the state of emergency. By opening the door to Public Interest Litigation (PIL), they provided civil-society organizations with a powerful lever for influencing government action. PIL enabled associations acting in the public interest to use the courts without pursuing a particular case.

The starting point was the case of People's Union for Democratic Rights (PUDR) versus Union of India (A.I.R., 1982, S C 1473), in which it was recognized that a third party could directly petition the court, whether through a letter or other means, and seek its intervention in a matter where another party's fundamental rights were being violated. In this case, referring to the Constitutional prohibition on forced labour and traffic of human beings, the PUDR submitted that workers who had been contracted to build the large sports complex at the Asian Games Village in Delhi were exploited. The PUDR asked the court to acknowledge that such work, under exploitative and overtly humiliating conditions, or work that was not even compensated by prescribed minimum wages, was a violation of fundamental rights.

Likewise, a petitioning of the Supreme Court was at the origin of the Right to Food campaign. The campaign began with a writ petition submitted to the Supreme Court in April 2001 by the People's Union for Civil Liberties (PUCL), Rajasthan. Briefly, the petition demanded that the country's gigantic food stocks should be used without delay to protect people from hunger and starvation. This petition led to a prolonged public interest litigation (PUCL versus Union of India and Others, Writ Petition [Civil] 196 of 2001). Supreme Court hearings were held at regular intervals, and significant 'interim orders' issued from time to time. The result was direct Supreme Court intervention in monitoring the various programmes set up by the Indian government to combat malnutrition.

Due to the court's action, problems were put on the government's agenda, that would have hardly emerged had they been raised using the regular means of representative democracy. But judicial responses have always been constrained by the strategic orientations of the executive, and the Supreme Court has challenged neither the large investment projects nor the reinforcement of the repressive arsenal created in the context of the government's war on terrorism.

The Movements at the Parties' Bedside: The NAC

The same types of constraint seem to have weighed on the National Advisory Council (NAC) for the implementation of the Minimum

Common Programme. This body was set up by the United Progressive Alliance (UPA) government around left-wing parties and Congress after their victory in the 2004 elections. It was composed of experts and personalities from civil society and had the mission of making proposals to ensure the implementation of the government's common programme. Militants had already been invited to forums in which government policy orientations were discussed. The Planning Commission and central-government ministries had extensive experience in this respect. But this was the first time that a body so close to decision-making and with such general competence was formed.

This convergence of civil activists and Congress was facilitated by the former Hindu nationalist government. Its wait-and-see attitude in the case of the Gujarat massacre was strongly condemned and caused some of the voluntary movements to move closer to the 'secular' political coalition formed by the Congress and the left. The political fate of the NAC was closely linked to that of its president, Sonia Gandhi. Having given up the idea of being prime minister, the president of the Congress could use this institution to claim the merit of having initiated important measures. Examples were the Right to Information Act and, especially, the National Rural Employment Guarantee Bill, passed unanimously by Parliament on 23 August 2005. In both cases, these bills were promoted within the NAC by senior social activists who had driven a national campaign on these topics. The laws that were promulgated did not entirely meet the demands advanced during these campaigns, and the final legislative result was severely criticized by some activists and these leaders.

However, this involvement of civil-society actors in circles close to government's decision-making bodies depended largely on the strategic position of the chairperson of the NAC. Sonia Gandhi's resignation from the NAC in March 2006 was rapidly followed by the withdrawal of active militants, such as Aruna Roy and Jean Drezes, from this institution – with the result that it suddenly seemed marginal.

Thus, although movements rooted in civil society have found new allies in the Indian state, their influence on the Indian political scene should not be overemphasized. Whenever the core strategies of the state are concerned, that influence is slim. Economic liberalization has been pursued without any major changes. The construction of dams has continued despite protest and, like the other major projects, has generated a steady flow of evicted persons. According to these movements, guarantees of compensation and reinsertion remain insufficient. Likewise, the rule of law is undermined by the lasting dread of terrorism in the country. The armed conflicts overwhelming Kashmir and the North-East of India, and the pressure of the Maoist armed struggle in the Central East have triggered the introduction of highly repressive legislation. However, political society remains largely insensitive to the alarm bells set off by these measures among human-rights movements.

CONCLUSION

If we consider only the discourse on civil society, the evolution of the Indian debate echoes more general tendencies. But when the place of civil society in political society is examined, the terms of the Indian debate differ profoundly from this broad trend. The hypothesis that civil society becomes a point of reference whenever established politics enter into crisis, is illustrated by the return of civil society after the state of emergency in the late 1970s. The framing of alternative references for relations between the state and civil society has borrowed much from the international discourse on good governance and, particularly, on the crucial role of voluntary associations in the empowerment of beneficiaries, in the activation of bureaucracies and in the defence of the environment. This discourse, which is close to a version of the 'third way model' for the states of the South, has been fiercely criticized by those social movements – oriented or not towards a radical transformation of society – which have actively participated in alter-globalization forums. Nevertheless, a shift in strategies can be witnessed among these groups. Although they still condemn the liberal development model, they tend to be more focused on means of civilizing the state, attempting to limit harmful impacts of globalization on the most disadvantaged groups.

The saga of social movements in India has received much attention on the international scene. However, this should not cause us to forget the modest role of this civil associational world in the reality of daily life in India. Even in a modern city like New Delhi, John Harris found associations only play a very minor part in the solution of citizens' problems (Harris 2005). In the same vein, a book entitled Democracy without Associations (Chibber 1999) generated much debate in India, but no one could question its testimony to the weakness of formally established organizations. It clearly indicates the fact that:

> for the lowest strata of Indian society, associational channels ... are not easily available: their repertoire, which has considerable range, stretches from acceptance of patronage of politicians to wary support of local toughs; from political mendicancy to spontaneous violence. All elements of this repertoire lie outside the definition of associational 'civility'.
>
> (Kaviraj 2001: 317)

Yet, the fragility of the third sector is just one difficult facet among others, of the challenge to incorporate civil society into Indian political society. Civil society embodies a people consisting of citizens, whereas Indian political society is structured around inherited and imagined communities. Hindu nationalists base the political collective on the Hindu majority's revenge over centuries of foreign domination (including the Mughal Empire). The Scheduled Castes and Other Backward Castes also want to use the law of numbers to repair the injustices from which they have suffered. Hence, the minorities are also mobilizing to claim their fair share of public benefits. The strive for these particular advantages sometimes even takes precedence over the quality of the service delivered by bureaucracies. Certain currents of civil society have not been insensitive to the charms of particularism and have argued around a mobilization of traditional identities to oppose the steamroller of globalization. The universalism of the right to vote has thus led to a confrontation between particularist groups for the sharing of the spoils of the state. The battle for public resources is intensifying as liberal policies for controlling public expenditures prevail. The new market prosperity is, nevertheless, enabling the middle and upper-classes to turn elsewhere, to find more attractive services and jobs in the private sector. Over and above these different particularisms, unity is sought through an activation of Indian or Hindu nationalism.

The place that particularist actors have in political society puts civil society into an awkward position. The unity that civil society could, promote would be founded on the creation of a common base of civil, political and social rights, cross-cutting boundaries of caste and tradition (Gupta 2003). In Indian political discourse, homage is ritually paid to the recognition of human rights in the constitution, in jurisprudence and even in the programmes of the different plans, aimed at meeting essential needs. But this definition of a common base is obscured by the dynamic of collective rights.

The consolidation of this common base depends, in turn, on the existence of a network of different, open and secular institutions. According to Andre Beteille (Beteille 2003: 202), it is the autonomy of these institutions that guarantees the possible vitality of civil society. Several observers have celebrated the 'silent revolution' (Jaffrelot 2003) that Indian democracy is said to have experienced with the growing movement of the untouchables. To be sure, greater participation by the working or poor classes in the elections is a remarkable feature of Indian democracy, yet it remains to be seen whether this 'revolution' will bring civil society and political society closer together.

References

Basu, T., Datta, P., Sarkar, S. and Sen, S. (1993), Khaki Shorts and Saffron Flags: *A Critique of the Hindu Right*, Hyderabad: Orient Longman Limited, 126.

Baxi, U. (2000), 'The avatars of Indian judicial activism: explorations in the geography of (injustice',in S.K. Verma and K. Kusum (eds) *Fifty Years of the Supreme Court of India*, Delhi: Oxford University Press.

Beteille, A. (2003), 'Civil society and its institutions', in C. Elliot (ed.) Civil Society and Democracy, a Reader, New Delhi: Oxford University Press, 191–210.

Chandhoke, N. (2003), *The Conceits of Civil Society*, New Delhi: Oxford University Press, 278.

Chathukulam, J. and John, M.S. (2002), 'Five years of participatory planning in Kerala: rhetoric and reality', *Economic and Political Weekly*, 37 (49): 4917–4926.

Chatterjee, P. (2001), 'Postcolonial civil and political society', in S. Kaviraj and S. Khilnani (eds) *Civil society: History and Possibilities*, Cambridge; Cambridge University Press, 165–178.

Chibber, P. (1999), 'Democracy without Associations: Transformation of the Party System and Social Cleavages in India', Ann Arbor: University of Michigan Press, 304.

Fung, A. and Wright, O.E. (2003), 'Deepening democracy: innovations in empowered participatory governance', *Politics and Society*, 29 (2): 5–41.

Government of India (GOI) Planning Commission (1978) 'Draft - VI five year Plan revised', New Delhi.

_______ (2006), 'Toward a faster and more inclusive growth. An approach to the 11th Five Year Plan 2007–2012', New Delhi, 109.

Guha, R. (ed.) (1983), Subaltern Studies: *Writings on South Asian Studies*, Oxford: Oxford University Press.

Gupta, D. (2003), 'Civil society or the state. What happened to citizenship?'in C. Elliot (ed.) – *Civil Society and Democracy*, A Reader, New Delhi: Oxford University Press, 211–237.

Harris, J. (2005), 'Political participation, representation and the urban poor: findings from Delhi', *Economic and Political Weekly*, 40 (11): 1041–1054.

_______ (2007), 'Antinomies of empowerment. Observations on civil society, politics and urban governance in India', Draft Paper for the Berkeley CSAS Conference on Local Governance and Empowerment May 2007, http://ias.berkeley.edu/southasia/demo-cracy07/docs/jharris.pdf (accessed November 2007).

Hasan, Z. (2000), 'Representation and redistribution', in F.R. Frankel, Z. Hasan and R. Bhargava (eds) *Transforming India: Social and Political Dynamics of Democracy*, New Delhi: Oxford University Press, 146–175.

Jaffrelot, C. (2003), *India's Silent Revolution*, New York: Columbia University Press.

Jobert, B. (1984), The testing of the alternative: two major innovations in Indian social policy', *Social Science Information*, 23 (6): 921-954.

_______ (1985), 'Populism and health policy: the case of Community Health Volunteers in India', *Social Science and Medicine*, 20 (1): 1–28.

Joseph, S. (2002), 'Society vs state? Civil society, political society and non party political process in India', *Economic and Political Weekly*, 26 (4): 299–305.

Kaviraj, S. (2001), 'In search of civil society', in S. Kaviraj and S. Khilnani (eds) *Civil society: History and Possibilities*, Cambridge: Cambridge University Press, 287–323.

Kothari, R. (1970), *Politics in India*, New Delhi: Little Brown Company and Orient Longman, 459.

_______ (1988), State Against Democracy: In search of Human Governance, Delhi: Ajanta Press, 308.

Landy, F. (2007) 'Vertical governance: brokerage, patronage and corruption. The case of the public distribution system of foodstuff', unpublished contribution to the APUG seminar, Mumbai and Hyderabad: University Nanterre, 29–30 May 2007, 27.

Planning Commission. Government of India (2005), 'PRIA Voluntary sector in India. Scale, impact and potential 'New Delhi, 9 September 2005, planningcommissin.nic.in/data/ngo/csw/csw_4.pdf(accessed October 2007.

Rudolph L. and Hober Rudolph, S. (1987), In pursuit of Lakshm: *The Political Economy of Indian State*, Chicago: University of Chicago Press, 529.

Samuel, P. (2006), 'Public Spending, outcomes and accountability: citizen report card as a catalyst for public action', *Economic and Political Weekly*, 41 (4): 333–340.

Shah G.(2002), 'Direct Action in India: A study of Bihar and Gujarat', in G.Shah (ed) *Social movements and the State: Readings in Indian Government and Politics*, London, Sage, 335–360 and 475.

Sheth D.L. (2004), 'Globalisation and New Politics of micro-movements', *Economic and Political Weekly*, 39(1): 45–58. Weiner, M. (1962) *The Politics and Scarcity*, Chicago: University of Chicago Press, 271.

Weiner, M. (1962), *The Politics and Scarcity*, Chicago: University of Chicago Press, 271.

12

Civil Society: Active or Passive? India

Rob Jenkins

OVERVIEW

This chapter examines civil society in the 'world's largest democracy'. Unlike most developing countries, India has maintained a democratic political system since emerging from colonial rule – a feat often attributed to the vibrancy of its civil society. After outlining some of the salient features of India's recent political history, this chapter examines: (1) controversies surrounding the size and composition of India's civil society; (2) issues relating to regional variations in the nature of associational life; (3) the question of whether states can help to spur the development of civil society; and (4) problems in understanding the contribution of civil society to improved governance, including consideration of civil society's darker side.

INDIA

INTRODUCTION

The Indian National Congress, the premier organization in the struggle for independence from British rule, was formed in 1885 by a group of English-educated lawyers and professionals. It was not until the 1920s, under the leadership of Mohandas K. Gandhi, that 'Congress' became a mass movement capable of pressing the colonial authorities for greater self-rule. This was also the period when, largely through Congress-related efforts, India's civil society began to flourish. The process was aided by the mobilizing efforts associated with the pre-independence elections to legislative councils. India's constitution of 1950 outlined the functions of its political institutions, including the division of powers between the central and provincial tiers of its

Box 1. Key dates in the history of independent India

1947	'Partition' of colonial India creates two independent states, India and Pakistan; more than a million people killed in accompanying Hindu-Muslim riots; Jawaharlal Nehru (of the Indian National Congress) becomes first Prime Minister
1950	Constitution ratified, confirming India as federal, democratic, secular, and committed to social justice
1967	Fourth General Election: under Prime Minister Indira Gandhi Congress loses power in several states
1975–9	Mrs. Gandhi's national 'Emergency' (1975–7); widespread protest action leads to electoral defeat for Mrs. Gandhi (1977) and India's first non-Congress central government (1977–9)
1984	Mrs. Gandhi assassinated by Sikh bodyguards; her son, Rajiv, becomes Prime Minister
1991	Rajiv Gandhi assassinated by Sri Lankan Tamil separatists; new Congress government of P.V. Narasimha Rao initiates economic liberalization programme
1992	Destruction of Babri Mosque by Hindu nationalist militants
1998	BJP assumes national power (in coalition); following year, BJP receives fresh electoral mandate (also in coalition)
2002–3	After a train carrying Hindus is burnt,thousands of Muslims are killed in Gujarat, with suspected state complicity
2004	Voters replace BJP-led coalition government with coalition headed by Congress

federal system. The constitution contained the usual liberal protections that make civil society possible (freedom of speech, of assembly, and so forth). But India's civil society was also shaped by other legal provisions, such as the 'reservation' of roughly one-fifth of parliamentary constituencies for members of the so-called Scheduled Castes and Scheduled Tribes. Within the Hindu caste system, a complex and ancient though evolving system of social stratification in which people's caste status is determined at birth, Scheduled Castes (now often referred to as Dalits) were marginalized and regarded as almost subhuman 'untouchables'. The mainly forest-dwelling Scheduled Tribes were similarly regarded as beyond the pale of civilized life.

Congress dominated the first twenty years of post-Independence politics. Its stranglehold over state-level (i.e. provincial) power was broken only at the 1967 general elections. Another decade elapsed before Congress first lost power at the national level in the 1977 general elections. By the late 1980s, not only was unchallenged Congress dominance a thing of the past; so was control over electoral politics by the richer, more powerful and better-educated groups in the Hindu social order – the so-called upper castes. Increasingly, parties appealed to members of the lower castes, particularly those just above the Scheduled Castes in the hierarchy, often recruiting a greater number of candidates from these communities. Parties constructed around lower-caste identity also emerged. From the late 1980s, regional parties – those confined mainly to a single state – began increasing their share of the vote.

To these trends, the 1990s added two others of great significance. The first was the ascendancy of the Hindu nationalist Bharatiya Janata Party (BJP). The BJP's primary pledges were to tear down the Babri Mosque in the north Indian town of Ayodhya (accomplished by BJP-affiliated militants in 1992), and to abolish legal provisions that permitted religious minorities to follow different sets of social practices concerning marriage, divorce, and other matters. The BJP began the 1990s as a pariah party with which almost no other mainstream grouping would ally; by 1998 it was leading the national coalition government. The BJP was aided by the 'regionalization' of party politics, through which single-state parties emerged as significant electoral players. In several states, regional parties proved more than willing to ally with the BJP in order to defeat their long-time local rival – the Congress. The BJP – which polling data have consistently shown as more popular among richer and higher-caste voters – also benefited from a backlash against the political assertiveness of traditionally subordinated groups among the lower castes.

The second key trend of the 1990s was the shift from a state-dominated economic policy framework to one giving greater scope to market signals. The programme of economic liberalization undertaken by a Congress government in 1991, but continued by successive governments from the left and the right, has unfolded much more gradually than similar reforms in other developing countries. But while much controversy remains concerning the impact of India's reforms, particularly on the poor, by the twenty-first century India's role in the world economy (and in international economic diplomacy) had clearly increased.

Key Points

- India's civil society first emerged with nationalist and electoral mobilization by Congress.
- Congress dominance was increasingly challenged from the late 1960s.
- The BJP's rise during the 1990s coincided with the regionalization of party politics.
- Since 1991 there has been significant economic liberalization.

SIZE AND COMPOSITION OF INDIA'S CIVIL SOCIETY

Whatever its shortcomings, India's democratic system is known, even to those without detailed knowledge of the country, as a site of lively political contestation, with all manner of civic groups endlessly aligning and realigning with one another on every conceivable issue – from how to reform affirmative action provisions in government employment, to the appropriate nuclear doctrine for a country in India's geostrategic position. Even during periods when India's democratic institutions were undergoing decay, observers (within and outside India) have always had great faith in the ability of India's vast and varied civil society to take up some of the slack (Kothari 1984).

It will therefore surprise many people to learn that considerable controversy has recently surfaced over whether India's civil society is so impressively diverse and prolific after all. In Democracy Without Associations, Chhibber (1999) turned conventional wisdom on its head, arguing that India's civil society was characterized by relatively small size and thin substance. The dearth of civic associations, Chhibber maintained, caused India's political parties to mobilize people on the basis of caste, sect, ethnicity, or linguistic group. In a vicious circle, the politicization of these 'ascriptive identities' – groupings to which people belong by birth, rather than bychoice – further shrank the space available for non-partisan civil society.

The Role of Ascriptive Identity

The claim that India's associational life was weak drew intense criticism. Particularly targeted was Chhibber's apparent insistence that 'informal' associations – those in which there are no office-bearers or codified rules – did not qualify for inclusion within a narrow definition of civil society. There is a long-standing argument over whether ethnicity-based organizations – such as caste associations, religious brotherhoods, and groups that seek to politicize linguistic identity – should be considered part of Indian civil society. But Chhibber's critics felt he had gone too far in the restrictive direction. One otherwise positive reviewer asked: 'is focusing on formal associations a reasonable indicator of the presence of solidarities between the family and the state' (Sethi 1999: 94)? In another review, the co-author of a key 1960s text that challenged the assumption that organizations had to be either modern or traditional (Rudolph and Rudolph 1967), argued that Chhibber was defining civil society too narrowly: 'Caste associations are anomalous; they are intentional associations, hybrids that combine voluntary with ascriptive characteristics'(Rudolph 2003).

These associations exemplify 'the modernity of tradition': in order to advance the interests of traditional caste groups, they sought access to modern means of social mobility and political influence. Caste associations, such as those representing various segments of the Jat community in north India, have done this by establishing scholarship programmes and student hostels, promoting internal reforms of the community's social practices (particularly around gender relations) and demanding representation in government service. Jat and other caste associations sometimes endorse candidates or parties at election time. But even when they do not, they are engaged in modern politics. In fact, contesting elections can alter the structure and meaning of caste itself – modernizing it, one could say. For instance, the geographical and social boundaries of a caste often broaden considerably as associations seek to increase their numbers, the currency of electoral democracy. Divisions among the various sections of what came to be known as the Maratha 'caste cluster' in western India are papered over in the name of constructing a more encompassing political identity for the group (Lele 1990).

Rudolph's main point, however, concerned the broader characterization of India's civil society: 'If caste associations, demand groups, issue and movement politics, and non-government organizations are taken into account, India could be 'read' as having a pervasive and extraordinarily active associational life, perhaps one of the most participatory in the world' (Rudolph 2003). Even if Chhibber's critics are largely right on the question of civil society's vibrancy – their case looks extremely strong on certain methodological points – Chhibber has still provided a valuable service by directing attention towards places where civil society's size or importance has been overstated, or where it is looking frayed around the edges. For foreigners who come into contact with elements of India's civil society it sometimes seems bigger than it actually is; there is a tendency to be impressed by the absolute numbers of associations involved, and the amount of noise they generate in English-language media, and to forget how unimpressive these numbers are given India's huge population. This is true of the trade union sector, for instance. Organized labour only exists in the outermost layer of Indian economic activity. Three per cent is a common figure cited as the proportion of the population that belongs to a union. And yet, even here caution is warranted. Many labour organizations are unregistered, and though this means they are less capable of obtaining full legal recognition, it also means that there may be more associational activity taking place in various hidden parts of India's vast hinterland than the statistics indicate.

As for civil society's frayed edges, Varshney (2004), among others, observes that, whatever its merits, India's civil society may be living on borrowed time. Many associations exist in theory, but are shells of their former selves, lacking organizational substance. In some regions, the better part of local civil society consists of associations founded during the movement for independence. This is an institutional inheritance from an earlier era of organization-building. It consists of many functional organizations affiliated with the Congress movement – women's leagues, student federations, and so forth, not to mention cooperatives of various sorts, many of which are so highly compromised by government interference that they appear, in fact, to constitute good examples of the weak civil society perceived by Chhibber.

Regional Variations in Civil Society

In addition, both the strength and effectiveness of civil society vary from state to state. The southern state of Kerala, for instance, is a land of civic bounty: there one can find reading clubs, cinema clubs, drama clubs, alongside the more familiar actors such as trade unions (Kerala's strong Marxist political tradition has ensured this), business associations, and so forth. In the eastern state of Orissa, on the other hand, civil society is extremely weak, and in some areas non-existent.

The memberships (and conceptual horizons) of most associations do not, generally, extend beyond state borders. Katzenstein et al. (2001: 245) argue that 'issue-based Indian social movements have remained substantially limited to the regions within which they operate ... even when the issues and interests they represent are national in their relevance'. There are good reasons for even functional associations (let alone 'movement' groups) to confine their work within the boundaries of their 'home' state. First, the sheer size of most states – in population terms alone – is usually sufficient to occupy the efforts of civic groups that deal intensively with public authorities. Second, in India's federal system states form a powerful tier of government. State governments make many important policy decisions, particularly in the era of economic liberalization. Third, most Indian parties are geared to the state level: they would prefer control over a state government to even the most senior cabinet positions in New Delhi, short of the prime ministership. Fourth, since India's federal system is organized along linguistic lines, there are natural barriers to the spread of many associational forms. Kerala's literature societies, for instance, find it hard to break out of their provincial boundaries. Associated cultural differences between states (not least the existence of distinct regional caste systems) further reinforce the federally segmented nature of associational life. Despite all these constraints, civil society's largely state-specific nature is undergoing profound change: the proliferation of national and international media (including the internet) has brought 'national organizing' within the grasp of an increasing number of associations.

The difficulty of pinning down the implications of these trends for the development of civil society is exemplified by the ambiguous impact of the so-called 'regionalization' of Indian politics alluded to earlier. Because political contestation is increasingly between single-state parties, one might expect a corresponding regionalization of civil society. There is some evidence of this: state-level units of national trade union federations are increasingly going their own way – or at least acting more autonomously (vis-a-vis their national leaderships) than in the past. However, over the past decade, these same regional parties have joined with national parties of the left and the right to form coalition governments in New Delhi. This has made regional parties key actors on the national political stage. Again, it would not be surprising to find civil society mirroring this crucial political trend, with national-level ministers from, say, Andhra Pradesh's Telugu Desam Party providing a much needed point of access to central government agencies for Andhra Pradesh-based civic groups. There is some anecdotal evidence to support this claim, but it requires systematic empirical study. If true, such a trend would represent a major shift from past practice. The state-wise organization of India's civil society has often impeded the emergence of effective national lobbies on controversial policy matters – notably agriculture. In the 1980s, an alliance was formed among farmers' organizations from Karnataka, Maharashtra, and Uttar Pradesh; it collapsed when each group became focused on events in its respective home state.

Key Points

- The reputed vibrancy of India's civil society has recently been questioned.
- One issue is whether associations based on ascriptive identity should count as part of civil society.
- Many of the civil society organizations formed during the independence movement are moribund.
- India's federal system means that the nature and effectiveness of civil society varies between states, which also tends to impede activism across state boundaries.

STATE FOSTERING OF CIVIL SOCIETY

While state-wise variations in the texture of civil society clearly exist, the reasons for these differences are much debated. For instance, while some attribute Kerala's diversified civil society to its high literacy rate, the nature of the Keralan state's interaction with civil society can also be seen to breed further civic associationalism. The People's Plan Campaign (PPC), a radical programme of democratic decentralization, was established by the state's Left Democratic Front coalition in the mid-1990s. The newly introduced system of political representation (and development planning) did not just create more state bureaucracy; it also catalysed a huge flowering of civil society. Whether entities such as 'user committees', 'women's groups', and 'neighbourhood groups' – voluntary associations that under the People's Plan had to be formed in order to obtain certain state benefits – qualify as bona fide manifestations of civil society is almost as long-standing a debate as the question of how to classify ethnic associations. Clearly, many such associations do spring up merely to obtain a specific benefit, and have no substantive influence over state functioning. Indeed, many get 'captured' by syndicates of 'contractors', the politically connected people – sometimes politicians themselves – who obtain contracts for development works. But there are indications that at least some of Kerala's 'state-fostered' associations have gone on to seek improvements in systems and procedures of governance (Isaac 2000).

Readers might be surprised that it is considered legitimate in India for state policy to be explicitly geared towards creating civil society groups; the two sides of the state-civic divide are usually conceived of as autonomous and separate. But two factors – one related to India, the other more general – make this less unusual. First, as we have seen, India's nationalist movement was a hothouse of association-forming activism. This introduced into India's liberal political culture the idea that civil society need not spring up organically. The 'fostering' of civil society, whether by parties or the state (and the Congress, as a bridging institution, straddled the two), became an accepted route through which new associational forms could emerge. The second relevant factor is the influence of aid agencies, which as a result of their work in developing countries where the public sphere is less fertile than in India, are accustomed to funding programmes that, by design, try to create civil society organizations that could improve accountability (Jenkins 2001).

Key Points

- One reason for variation between states is the role of state governments in fostering civil society.
- Opinions differ on whether state-fostered associations should qualify for inclusion within civil society.

CIVIL SOCIETY AND THE PROMOTION OF BETTER GOVERNANCE

Despite these hopes, the Indian case demonstrates that the role of civil society in promoting better governance is ambiguous at best. This can be illustrated with examples of civil society groups that have sought to combat corruption and tried to prevent communal violence.

Chandhoke (2003: 184) argues that 'legal and bureaucratic languages ... even as they penetrate civil society, are embedded in the power of the state'. The language, and indeed practice, of legal-bureaucratic rationality has become a much more prominent focal point for the actions of certain civil-society actors in India. It has long been the operating idiom of the professionalized sector of civil society – for instance Non-Governmental Organizations (NGOs), the policy advocates working in obscure areas of technical competence – but only during the past decade has the 'mass movement' sector of civil society fully embraced the language and practices of legal-bureaucratic rationality.

The rise of public-interest litigation in India has arguably triggered an interest by social movements in adopting, almost mimicking, legal processes. This has taken the form of procedurally complex public hearings – of which the approach taken by Mazdoor Kisan Shakti Sangathan (MKSS), detailed below, is but one version. People's hearings are held where voluntary groups feel compelled to substitute for authorities that fail to provide information or consult with citizens, especially on controversial infrastructure projects deemed likely to have damaging environmental impacts, such as the Enron power project in Maharashtra. The logistics of collecting evidence, both for one-off civil society led hearings as well as for the researching of faux-official 'status reports' on incidents of police violence, are formidable and represent a 'legalization' of social action. Instead of demanding an inquiry, these civic groups conduct inquiries themselves, and if sufficiently successful in conveying their evidence to a larger constituency, can be in a strong position to demand inclusion in state investigations.

Civil society activism geared towards combating corruption tends to produce organizational hybrids – not in the sense of sharing modern and traditional characteristics, but in so far as they expand beyond their conventional roles. Rather than merely mobilizing voters during elections, and pressing governments to live up to their campaign promises between elections – that is, providing vertical accountability – many civic associations have insinuated themselves into horizontal channels of accountability, which traditionally involve state agencies (auditors, ombudsmen, judiciaries) monitoring other branches of the state (executive ministries, parastatal organizations). By combining their conventional role within vertical channels of accountability with participation in horizontal channels of accountability (from which non-governmental actors were once completely excluded), some civic associations have undergone a process of hybridization (Goetz and Jenkins 2004).

Based in the state of Rajasthan, the Mazdoor Kisan Shakti Sangathan (MKSS), or Workers' and Farmers' Power Organization, embodies this trend. The MKSS immediately presents the question of categorization. Is it a movement, as its leaders claim? Ironically, this claim is both bolstered and undermined by the MKSS's participation in the National Alliance of People's Movements (NAPM) – a 'movement' group, as its name suggests, but also an increasingly organized force in mainstream, institutionalized Indian politics. Is the MKSS a union? The 'Worker' part refers to day-labourers on employment-creation schemes, so it qualifies in one sense, but does not engage in the kind of collective bargaining conventionally recognized as trade unionism. Is it a party? Not really, but it has run, sometimes successfully, a few candidates in village elections.

Regardless of how it is classified, the MKSS's great innovation has been to use financial information from government documents as the catalyst for a participatory auditing exercise. This involves ordinary villagers cross-checking information from official files against what has actually been constructed by public works programmes on the ground. Part of the process is questioning workers on employment schemes to see how much they were actually paid, a sum that is almost always less than what financial records showed officials to have claimed on their behalf from the state exchequer. By exposing these discrepancies, in public, and based on people's own energies and testimonies, some corrupt officials and local notables have been forced to apologize and return stolen funds – major if isolated victories. A minor deterrent effect has been felt in some localities close to where the MKSS is active (Jenkins and Goetz 1999).

But the odds against long-term impact are huge. This may be partly why the MKSS has branched out into at least two other areas of work. First, it has sought to make use of new rules requiring candidates to declare their financial assets and whether they have criminal records. During state-level elections in 2003, the MKSS and other civic groups publicized this information in a form accessible to voters (Khera 2004). Second, the MKSS has participated in public-interest litigation against government agencies that have failed to use public grain stocks to alleviate famine in various parts of India. This has involved monitoring activities in coordination with commissioners appointed by the Supreme Court to obtain evidence of government compliance and non-compliance. Such state-civil society partnerships are often criticized for neutralizing civil society. But in this case there appears to be a genuine difference in the quality of the partnership: the litigants, MKSS among them, are engaged as active demanders of accountability, driving the advancement of rights, rather than as subcontractors delivering public services.

The role of civil society in communal relations is another area where the lines between traditional and modern, and between state and civil society, are blurred. It is also an area in which we are reminded of the distinction between civil and uncivil forms of associationalism. On the one hand, civil society organizations and the state seem – in some instances – excessively intertwined. In 2002–3, the state of Gujarat suffered India's worst communal rioting since partition. Thousands of Muslims lost their lives, and tens of thousands lost their homes. A pivotal player in these events was the 'voluntary sector' organization, the Rashtriya Swayamsevak Sangh (RSS), or National Volunteers' Association, which is the ideological core of the Hindu nationalist movement, the then ruling BJP being its political expression. The RSS's presence within organs of the state administration – among elite civil servants, the police, paramilitary units – was a crucial influence on the grisly outcome.

On the other hand, one of the few mechanisms that appear to have been effective at combating communal violence is something very similar, in terms of breaching the state-civil society divide. Varshney (2004: 206) has argued that under certain circumstances, in order to prevent communal violence, 'Civil society organizations, for all practical purposes, become the ears and arms of the state'. While this may sound sinister, Varshney is in fact referring to a positive version of state-civil society partnership with a proven ability to tackle small, localized communal flare-ups before they erupt into widespread violence.

Varshney's study of civil society and communal violence in Kerala and Uttar Pradesh (UP) addresses the question of why UP suffered so much Hindu-Muslim violence, compared to Kerala, which during the early part of the twentieth century had been a communal tinderbox. The conventional wisdom has interpreted the statistical correlation between statewide levels of illiteracy and the propensity towards communal rioting as implying a causal relationship. Fewer illiterates in Kerala, in other words, means fewer chances to manipulate communal passions. Varshney suggests that states are the wrong unit of analysis for this particular problem. Communal violence is a local (primarily urban) phenomenon, and when data on development and communal violence are aggregated at the city or town level (instead of at the state level), the correlation between social high literacy and communal peace disappears. What does correlate, inversely, with lower levels of communal violence is the degree of local civil society organizing that spans the Hindu-Muslim divide – that is, the existence of inter-communal associations that can act as an unofficial institution for defusing disputes and preventing escalation into full-scale rioting.

Key Points

- Evidence that civil society organizations improve governance is ambiguous.
- The MKSS's efforts to combat corruption provides a good illustration.
- Some civil society organizations foment communal violence but other cross-communal organizations may contain it.

CONCLUSION

The complex nature of India's associational life has spurred debates about its size and composition, its regional variations, its relations with the state, and its capacity to improve governance. The difficulty of resolving these issues demonstrates both the protean nature of India's civil society in particular, and the ambiguity of concepts used to analyze civil society more generally. Indian civil society challenges conventional analytical categories separating modern and traditional identities, civil and uncivil expressions of the associational impulse, and vertical and horizontal forms of accountability. India's civil society tends to revise and reconstitute itself with remarkable frequency. Though the exact nature of the impact is unclear, it is hard to deny that this process is being affected by globalization. Many Indian civic organizations have received a boost from their connections abroad—largely through transnational social networks connecting members of the Indian diaspora. In some cases, such linkages illustrate other trends discussed in this chapter. For instance, the reportedly large role played by overseas Indians in fund-raising for the Vishwa Hindu Parishad or (World Hindu Council), another RSS-linked group, suggests not only that India has not bucked the world wide trend towards mobilizing so-called traditional identities through modevu mean, but also that its civic associations are unafraid of deploying uncivil methods to obtain their objectives.

References

Chandhoke, N., *The Conceits of Civil Society* (Delhi: Oxford University Press, 2003). Uses the case of India to advance theoretically informed arguments about the way in which the idea of civil society has been deployed in much contemporary scholarship.

Jaffrelot, C., *India's Silent Revolution: The Rise of the Lower Castes in North India* (London: Hurst and Co., 2003). Sensitively analyses the emergence of socially marginalized groups into the mainstream of party politics, a process both reflecting and profoundly influencing the nature and development of India's civil society.

Jeffrey, R., *India's Newspaper Revolution: Capitalism, Politics* and the Indian-Language Press, 1977–99 (Delhi: Oxford University Press, 2000). Charts, in fascinating detail, both encouraging and disturbing trends in the development of one of the key elements of any functioning civil society – the press.

Mahajan, G., 'Civil Society and Its Avatars: What Happened to Freedom and Democracy', *Economic and Political Weekly*, 15–21'May

1999 (available at www.epw.org.in). Excellent account of the relationship between thinking about civil society in the West and in India.

Sainath, P., *Everybody Loves a Good Drought: Stones from India's Poorest Districts* (New Delhi: Penguin, 1996). An excellent collection of reportage on the plight of India's most vulnerable citizens, showing both their need for strong associations to represent their interests and how sometimes oppressive forms of civil society contribute to the problem.

Varshney, A., *Ethnic Conflict and Civic Life: Hindus and Muslims in India* (New Haven: Yale University Press, 2002). Combines statistical sophistication and conceptual rigour to examine the role of some forms of civil society in defusing communal conflict.

13

Religion in the Public Sphere

K.N. Panikkar

Unless the secular character of the public sphere is retrieved, the religious character that it has come to have could impinge on the functions of the state.

On March 15, 2007, Jurgen Habermas delivered a lecture at the University of Tilberg in the Netherlands, on 'Religion in Public Sphere,' an expanded version of which has appeared as a chapter in his latest work, *Between Naturalism and Religion*. In the debate that followed the lecture, the most important issue that was raised related to the relationship between modernization and secularization.

For a long time it was held that a close link existed between the modernization of society and the secularization of the population. Consequently, it was argued that the influence of religion declined in post-enlightenment society. This assumption, Professor Habermas suggests, was based on three considerations. First, the progress in science and technology made causal explanation possible and more importantly, for a scientifically enlightened mind it was difficult to reconcile with theocentric and metaphysical worldviews. Secondly, the churches and other religious organizations lost their control over law, politics, public welfare, education and science. Finally, the economic transformation led to higher levels of welfare and greater social security. The impact of these developments, it is argued, has led to the decline of the relevance and influence of religion.

Opposed to the modernization-secularization paradigm is the view that the influence of religion in the public sphere has not only declined, but in fact, has increased. It is held by many scholars that the modernization thesis has lost its validity in the contemporary world, as there are tendencies which suggest that there is a worldwide resurgence of religion. Such an impression is based on three factors: missionary expansion, fundamentalist radicalization and the political instrumentalization of the potential for violence. On the whole, although 'data collected globally still provides surprisingly robust support for the defenders of secularization thesis,' Professor Habermas terms secular societies as 'post-secular' in which 'religion maintains a public influence and relevance.' At the same time, he held the view that 'the secularist certainty that religion will disappear worldwide in the course of modernization is losing ground.' It is not only that this expectation has not been realised, religion has emerged as a powerful influence in the public sphere all over the world. This is particularly so in India.

A national survey conducted by the Centre for Developing Societies, New Delhi, testifies to the growing influence of religion in Indian society. According to this survey, four out of 10 people are very religious and five out of 10 are religious. That is to say that 90 per cent of the respondents claimed to be religious – performing rituals, visiting places of worship and undertaking pilgrimages. Among them, 30 per cent claimed to have become more religious during the last five years. An increase in the number of religious institutions is also an indication of the greater hold of religion on society. Enlightenment and modernity in India have not led to the decline of the influence of religiosity. If anything, it has only increased.

The public sphere emerged in Europe in the eighteenth century within the bourgeoisie society as a discursive space in which private individuals came together to discuss matters of public interest. The separation of powers of the state and the church and the enlightenment virtues of reason and humanism, and the economic changes brought about by the Industrial Revolution, contributed to the formation of the public sphere and shaped the transactions within it. The existence of the public sphere was contingent upon the access of all citizens to, and protection of individual rights by, the rule of law. In essence, the character of the public sphere as it evolved in Europe in the eighteenth century was secular and democratic.

The formation and development of the public sphere in India during the nineteenth and twentieth centuries had a different trajectory. This was primarily because India was under colonial domination and Indian society did not have the necessary independence to shape its destiny.

The political, economic and intellectual conditions were qualitatively different from the one in which the public sphere in Europe took shape. The passage to an uninhibited state of enlightenment and modernity was not part of its experience. The constraints of colonialism warped the economic development, inhibited the efflorescence of renaissance and enlightenment, suppressed democratic aspirations and tried to undermine secular consciousness. Yet, within these constraints emerged what has come to be described as colonial modernity, which was at best a caricature of what was witnessed in Europe. The contradictions within this modernity, existing as an island in a traditional pool, induced the Indian intelligentsia to seek an alternative, the endeavours of which were articulated through the highly restrictive transactions in the public sphere.

For a variety of reasons, the ability of the agencies which contributed to the formation of the public sphere in India – such as the media, voluntary organizations and social and religious movements – to constitute a public sphere was restricted. Unlike in Europe the public sphere in India was not the product of a free bourgeois society; it took shape within the political, social and economic parameters set by the colonial government. Its social base was very weak, consisting of the nascent middle class emerging out of the structures of colonial governance. The media were constantly under the surveillance of colonial rule; the reach of the voluntary organizations was limited and the social and religious movements could not transgress their respective caste and religious boundaries. As a consequence, the public sphere was not vibrant, nor could it acquire a fully democratic and secular character. This in a way emerged out of the ambivalence of the colonial state: its liberal pretensions on the one hand and authoritarian compulsions on the other. As a result, it could not but monitor the transactions within the public sphere.

The legacy of colonial rule imparted to the public sphere in independent India an internally contradictory character. In terms of conception and constitution the public sphere was democratic and secular, but it was not so in practice. Several sections such as women and Dalits were excluded, and by and large it remained a preserve of the educated upper castes. Moreover, either created or controlled by the colonial bureaucracy, their democratic rights were considerably restricted. Yet, the public engagements within the public sphere indicated a continuous struggle for democratic ideals and practice.

As an institution mediating between civil society and the state, debating issues of public interest, the public sphere is secular in character. In India, however, the public sphere reflected the co-existence of the secular and the religious. The media were essentially secular, but an undercurrent of religious consciousness was reflected in their concerns. For instance, the contributors to the Letters to the Editor column of Bombay Gazette in the nineteenth century described themselves with their religious-denominational descriptions – Hindu, Muslim, Parsi and so on. They were all debating public and secular issues, but while doing so carried with them their religious baggage. The religious identity was true of voluntary associations also as was evident from their denominational names. Many of them were organized on religious terms.

If religion is a private matter, as considered by the Indian state, would it be proper to allow it to be active in the public sphere? The Indian state has not successfully resolved this contradiction. The official policy of equal recognition of all religions has only led to the reinforcement of this contradiction, because it has opened up more and more public space to all religions. As a result, what has become prominent in the public sphere is not secular reason but religious celebration. The public sphere has succumbed to the celebration of religiosity, based on rituals and superstitions.

Two conclusions are in order about the transactions in the public sphere in India. The universal experience of the modernization-secularization connection appears to be true of India. It is particularly so because the renaissance, enlightenment and scientific revolution being either borrowed or weak, the capacity of modernization in India to impact on secularization and marginalization of religion is itself not pronounced. Instead, religion remains a powerful force in civil society. Secondly, the use of religion for political ends has substantially increased during the last few decades. Such a development has serious implications for a secular state and society. Retrieving the secular character of the public sphere is therefore imperative; otherwise its religious character is likely to impinge upon the functions of the state.

(These are excerpts from the valedictory address delivered at the Silver Jubilee celebration of the Department of Christian Studies, University of Madras).

14

Overview of Civil Society

G.K. Rathod

DEFINING CIVIL SOCIETY

The concept of the civil society is elusive and there is still confusion over its constitution. Civil society is not necessarily a neutral arena for it is also a site of contestation depending on the directions of the pressures and is always part of a project to shape the social relation, cultural forms and modes of thought of society. It is also argued that democracy requires a strong and vibrant civil society not for its formation but for its consolidation and stability. Therefore, civil society should be vigilant for two reasons: First, it bears the responsibility to challenge the government when government escapes unscathed after narrating lies and doing wrong. Second, it is its duty to make use of all opportunities to exert pressure upon government to benefit the people. Apart from being citizens of the state, they are members of many other spheres and in such places they acquire political competency, learn to compromise, make friends and explore new ideas. However, civil society refers to the arena of un-coerced collective action around shared interests, purposes and values. As civil society is a dynamic, innovative source for articulating new projects and generating new values and collective identities, the revival of civil society is valuable to reassert the ideas in modern societies. Civil society offers opportunity to realize freedom, equality and solidarity in present social and political situations. It is oriented towards conflict, discourse and compromises. Several versions of civil society have been suggested by a classical scholar. One, based on the rule of law and civility; second, encompassing all organized social life between state and the family;

third, represented by social movements and civic activists; fourth, including charities and voluntary association; and fifth, nationalist and fundamentalist movements.

Blaney and Mustapha Pasha noted that the common employments of the concept ignore the theoretical and historical specificity of civil society: civil society is used to label any group or movement opposed to the state, regardless of its intent or character, or used too generically that it is indistinguishable from the term 'society'. Instead, they argue that civil society is a sphere of social life, involving a stabilization of a system of rights, constituting human beings as individuals, both as citizens in relation to the state and as legal persons in the economy and the sphere of private association. The renewal of civil society is also the object of growing popular movement. This movement has several objectives. It reflects a search for a new citizenship that is less self-interested, more civil and more civically engaged.

SOME CHARACTERISTICS OF CIVIL SOCIETY

Civil society is socially autonomous and self-sustaining because it generates its own norms within itself different from any other societies and institutions. Its human networks exist independently of the state. Civil society declares moral and political autonomy of a society of citizens. Since it is self-regulating body, there is no control of government over its functioning. It is our ideal of what civil society autonomy should be. But in reality, the existing civil societies are not so autonomous of the state. The state has in the present century acted as the most serious threat to the institutions. Cohen and Arato suggested to thematize a programme that seeks to represent the value and interest of social autonomy in the face of both the modern state and capitalist economy. Social autonomy requires certain political conditions. The western tradition of parliamentary liberal democracy has always maintained the primacy and autonomy of civil society in its relation to the state. Interventions are necessitated by the fact that civil society did not function in a democratic framework. Civil society tried to assert its autonomy (T.K. Oommen). Any modern civil society must be a society of spontaneous order. This order emerges out of social interactions not coordinated by command. This means it consists of those institutions and practices which are a result of human actions but not the result of some specific intention. The institutional pluralism is another feature of civil society. A modern civil society comprises institutions of all kind – religious, voluntary associations, charity trust, etc. No society is without existence of institutions. But only some institutions contribute to the health and well-being of civil society. The well-being of civil society depends upon the emergence of open and secular institutions.

Civil society, according to Keith Tester, can be read as both the condition of possibility and the product of continuing modernity. Civil society was all that it was said to be. It was an existing image which could be examined to explain what it was that made the social world social. He clarified that it collapsed because of the implication and consequences of its antinomies. Civil society has the potential of making all our social relationships rather less than totally obvious. It is part of a larger society but an independent arena of society outside the state. This is a realm where people come together and form more or less voluntary associations. This means civil society is essentially an arena of self-regulating voluntary associations.

ORIGIN OF CIVIL SOCIETY

A return of civil society concept inspires us to know its origin from various sources of the subject. Civil society is an old idea and its origin can be found in classical heritage that understood it as politically organized commonwealth. Civility described the requirement of citizenship rather than private sensibility or good manners. Aristotle's civil society was still a political association that improved its citizen and he also insisted on respect for multiple associations in which life is lived. Cicero and other developed a broader notion of civil society and conspired to make liberty a mark of virtue and civility. According to Cicero the State is natural because the individual cannot live solitary life and is inclined to live in a civil society. St. Augustine quoting Cicero with approval defines civil society or the commonwealth as an assemblage (of men) associated by a common acknowledgement of right and by a community of interest (T. Metzer). Christianity provided the basis for common spiritual fellowship by articulating a relatively consistent theory of the State and civil society as a Christian commonwealth. Civil society was divinely ordained and its integral function was to strengthen Christianity. According to John Locke, gradually, due to some reason, men decided to establish civil society in contrast to the state of nature. He further added that civil society provided a stable set of positive laws. As Burke puts it, if civil society is to be made for the advantage of man, all the advantages for which it is made become his right. German thinker Kant conceptualized civil society in light of French Revolution. For him, civil society meant a political project of emancipation against the absolutist state. The public sphere lies at the heart of Kant's civil society. Hegel was also absolutist who defined civil society as per the logic of spheres but combined this approach with a logic of action that was based on educative force of institutions of civil society where the individual learns the value of group action, social solidarity and dependence of his welfare on others. Tocqueville's astonished description of the number and variety of voluntary associations in America seems to announce the definitive triumph of society – not only over a self-centered individualism, but over the state le monde politique as well. He clearly thought that civil associations have an important role to play in combining the disempowering effects of democratic equality.

CIVIC VIRTUE

Civic virtue refers to the personal role that a person may occupy – the role of a citizen. Someone exhibits civic virtue when he or she does what a citizen is supposed to do. It is performance of role or exercise of a certain skill. Civil society is synonymous with a search for civility. The very promises of civil society suggest that public discussion be civilized and civilizing. What is civil society? Again beyond the common usage, it is about the virtue of the citizens. It is about good manners that enable people to accept one another as members of a common order and treat one another with due regard for social well-being and what is accepted as moral rights. This is where a normative social society can find its footing for the long journey ahead. How does one teach people to be polite? Civility is usually understood as politeness, good manners and courtesy, etc. Edward Shills explicitly distinguishes civility as good manners in direct relationships of individuals from what he calls public civility though he does not deny that these two relate to each other at some point. In his view, 'civility is an attitude and a mode of action which attempts to strike a balance between conflicting demands and conflicting interests'. It is also a policy of action on behalf of the whole society as well as the procedure of political or public action. This attitude and the way of action is derived from collective self-consciousness of actors toward their membership of civil society and their attachment to an ideal of civil society. Shills points out that the civil society 'is constituted by collective self-consciousness in which the important referent is the civil quality of its participants, that is, their being members of a society under a common authority, common laws and living in a common, more or less bounded territory. Each participant in the civil collective self-consciousness sees his fellow participants as fellow-citizens, not as fellow-kinsmen. Participants in a common civil collective self-consciousness engender a sense of obligation to the other participants simply by virtue of their quality as members – mainly anonymous members – of the same civil society'. There is more to this emphasis than the mere appreciation of good manners as matter of form. Civility ensures that there is free and frank exchange of opinions among persons with divergent political attachments and, indeed, with divergent conceptions of the good society. Civility manifests citizen's commitment to cooperate with each other in a spirit marked by genuine reciprocity and mutual respect. It is a personal virtue that leads citizens to seek to live together cooperatively. This kind of virtue is grounded in the belief that all fellow citizens are free and equal. All are entitled to participate in determining what the cooperative arrangements of social life will be, especially the most important institutions of government and the rights and duties they respect. Civility indeed respects the freedom and equality that advocates of tolerance are so concerned to protect. But it begins from recognition that freedom and equality can only be achieved through mutual cooperation, interaction and interdependence. Citizens in pluralistic society learn through the virtue of civility to understand the meaning of the common good in its many aspects and seek to pursue the common good. Thus, in turn it leads to a deeper understanding of how to live well together.

CIVIL SOCIETY AND THE PUBLIC SPHERE

Both the concepts of civil society and the public sphere are fluid, problematic, and open to various sometimes conflicting interpretations. Although the concepts are closely related in contemporary debates, especially among writers drawing on Habermas, they have different origins and connotations (Saligman, 1995).The ideas of public disputation and face-to-face contact refer to homogeneous society, while civil society implies more complex, organic and differentiated orders. Civil society like public sphere originiate in Greek and Roman political philosophy but is more closely identified with eighteenth century political philosophy. Public sphere is not merely conceptual but has specific historical referent linked to the Enlightenment's emerging condition and theory of civil society.

Cohen and Areto employ Habermas's system-lifeworld distinction to locate civil society as the sphere of social interaction between economy and the state, composed of all the ultimate spheres (especially the family) the sphere of association, social movements and forms of communication. Civil society then refers to the institutionalized component of life-world. The institutions of civil society anchor the communication structure of the public sphere in the society component of life-world. Cohen and Areto (1992) argue that the new public spheres in Eastern Europe could provide a model for more general ideal of civil society that is appropriate in the West too. Civil society and public sphere are best viewed as multiple processes rather than homogeneous communities.

The basic components of Habermas's critical liberalism are the following: Civil society is the site of resistance and emancipation; the arena of action is the public sphere; the type of action is democratic deliberation. The public sphere is an important extension of civil society. It is where the ideas, interests, values and ideologies form within the relations of civil society that are made politically efficacious. Basic constitutional guarantees alone cannot preserve the public sphere and civil society from deformation. The communication structure of public sphere must rather be kept intact by an energetic and active civil society. Not the state but members of civil society bear responsibility of sustaining of an effective democratic public sphere. Now, it is civil society that is supposed to reinvigorate the public sphere – civil society is also considered broader than the public sphere.

Civil society is generally regarded as combining a public sphere along with an associational one. It is inclusion of the public sphere that most clearly distinguishes civil society from non-profit sector, two concepts that otherwise overlap to a great extent (Helmut Anheier). Civil society included institutions that encouraged debate among private persons on matters of common concern. It was an operationalization of civil society's capacity for self-organization. Mutually dependent private individuals can achieve self-determination that is fundamental to the motivation of the modern public. In its role as the 'public sphere', civil society becomes the arena for argument and deliberation as well as for association and institutional collaboration (Michael Edward). The public sphere is thus crucial dimension of civil society. Civil society without a strong public sphere lacks opportunities for participation in collective choice. While freedom of speech and association is a necessary condition for a strong public sphere, they are not enough. Basic constitutional guarantees alone cannot preserve the public sphere and civil society from deformations. The communicative structure of the public sphere must rather be kept intact by energetic civil society (Habermas). Not the state, but civil society bears the responsibility of sustaining an effective democratic public sphere.

Civil society and public sphere are not precisely equivalent concepts. It is important to keep the idea of 'public' distinct from community or even civil society in general. Civil society is an arena of purely private associations. Such associations are not accessible to everyone nor do they directly concern everybody. Thus, in civil society people come together for restricted, personal ends. A public sphere on the other hand consists of intercommunicating spaces available in principle to everybody and into which people may bring issues that concern everybody (Rajeev Bhargav). Though civil society and the public sphere differ from each other in respect of their functions, the concept of civil society is central to understand the development of civil society. Because the public sphere is central to strengthen civil society. All relevant public issues, opinions, values and interests are expressed in the public sphere. But to create ideal public sphere, some fundamental laws are required for mass communication. Theories of public sphere provide a powerful framework for interpreting the role played by civil society in social change.

The public opinion is not a result of public deliberation. In a fully realized public sphere, a common mind on the common good is actively generated in publicly accessible site through discussion and dialogue. Habermas's public sphere of civil society, was an arena of deliberative exchange in which rational-critical arguments rather than mere inherited ideas or personal statuses could determine agreements and actions. It was an operationalization of civil society's capacity for self-organization, one that emphasized plurality and reason. It was a social formation that depended in various ways on civil society for support (Craig Calhoun). When the terms of civil society and public sphere are taken up for theoretically serious use, it is crucial to keep them distinct and analyse the relationship between social institutions and discourse.

By the public sphere, Hebermas means an arena of rational discourse and influence which is independent of government and big business. The public sphere is accessible to the citizenry and is the space in which public opinion is found. Habermas argues that the public sphere provides an axis of defense against manipulation and propaganda. The demand for 'free speech' produced the movement for a free press and parliamentary reform. By the mid-nineteenth century the public sphere was constituted with the features of open debate, open reportage, critical scrutiny and public accountability.

In recent years, leading public figures, such as Richard Nixon, Robert Maxwell, Jonathan Atiken, etc., have been found guilty of misleading the public in order to achieve their narrow self-interest. This reinforces Lyotard's argument that today a rational politics is no longer admissible. The pragmatic Kant separates ethnic from politics. Politic is operative in the public sphere, which is a sphere that regulates self-interest else self-interest will defeat itself. The public sphere is centrally concerned with the processes of opinion and with formation and therefore it prevents people from voting a wrong party who is contesting elections for special interest because public sphere works towards public interest against vested interest. Thus, conversation in the public sphere can provide a reasoned justification for major decision. Public sphere is meant for consensus-making which in turn helps in social progress. It provides venues for deliberating over norms and values (Michael Edwards).

It is a metaphorical term that is used to describe the virtual space where people can interact and it is the virtual space where the citizens of a country exchange ideas and discuss issues, in order to reach agreement about 'matter of general interest' (Habermas 1997). The public sphere is a vital part of democratic societies. The concept of the public sphere is useful for understanding how societies are organized in the historical period called modernity and how liberal societies function. It is useful for writers who believe that politics is more than simply what happens in parliament, as it makes us think about 'a broader sense of political practice as the constitution of ways of living together' (Calhoun, 1996). To sum up, the term 'public sphere' is a shorthand for speaking about many issues and their interconnections.

In modern time, serious threats to the public sphere have emerged and there is concern about the public sphere in Western countries at the start of the twenty-first century that it is too trivialized; it is too commercialized and it is too fragmented. Craig Calhoun suggests that though the public sphere has been challenged and compromised it has not lost its importance. The success of public sphere depends upon: the extent of access, the degree of autonomy, the rule of law, the quality of participation and rational-critical discourse. In rational-critical discourse, everyone has ability for equal participation and the supreme communication skill is the power of argument. Participation in the public sphere is open to all those who engage in the mutual deliberation what counts as equal and common in their perspectives, experiences, needs and problems. Each will be allowed to try to demonstrate the reasonableness of his needs and his points of view. The give and take of argumentation and debate is an essential tool in building the democratic solidarities of public. However, this ideal of the public sphere has never been fully achieved by most accounts.

CIVIL SOCIETY AND NATIONALISM

Individual liberty and collective independence were merged in the ideology of nationalism. As an ideology, nationalism means a mobilization, a movement or a state-sponsored legal practice for attaining and maintaining autonomy, unity and identity for a population, which some if its members deem to constitute an actual or potential 'nation' (Smith). The emergence of the nation state gave rise to the idea that loyalty was due to the nation and that demands for loyalty were based on law not on faith. For many historians, nationalism is an ambivalent phenomenon. It carries a democratic, emancipatory promise but it invariably also has an aggressive side to it. Some scholars speak of the 'values of nationalism'. Nationalism is associated with the struggle for self-rule in India and with the ambitious project of liberalization from home-grown injustices.

Men and women actively engaged – in state, economy, and nation and in many other settings too. The preferred setting is the nation, within which we are loyal members, bound to one another by blood and history. To form a true nation Friedrich Schlegel demanded that all its members be held together by ties of blood, of descent from the same ancestors. Nationalism has often been a leftist ideology, historically linked to democracy and even to socialism. The quality of nationalism is also determined within civil society. Civil society is a project of projects (Michael Walzer). To the extent nationalism instills people with a sense of belonging and a security in themselves and each other. Because of its ambiguous and variable nature, nationalism has a complicated relationship with the civil society. Civil society and the nation began as allies. Nationality provided the cohesion that might otherwise have been lacking in nascent civil societies. Christopher Byrant contends that national society need not be the enemy of civil society. Civil society is aligned with civic nation insofar as it is conceived of as inclusive, he claims. Traditional national identities can be called into question because they are artificial constructions, created by capitalism as a way of binding people together under the authority of national elite. The problem facing us today is absence of any systematic means through which a wider coherence can be imposed upon society. Being narrow in character, the ideology of Cultural nationalism in India is hostile to the society as civil societies can be organized in ways that are not healthy for civil society itself. Nationality provides a home, a place its members call their own. They grow up and are educated within it, and are deeply shaped by its values and ethos. A space structured by its members gives intensity and depth to their relations with each other and forges common bonds. According to the idea of self-determination, citizens should be able to choose freely the conditions of their own associations, leading to their choices of form and direction of their polity. Authors of civil society have shown that the defence of 'the nation' and the struggle for an open civil society and political democracy against arrogant despotism are identical. As doctrine of national self-determination has been subject to crisis, a more complex understanding of the relationship between civil society and national identity and nationalism, and greater clarity in turn, about the nature of citizenship is necessary. A theory of civil society should be revised in this sense. It is presumed that there is an affinity between self-determination and democracy and therefore, a sense of national identity is essential to the formation and survival of a vibrant, confident civil society. This claim can be affirmed by an ideal national identity, where people consider themselves bound together because they speak a common language; because they inhabit or are closely familiar with a defined territory. The political conception of 'the nation' defines and includes those citizens who are entitled to participate in politics and to share in the exercise of sovereignty and it has fundamental implication. National identity has its importance for revised theory of civil society. It can infuse citizens with a sense of purposefulness, confidence and dignity by encouraging them to feel at home.

Edward Shills vindicates the phenomenon of the nation and argues that civil society could not exist without it. The nation, although related to nationalism, is by no means identical with it. Extreme forms of nationalism are generally iniquitous and in many cases severely damaging to the societies in which they occur. The same structure does not apply to the nation.

Like other ideologies, nationalism is power-hungry and scavenger. It is a pathological form of national identity. In contrast to national identity whose boundaries are not fixed and whose tolerance of difference and openness to other forms of life is qualitatively greater than nationalism. Nationalism seeks to repress internal difference. In extreme cases, nationalism becomes a continuation of totalitarianism by other means.

It is necessary that the nation should be open to democracy and diversity. In power, extreme nationalists do not just repress other people, they repress the diversity and creativity of people. Nationalism is benign only when it does not tend towards this pseudo-democracy of sameness. And this is where civil society comes in. Civil society is the locus of diverse groups and individuals and more importantly of their contact with each other. In civil society, the exchange not only of goods but of ideas can take place. If democracy is to flourish, nationalism must not become the enemy of difference (Craig Calhoun).

CIVIL SOCIETY AND ITS PLACE IN POLITICS

Politics is clearly central to the discussion of civil society. The very first paragraph of his book 'Politics' established Aristotle's understanding that Politics is the most comprehensive of all multiple spheres in which people live. In his view, civil society is politically organized community. Until early 1980, debates on civil society were largely confined to the history of ideas in Western political philosophy. With the third wave of democratization, discussion on proper relation between individuals, services, state and market came to the fore, sparking wide spread debate over the meaning of civil society and its place in politics. Role of civil society organization is advancing change in the direction of open politics.

The origin of civil society can be found in a classical heritage that understood it as a politically organized commonwealth. Reflecting the general domination of political category, civility described the requirement of citizenship rather than private sensibility or good manners. Aristotle's civil society was still apolitical association that improved its citizens. Machiavelli realized that it is difficult for him to theorize civil society outside a purely instrumental understanding of politics. Civil society was no longer understood as a universal commonwealth but came to mean political democracy and rule of law. Civil society is theorized in contemporary political discourse by focusing on the experience of Eastern Europe.

The 1848 revolution that swept across Europe failed to dislodge the grip of the German aristocracy on power. But the seeds of change had been sown in the civil society. During the 1850, civil society flourished in Germany. It was a process that produced several important outcomes. Political parties, liberal and socialist found their feet in the associational life of civil society. At the local level, civil society became an instrument for participation in governance through social engagement. A welfare model was being shaped in Germany that was to involve a shared responsibility between the state and civil society for the poor. This process was augmented by German unification in 1871 (Anheier and Seibel).

The revival of 'civil society' since 1980s has been intimately linked to questions of democratic renewal; civil society has served as a bridgehead of democratic reform. Civil society has transmuted from a social theory to a political theory. The line of enquiry has been from social to political. In this case, the revival of civil society as a ubiquitous category of current debate is less renaissance than a mutation, reworking of its diverse social, cultural and political meaning in European history (Frank Trentmann).

Political institutions have had a long history of recognizing and influencing every civil society's volunteer associations, interest groups and social movements. On one hand, in order for civil society to develop fully and to be maintained in the long run it needs political institutions than supply the criteria of a constitutional state and the rule of law, permit democratic participation, set legal conditions, intervene to protect, foster and reconcile it citizens. On the other hand, it is civil society that influences constitutional state and the rule of law, the dynamic part of civil society supplies polity with necessary energy and mobility. The access of civil initiative, social members and organizations to the political system is therefore, a central condition of the functioning of civil society (Eisenstadt Shmuel). Reviving civil society requires the breadth of thought and action that only politics and an orientation towards state can provide. With paradigm shift concerning civil society from traditional civility to modern politics, a new political trend towards civil society has been set and in many countries, civil society and social movement are coming to play a significant political role. Both civil society and political society play a political role to seek to influence policy decisions. But the political role of civil society is indirect in these circumstances, political struggle over state policy is highly required to revitalize civil society.

CIVIL SOCIETY AND THE GOOD SOCIETY

Good society consists of various conceptions. The criteria of good society differs under different conditions. Many individuals have the same conception yet it could be possible for them to agree on basic characteristics of civil society. Civil society cannot grow under totalitarian regime where one single and uniform conception of good society is imposed by regime itself. Civil society has more chances to grow in liberal, pluralist and secular regimes. Moreover, liberal, pluralist and secular regimes can accommodate diverse consequences of good society (Andre Beteille). Thus, according to writings on civil society, the idea of civil society is not closest to that of good society. However, medieval thought continued equating civil society with 'politically organized commonwealths'. Ferguson insisted that a public spirited citizenry was essential for maintaining a good society. Theories of good society help to keep our gaze on the goal and challenges that motivate the search for freedom and human progress; theories of associational life help to explain how to meet those challenges through medium of non-state action, which is always necessary but not sufficient; theories of public sphere connect the two together by providing a framework for argument and negotiation around social goals and strategies required to reach them. Civil society and good society are constitutive of each other (Michael Edward).

Robert Bellah raised some questions about good society. What we mean by good society, how would we define it, how we recognize it, if a good society for whom and good society in whose opinion? And he answered that there is no pattern of a good society that we or anyone else can simply discern and then expect people to conform to. The common good is crucial to civil society. As Dennis McCann has put it, the common good is the pursuit of the good in common.

'Pluralism does not contradict the idea of a good society, for the latter would be one that would allow a wide scope for diversity and would draw on resources from its pluralistic communities in discerning those things that are necessarily matters of the good of all. An interdependence enables everyone to participate in the goods of society, without which the search for good society is surely illusory. Freedom is an essential ingredient in a definition of a good society. Freedom must exist within and be guaranteed by institutions and must include the right to participate in the decisions that affect our lives. Indeed, the great classic criteria of a good society – peace, property, freedom and justice – all depend today on a new experiment in democracy, a newly extended and enhanced set of democratic institutions, within which we citizens can better discern what we really want and what we ought to want to sustain good life for ourselves and the generation to come'. (Robert Bellah).

The role played by societal institutions in a good society is different from that which they play in the civil society. However, these terms of civil and good society are by no means oppositional. The good society is simply a more expansive concept. Thus far from being uncivil, it fosters additional virtues beyond merely civil. To put it differently, the two concepts are like concentric circles, with the small circle representing the domain of civil society and the larger that of the good society (Amitai Etzioni).

SOCIAL ORDER

From the eighteenth century through the nineteenth, the concern to all social philosophers was the possibility of positing unified vision of the social order that at the same time recognized the legal, moral and economic autonomy of its component parts. The ideal of civil society emerged at the beginning of this period as just such a situation. Proper relation between individual remained, however, as the defining problem of social thought (A.B. Seligman). Securing social order through formation of any government invariably requires a direct consent of those who are to be governed. Social order is a state of affair in which people are safe from physical attach. Social order includes security of property, day-to-day social life, conformity to social norms and cooperative behaviour. For Vaclav Havel, civil society was social order towards which all modern democratic societies are gradually working.

For social order to arise and maintain, two separate problems must be overcome. People must be able to coordinate their action and they must cooperate to attain common goals. If people are to leave together, they must not only be able to interact productively – to do things, help rather than hurt others. Thus, highly ordered- society have a remarkable capacity to sustain cooperation. If citizens have real powers, indeed, they are able collectively to choose institutions, not only policy to participate in the creation of the social order in which they live.

Civil society, in Gramsci's thinking, is realm in which the existing social order is grounded; and it can also be the realm in which a new social order can be founded. His concern with civil society was, first to understand the strength of the status quo, and then to devise a strategy for its transformation. The emancipatory potential of civil society is the object of his thinking.

Civil society has become a crucial battleground for recovering citizen control of public life. It seems that very little can be accomplished towards fundamental change through the state system, as it now exists. That system might be reconstructed on the basis of a reinvigorated civil society which could only come about through a long term position of war. Ultimately, more importantly, pursuit of the primary goal of resurrecting a spirit of association in civil society together with a continuing effort by the organic intellectuals of social forces to think through and act towards an alternative social order at local, regional and global level. The modern ideas of civil society developed by Locke, Ferguson, Smith and Hutcheson were all attempts to posit solution to the new problem of social order that emerged (Seligman).

PUBLIC GOOD/COMMON GOOD

Civil society always aims at the realization of some common goods and is politically about humanity's desire to nurture a public sphere for the common good. But there the political contestation begins. Common good consists of specific moral and social goods such as justice, compassion and consideration for all – they are desired and deserved by all human beings by virtue of their being human. The common good cannot be achieved by simply imposing one's way by means of will or force of personality. A definition that separates a democratic, virtuous civil society acting in public interest from non-democratic, uncivil one, selfishly promoting narrow interest is more normative than analytical. The idea of common good and the public interest obfuscate the reality that all societies are made of groups with different and often conflicting interest and that all groups are equally part of society, whether their goals conform to a specific idea of civil or not. The concept of 'public' – a whole polity that cares about the common good and has the capacity to deliberate democratically – is central to the thinking on civil society. The development of shared interests, a willingness to cede all are crucial attributes for effective governance and practical problem solving (Michael Edwards).

The concept of public or common good has two dimensions. The first consists of feelings and emotions. Here, public, or common good means the feeling of togetherness, the mutuality under strong leadership. Apart from the rather oxymoron concept of common good, there appear third concept of common or public good related to common, local concern.

The most inclusive formation seems to view civil society as individual and collective initiatives towards common public good (Tandon and Mohanty 2002). This definition includes both individual efforts at promoting common public goods, as well more collective one. Public goods are constantly changing and evolving; differing priorities are attached to the various public goods by different stakeholders. Apart from government, civil society is a private domain that serves the public goods. Some examples of NGOs that comprise civil society are independent labour unions, churches, media, etc. It is clearer if, we call public goods as 'collective goods'. Collective goods are non-rival, meaning the use by one person does not reduce the use by another. We can divide goods into those that are excludable and that other are not excludable. Excludable means that it is physically possible to prevent a person from using the goods. Very few produced collective goods are excludable.

Civil society is a public sphere. This is 'civic' space where deliberations, ideas and contestations about relevant public goods are held (Edward, 2004). Two basic themes are linked to the idea of 'Public'. First, the notion of public goods provided by collective rather than individual action and usually shared. Publicness is also a matter of the existence of public goods. There are goods which must be shared if they are to exist at all, like clean air; goods which we believe normatively should be shared like equal opportunity for citizens; goods which constitute a public by being shared, like open communication. (Craig Calhaun).

Rajesh Tandon defines civil society as a collection of individual and collective initiatives working towards the 'common public good'. He also articulates that in a democratic polity, civil society contributes towards governance by influencing the definition and prioritization of public good. There are different interest groups that influence the defining common public good. In a diverse society like India it is not possible to have a definition of public good that is uniformly applicable. He also points out that civil society influences the definition of public good through challenging and contesting dominant priorities and these challenges educate society on advantages and disadvantages of pursuing approaches towards public good.

PUBLIC ACTION

Political action means action to attain a purpose by use of political power or by activity in political channel. But mutual trust is a basic condition for political action and somehow we find more of that in democracies than in autocracies. Public action means civic engagement. State is weak without high degree of civil participation. Public action is one of the conditions of modern democracy. Civil society has vital role to play in good governance. Now this is time to change traditional public action of representative government into direct public action. To change its image, civil society should get involved directly in public action rather than citizen protest and social movement. Through public debate, civil society actors achieve public goods. Therefore, they are required to be involved in decision making process and its implementation.

Sunil Khilani explains his views in the Indian context that an optimistic faith in the power of 'public action' has two aspects: First, public pressure groups must continue to politicize issues and should aim to influence the state to act accordingly. Secondly, economic development might also be advanced by social movements, NGOs and self-help organizations that constitute what now tends to be called 'civil society'. The domain of public action is vibrant in India today; but by definition it is at its strongest and most effective when it is most loyal and particular in its concern.

Amartya Sen has accorded a central role to public action, thus narrowing the gap between academic work and the actual world, between elegant theories and their possible impact on the actual lives of citizens. Public action refers not merely to activities of the state but also to social action taken by the members of the public such as participation in families, community, political protests, the media, democratic practices and social members. Public action can sometimes be collaborative in nature with respect to government policy. For example, the cooperation of the public is crucial to the success of literacy campaigns, health and hygiene programme, famine and disaster relief and land reforms. But public action can also assume a critical role through journalistic pressures, political activism and informed criticism. This enables people to be vigilant and scrutinize policies both at the initiation and implementation stage. The liberal form is related to the construction of a right structure to forms of collective action aiming to secure accountability and the rule of law. Civil society triggers social action only when political society fails to fulfil its proper role within the liberal order. With the representative democracy and the bureaucracy having failed in implementing the government policy, the role of civil society has changed to the effect that it should be involved in public action not for protest but for policy implementation.

Contributors

1. **G.K. Rathod** is Ex-Deputy Secretary and Law Officer in Gujarat Government at Gandhinagar (India).
2. **Bhikhu Parekh** is Professor of Political Philosophy at the University of Westminster, UK. A Political Theorist of international renown, he is fellow of the British Academy, and receipient of a Distinguished Global Thinker Award and the Sir Isaiah Berlin Prize for lifetime contribution to political philosophy. He is a Labour member of the House of Lords and President of the Academy for Social Sciences.
3. **Craig Calhoun** is President of the Social Science Research Council and University Professor of the Social Sciences at New York University. His most recent book is *Nations Matter: Culture, History and the Cosmopolitan Dream.*
4. **Robert C. Post** is Alexander F. and May T. Morrison Professor of Law at the University of California, Berkeley. He is the author of *Constitutional Domains* and editor or coeditor of several other books.
5. **Nancy L. Rosenblum** is Professor of Government at Harvard University. She is the author of *Membership & Morals (Princeton)*, Another Liberalism, and editor of Obligations of Citizenship and demands of Faith (Princeton).
6. **Ellen Meiksins Wood** is Professor of Political Science at York University, Toronto. She is the author of *The Pristine Culture of Capitalism* (1991), *Peasant-Citizen and Slave* (1998), and *The Retreat from Class* (1986) which won the Deutscher Memorial Prize.

7. **Baogang He** is Associate Professor in the School of Government, University of Tasmania. He is the author of *The Democratization of China* (Routledge, 1996), *The Democratic Implication of Civil Society in China* (Macmillan, 1997), and co-authors (with Yingjie Guo) of *Nationalism, National Identity and Democratization in China* (Ashgate, 2000). He has co-translated several books into Chinese (including John Rawls's *A Theory of Justice*) and has published widely in English-language journals.
8. **Marrina Ottaway** is Senior Associate in the Democracy and Rule of Law Project, of the Carnegie Endowment for International Peace, Washington, DC, USA.
9. **Jean L. Cohen** is Professor of Political Science at Columbia University. She served as Assistant Professor of Social Science at Bennington College from 1980–1983 and as Assistant Professor of Sociology at the University of California, Berkeley (1984). Cohen is also Associate Editor of the journals Constellations and Dissent. Jean L. Cohen serves on the Editorial Advisory Board of the Council's journal, Ethics & International Affairs. *Civil Society and Political Theory*, co-authored with Andrew Arato, is viewed by many as a seminal text on contemporary civil society.
10. **Kai Nielsen**, Ph.D. (Calgary) is professor emeritus in the department of philosophy at the University of Calgary and adjunct professor of philosophy at Concordia University. His books include *Ethics without God, Why Be Moral*? and *Naturalism without Foundations.*
11. **Michael Edwards** is Distinguished Senior Fellow at Demos, New York. Visiting Senior Scholar at the Wagner School of Public Service, New York University and Senior Visiting Fellow and Simon Fellow at the Brooks World Poverty Institute at Manchester University.
12. **Bruno Jobert** is senior researcher at the CNRS. He works in PACTE, a research centre attached to the Institut d'Etudes Politiques of Grenoble. He has worked on the role of discourses and ideas in public policies.

13. **Rob Jenkins** is Professor of Political Science, Birkbeck College, University of London, UK.

14. **K.N. Panikkar** is Vice-chancellor of Kerala State Higher Education Council. He was professor of Modern History at the Centre for Historical Studies, Jawaharlal Nehru University and he is currently the General President of Indian History Congress.